Yo

Recognition, Responsibility, and Rights

feminist constructions

Series Editors: Hilde Lindemann Nelson and Sara Ruddick

Feminist Constructions publishes accessible books that send feminist ethics in promising new directions. Feminist ethics has excelled at critique, identifying masculinist bias in social practice and in the moral theory that is used to justify that practice. The series continues the work of critique, but its emphasis falls on construction. Moving beyond critique, the series aims to build a positive body of theory that extends feminist moral understandings.

Recognition, Responsibility, and Rights

Feminist Ethics and Social Theory

Edited by
Robin N. Fiore and
Hilde Lindemann Nelson

ROWMAN & LITTLEFIELD PUBLISHERS, INC.
Lanham • Boulder • New York • Oxford

ROWMAN & LITTLEFIELD PUBLISHERS, INC.

Published in the United States of America
by Rowman & Littlefield Publishers, Inc.
A Member of the Rowman & Littlefield Publishing Group
4720 Boston Way, Lanham, Maryland 20706
www.rowmanlittlefield.com

PO Box 317
Oxford
OX2 9RU, UK

British Library Cataloguing in Publication Information Available

Library of Congress Cataloging-in-Publication Data

Recognition, responsibility, and rights : feminist ethics and social
theory / edited by Robin N. Fiore and Hilde Lindemann Nelson.
p.   cm.—(Feminist constructions)
Includes bibliographical references and index.
ISBN 0-7425-1442-0 (alk. paper)—ISBN 0-7425-1443-9 (pbk. : alk.
paper)
2. Feminist ethics. I. Fiore, Robin N., 1953– II. Nelson, Hilde
Lindemann.   III. Series.
BJ1395 .R43   2003
170'.82   dc21   2002011455

Printed in the United States of America

♾ ™ The paper used in this publication meets the minimum
requirements of American National Standard for Information
Sciences—Permanence of Paper for Printed Library Materials, ANSI/
NISO Z39.48-1992.

Contents

Recognition, Responsibility, and Rights: An Introduction

Robin N. Fiore

> Until we understand the assumptions in which we are drenched we cannot know ourselves.
>
> —Adrienne Rich

As Catharine MacKinnon famously declared: "a woman is not yet a name for a way of being human" (MacKinnon 1993, 91). That is, in defining what it is to be human, and thus what violates the dignity and integrity of such a being, women have been excluded as authors and as agents. If women are included in mainstream political and moral theory, it is derivatively—just in case they relevantly resemble men or figure in men's interests. The past two decades of feminist scholarship has convincingly established the failure of such ethics and politics to address the full range of human needs and interests.

However, the necessity for self-consciously feminist revisioning of moral theory goes beyond the fact that women's experiences and women's voices have been neglected. Standard philosophical conceptions are, as Robin Dillon puts it, "imbued with patriarchal poison" (Dillon 1995), their very ground inimical to emancipatory political goals. Feminist revisioning is thus "an act of survival" for women, according to Adrienne Rich, a refusal of "how we have been led to imagine ourselves" in a culture controlled by males (Rich 1979).

This collection advances the feminist project of remapping the moral in ways that emphasize feminist commitments to theory that acknowledges the diversity of women and engages "the living contexts of moral action"

(DiQuinzio and Young 1995). In what follows, feminists offer ground-breaking analyses of gender with respect to the key ethical concepts—recognition, responsibility, and human rights—and the social and institutional practices that are shaped by those concepts. My aim in this introduction is to prepare readers by briefly discussing the three title themes. I do not offer comprehensive analysis; that is for the individual chapters. I do, however, wish to call attention to the ways in which the concepts are intertwined. Modern Western philosophical efforts tend to focus on distinguishing core concepts and are apt to overlook conceptual interdependence (Hirschmann and Stefano 1996). In contrast, feminist moral theorizing takes as one of its basic tasks "seeing more clearly how the mesh between social positions, identities and responsibilities works" (Walker 1998).

RECOGNITION

The moral demand for recognition is associated with the dialogical model of human individuation, the view that practical identity is socially consti-tuted in and through relations with other persons and with public institu-tions, by recognition or its absence, or by "misrecognition" on the part of others. Moreover, persons may be harmed by representations of them-selves that are distorted, demeaning, or stigmatizing. To the extent that persons are unable to resist derogatory interpretations of their cultures or malignant misrecognitions of themselves, they risk being "imprison[ed] . . . in a false, distorted and reduced mode of being" (Taylor 1994).

The idea of recognition figures prominently in political theory, most commonly in connection with multiculturalism. While acknowledging the importance of the politics of recognition, feminist philosophers have argued for the need to make distinctions among different failures of rec-ognition; problems of recognition in multicultural contexts are not analo-gous to the problems of recognition for women (Wolf 1994).

Axel Honneth distinguishes three forms of "disrespect" that can deprive persons of the recognition that is constitutive of human dignity and integrity (Honneth 1990). The first, exemplified by rape and torture, damages persons' "most fundamental form" of practical relationship to the self—their self-confidence in matters of control over their physical body. The second, according to Honneth, affects persons' "normative understanding of self." This form of disrespect consists in depriving per-sons of the equal right to participate in their society's "institutional order"—either by "the denial of rights or by social ostracism." A person denied legal rights that others possess is not recognized as being equally morally accountable, that is, capable of equal moral agency. The third form of disrespect devalues certain patterns of self-realization—individual or collective lifestyles—denying individuals social acceptance and contributing to a loss of self-esteem. Moreover, according to Hilde Nelson, these latter two forms of disrespect can deprive people of opportunities to occupy roles or maintain relationships that are necessary to preserve crucial aspects of their identity. The "mother" identity, for example, is no longer available if one is denied custody of one's child on the grounds that one is a lesbian (Nelson 2001).

For feminists, due recognition is responding to others on the basis of their self-conception, attending to those features of their lives that they regard as identity constituting, rather than treating them according to one's own favored way of seeing them (Spelman 1977). Challenged by the diversity of the category "women" and the multiple forms oppression can take, feminists developed various approaches to "complex identities." Legal theorists working on civil rights issues were among the first to recognize the distortions imposed on identity as a result of regnant theoretical frameworks. Seeing the interdependence of rights and recognition led to the development of "intersectional" analytical frameworks that attempted to encompass the multiple burdens of Black women and lesbians, to name just two of the many possible intersections that are marginalized under homogenizing, single-axis analytical structures (Crenshaw 1991).

RESPONSIBILITY

Responsibility, as feminists deploy the concept, is not exhausted by traditional philosophical issues of free will and the possibility of moral judgments, of holding people accountable. For feminists, it involves human practices of responsiveness to particularity and context, of being accountable, that is, *taking* as well as *assigning* responsibility. Responsibility as feminists construe it is a more flexible analytical concept, better suited to pluralistic and socially stratified societies. As Margaret Urban Walker puts it, "We are not all responsible for the same things, in the same ways, at the same costs, or with similar exposure to demand or blame by the same judges" (Walker 1998).

Beginning with Carol Gilligan's influential work in moral psychology, *In a Different Voice* (1982), feminist ethicists have led the way in developing normative analyses that center on an ethic of responsibility, of interpersonal responsiveness rather than classic considerations of duty or virtue or the general welfare. Instead of construing personal moral responsibility solely in terms of reflective self-governance according to abstract principles, feminists understand responsibility as both relational and particular. "Specific moral claims on us arise from our contact or relationship with others whose interests are vulnerable to our actions and choices. We are obligated to respond to particular others when circumstance or ongoing relationship render them especially, conspicuously, or peculiarly dependent on us" (Walker 1998, 107).

In Paul Benson's work on self-worth and moral agency (Benson 2000), responsibility is connected with recognition. Benson criticizes traditional theories of responsibility for their narrow focus on agents' powers, capabilities, and decision-making processes. In proposing a "self-worth condition" of responsibility, Benson argues that for persons to be held responsible they must be seen as having a certain moral status, of being eligible to participate in moral exchanges by giving suitable responses, such as giving reasons, admitting fault, and so on. People who have internalized oppressive norms that exclude them from recognition as fully accountable moral agents have been made to feel unworthy to answer for their actions. These socially instilled attitudes that damage self-worth constrict their ability to exercise their moral agency.

RIGHTS

In the dominant Western view, human rights are conceived of narrowly in terms of state violation of civil and political liberties. Abuses that women experience *because* they are women, or that are not directly the result of state action, are not counted as wrongs against humanity. Among these are "honor" killings, genocidal rape, female genital mutilation, dowry-related violence, forced prostitution, wife battery, rape, and denial of reproductive health care and prenatal care. Feminists continue to challenge the idea that explicit state sanction is a necessary condition of holding the state and public institutions accountable. That "law's absence" contributes to the abuse of human rights can be seen, for example, in the way that systematic nonprosecution of violence against women maintains their subordination.

Another problem with prevailing notions of rights is their typically androcentric construction. As MacKinnon succinctly expresses it, "What happens to women is either too particular to be universal or too universal to be particular, meaning either too human to be female or too female to be human" (MacKinnon 1993). Feminists have shown that human rights considerations have uniquely gendered implications for women. For example, in refugee camps, food is often distributed through men who are designated as "leaders," a process that allows them to gain sexual control over women in exchange for food (Bunch 1990).

I have discussed the conceptual cross-fertilization between rights and recognition; here I want to cite a little-remarked connection between rights and responsibility. Rights, as Martha Minow understands them, are the outcome of continual renegotiation regarding what the law requires and allows in particular human communities. As "tools of continuing communal discourse," rights are the responsibility of the community that produces them. For this reason, Minow argues, a claim of rights effectively summons the "community" (Minow 1990, 309). For feminists, the community is inescapably global.

The chapters in this volume build on this body of feminist work and push it in exciting new directions. The first part of this collection presents new feminist work on recognition that responds to the challenges of intersectionality by reflecting on the usefulness of the concept of gender itself. The chapters in the second section speak to the possibilities of an ethic of responsibility as they address a variety of practical problems. In the final section of this volume, the global commitments of feminism are worked out in ways that transform and enlarge the idea of human rights to encompass living lives of dignity.

•

I

RECOGNITION

1

Lived Body versus Gender: Reflections on Social Structure and Subjectivity

Iris Marion Young

In her thorough and provocative essay, "What Is a Woman?" Toril Moi (1999) argues that recent feminist and queer theorizing has brought us to the end of a constructivist gender rope. While feminist theory of the 1970s found a distinction between sex and gender liberating both for theory and practice, subsequent feminist and queer critiques have rightly questioned the distinction. By destabilizing categories both of biological sex and gender identity, recent deconstructive approaches to feminist and queer theorizing have opened greater possibilities for thinking about a plurality of intersecting identities and practices. Deconstructive challenge to the sex/gender distinction has increasingly abstracted from embodiment, however, at the same time that it has rendered a concept of gender virtually useless for theorizing subjectivity and identity. At this theoretical pass, Moi proposes that we throw over the concept of gender altogether and renew a concept of the lived body derived from existential phenomenology, as a means of theorizing sexual subjectivity without danger either of biological reductionism or gender essentialism.

Moi is not alone in proposing that feminist and queer theory question the usefulness of a concept of gender even more deeply than have deconstructive critiques, and I will refer to other recent writings that make similar points in the course of my discussion. I concentrate on Moi because her analysis of the evolution of our troubles with gender is so thorough,

3

and because I find attractive her proposal that feminist and queer theory adopt a concept of the lived body to do the work that she argues the category of gender does not do well. I find Moi's argument incomplete, however. While she is correct that gender is a problematic concept for theorizing subjectivity, there are or ought to be other aspects of feminist and queer theorizing that cannot do without a concept of gender. By reflecting on Moi's account of recent feminist and queer theorizing, we discover that these aspects, which concern social structure more than subjectivity and identity, have been relatively neglected. The oppression of women and people who transgress heterosexual norms occurs through systemic processes and social structures that need description using different concepts from those appropriate for describing subjects and their experiences. Moi's proposal to reconstitute a concept of the lived body helps for the latter, but for the former we need a reconstituted concept of gender.

THE SEX-GENDER DISTINCTION

Early feminist appropriations of what until then had been an obscure psychological distinction between gender, as referring to self-conception and behavior, and sex, as referring to anatomy and physiology, were very theoretically and politically productive. At this theoretical moment challenging the conviction that "biology is destiny" was an important feminist project. In order to argue for opening wider opportunities for women, we needed ways to conceptualize capacities and dispositions of members of both sexes that distanced behavior, temperament, and achievement from biological or natural explanations. A distinction between sex and gender served this purpose. Feminists could affirm that of course men and women are "different" in physique and reproductive function, while denying that these differences have any relevance for the opportunities members of the sexes should have or the activities they should engage in. Such gender rules and expectations are socially constituted and socially changeable. Much of this early second wave feminist theorizing invoked an ideal of equality for women that envisioned an end to gender. "Androgyny" named the ideal that many feminists theorized, a social condition in which biological sex would have no implications for a person's life prospects, or the way people treated one another (including, importantly, in the most consistent of these theories, one's choice of sex partners). These androgynous persons in the transformed liberated society would have no categorically distinct forms of dress, comportment, occupations, propensities toward aggression, or passivity, associated with their embodiment. We would all be just people with various bodies.[1]

This appeal to an ideal of androgyny was short lived. Some of the turning point texts of feminist theory in the late 1970s and early 1980s turned instead to accounts of the social and psychological specificities of femininely gendered identity and social perspective derived from gender roles. While not at all explained by biological distinctions between men and women, nevertheless there are deep social divisions of masculine and feminine gendered dispositions and experience that have implications for the psychic lives of men and women, their interactions with one another, their dispositions to care for children, or exercise authority. Nancy Chodorow, Carol Gilligan, Nancy Hartsock, and others developed theories of feminine gender identities as expressing a general structure of subjectivity and social standpoint in significant ways defining the lives and possibilities of most women.[2]

No sooner had such a general account of feminine gender identity emerged than it came under attack as "essentialist." These accounts assume mothering as defining the experience of most women. They fail to inquire about the differences that race or class positioning make to caring practices, and they assume that women are or wish to be in relationships with men. They extrapolate from the historical specificity of twentieth-century affluent urban nuclear families and occupational structures, ignoring historical and cross-cultural specifications in the organization of family and work. Although the criticisms were not always voiced in the fairest way, most feminist theorists took their points to heart.

Queer theory broke into this dissolution of gender theory, in the person of writers such as Diana Fuss and Judith Butler. Because Moi focuses on Butler's subversion of the sex-gender distinction, and I will support Moi's conclusion in specific respects, I will follow Moi in this focus.

In *Gender Trouble*, Butler questioned the motive of feminist theory to seek a theory of gender identity. Feminists believe they need such a general theory of gender, she argued, in order to know what is the subject of feminist politics. Feminism has no meaning as a specific transformative social movement, it is thought, without an account of the "agent" of change, the subject to be liberated; that subject is "woman," and "gender" is the concept that displays what a woman is. As gendered, "women" are distinct from the biological sex, female. Butler argued, however, that the feminist distinction between sex and gender nevertheless retains a binarism of stable categorical complementarity between male and female, which reproduces a logic of heterosexual normativity. The very distinction between sex and gender ought to be put in question in order to challenge any reliance on a distinction between nature and culture, or any conception that subjects have inner lives to which an idea of stable gender identity corresponds. Gender is nothing other than a social performative. The discursive rules of normative heterosexuality produce gendered performances that subjects reiterate and cite; the sexing of bodies themselves derives from such performatives. In this process of reiterated gender performance some persons become constituted as abject, outside the heterosexual binary. Radical politics, then, consists in troubling the gender binaries and playing with gender citation.

In response to the critical reaction of some commentators that her theory of gender as performance makes bodies and sexual identity simply a product of discourse, in *Bodies that Matter,* Butler argues that the materiality of sexed bodies is itself socially constituted. She insists that such production of bodies is not "idealist," and that a valuation of "materialism" over "idealism" itself relies on a questionable binary logic.

Moi does not refute Butler's arguments, which she takes to be cogent, given their terms and methods. She argues, nevertheless, that ideals of subjectivity and sexuality have become increasingly abstract in this train of theorizing that begins with the sex-gender distinction and ends deconstructing a material-ideal dichotomy. It is not clear at this point what lived problems the theory addresses or how the concepts help people understand and describe their experience. Butler successfully calls into question the logic of the sex-gender distinction, yet her theorizing never goes beyond these terms and remains tied to them. This line of critique, Moi argues, calls for throwing off the idea of gender altogether as useful for understanding subjectivity and identity. Queer theory and practice bend gender meanings, aiming to loosen them from the normative polarities of hegemonic masculinity and femininity. Moi suggests that queer and feminist theorists should make a break with gender altogether.

THE LIVED BODY

The lived body is a unified idea of a physical body acting and experiencing in a specific sociocultural context; it is body-in-situation. For existentialist theory, *situation* denotes the product of *facticity* and *freedom.* The person always faces the material facts of her body and its relation to a given environment. Her bodily organs have certain feeling capacities and function in determinate ways; her size, age, health, and training make her capable of strength and movement in relation to her environment in specific ways. Her skin has a particular color, her face determinate features, her hair particular color and texture, each with their own aesthetic properties. Her specific body lives in a specific context—crowded by other people, anchored to the earth by gravity, surrounded by buildings and streets with a unique history, hearing particular languages, having food and shelter available, or not, as a result of culturally specific social processes that make specific requirements on her to access them. All these concrete material relations of a person's bodily existence and her physical and social environment constitute her *facticity*.

The person, however, is an actor; she has an ontological freedom to construct herself in relation to this facticity. The human actor has specific projects, things she aims to accomplish, ways she aims to express herself, make her mark on the world, transform her surroundings and relationships. Often these are projects she engages in jointly with others. *Situation*, then, is the way that the facts of embodiment, social and physical environment, appear in light of the projects a person has. She finds that her movements are awkward in relation to her desire to dance. She sees the huge city with its thousand-year history as an opportunity for learning about her ancestors. "To claim that the body is a situation is to acknowledge that the meaning of a woman's body is bound up with the way she uses her freedom" (Moi, 65).

How does Moi propose that the idea of the lived body might replace that of gender and the distinction between sex and gender? Like the category of sex, that of the lived body can refer to the specific physical facts of bodies, including sexual and reproductive differentiation. "Woman" and "man" name the physical facticity of certain bodies, some with penises, others with clitorises and breasts, each with differing experiences of desire and sexual feeling. A category of lived body, moreover, need not make sexual difference dimorphous; some bodies have physical traits like those of men in certain respects and those of women in others. People experience their desires and feeling in diverse ways that do not neatly correlate with sexual dimorphism or heterosexual norms. As a lived body, moreover, perceptual capacities and motility are not distinct from association with sexual specificity; nor is size, bone structure, or skin color. Most important for the proposal Moi makes, the concept of the lived body, unlike the concept of sex, is not biologistic. It does not refer to an objectivist scientific account that generalizes laws of physiology and function. A scientific approach to bodies proceeds at a significantly higher level of abstraction than does a description of bodies as lived. The idea of the lived body thus can bring the physical facts of different bodies into theory without the reductionist and dichotomous implications of the category of "sex."

The idea of the lived body, moreover, refuses the distinction between nature and culture that grounds a distinction between sex and gender. The body as lived is always enculturated: by the phonemes a body learns to pronounce at a very early age; by the clothes the person wears that mark her nation, her age, her occupational status; and in what is culturally expected or required of women. The body is enculturated by habits of comportment distinctive to interactional settings of business or pleasure; often they are specific to a locale or group. Contexts of discourse and interaction position persons in systems of evaluation and expectations that often implicate their embodied being; the person experiences herself as looked at in certain ways; described in her physical being in certain ways, she experiences the bodily reactions of others to her, and she reacts to them. The diverse phenomena that have come under the rubric of "gender" in feminist theory can be redescribed in the idea of lived body as some among many forms of bodily habitus and interactions with others that we enact and experience. In such redescription we find that Butler is right in at least this respect: it is a mystification to attribute the ways of being associated with the category "gender" to some inner core of identity of a subject, whether understood as "natural" or acquired.

In a recent essay Linda Nicholson similarly proposes that feminist and queer theory focus on the sociohistorical differentiation of bodies as lived, rather then maintain a distinction between biological sex and embodiment and gender as historically variable. To the extent that this distinction between sex and gender remains, feminist theory continues a "biological foundationalism," as distinct from biological reductionism. The study of sexuality, reproduction, and the roles assigned to men and women should consist in reading bodies themselves and not presume a nature/culture distinction that considers gender as "merely cultural."[3]

The idea of the lived body thus does the work the category "gender" has done, but better and more. It does this work better because the category of the lived body allows description of the habits and interactions of men with women, women with women, and men with men in ways that can attend to the plural possibilities of comportment, without necessary reduction to the normative heterosexual binary of "masculine" and "feminine." It does more because it helps avoid a problem generated by use of ascriptive general categories such as "gender," "race," "nationality," "sexual orientation," to describe the constructed identities of individuals, namely the additive character that identities appear to have under this description. If we conceptualize individual identities as constituted by the diverse group identities—gender, race, class, sexual orientation, and so on—there seems to be a mystery both about how persons are individualized and how these different group identities combine in the person. With the idea of the lived body there is no such puzzle. Each person is a distinctive body, with specific features, capacities, and desires that are similar to and different from those of others in determinate respects. She is born in a particular place and time, is raised in a particular family setting, and all these have specific sociocultural histories that stand in relation to the history of others in particular ways. What we call categories of gender, race, ethnicity, and so forth are shorthand for a set of structures that position persons, a point to which I will return. They are not properly theorized as general group identities that add together to constitute individual identities. The individual person lives out her unique body in a sociohistorical context of the behavior and expectations of others, but she does not have to worry about constituting her identity from a set of generalized "pop-beads" strung together.[4]

By means of a category of the lived body, then, "One may arrive at a highly historicized and concrete understanding of bodies and subjectivity without relying on the sex-gender distinction that Butler takes as axiomatic" (Moi, 46). The idea of the lived body recognizes that a person's subjectivity is conditioned by sociocultural facts and the behavior and expectations of others in ways that she has not chosen. At the same time, the theory of the lived body says that each person takes up and acts in relation to these unchosen facts in her own way.

> To consider the body as a situation . . . is to consider both the fact of having a specific kind of body and the meaning that concrete body has for the situated individual. This is not the equivalent of either sex or gender. The same is true for "lived experience," which encompasses our experience of all kinds of situations (race, class, nationality, etc.) and is a far more wide-ranging concept than the highly psychologizing concept of gender identity. (Moi, 81)

IS THE LIVED BODY ENOUGH?

Toril Moi argues that a concept of the lived body serves feminist theoretical purposes better than a concept of gender. She defines those purposes as providing a theory of subjectivity and the body and providing an understanding of what it means to be a woman or man in a particular society (Moi, 4, 36, 14). Feminist theory, she says, ought to become a project of dispelling confusions concerning bodies, sex, sexuality, sexual difference, and the power relations among women and men, heterosexuals and homosexuals (120). This last phrase about power relations is extremely vague. Depending on how it is specified, the scope of theorizing power relations might fall beyond what I take as Moi's major emphasis in defining the tasks of feminist theory. She defines this theory as focusing on subjectivity, who one is as an agent, the attributes and capacities one has for experience, the relations with others that contribute to one's sense of self. Nicholson also seems to consider that the theoretical function that a concept of gender has meant to serve is that of theorizing self-identity and the social constitution of the human character.

Recent discussions questioning the stability of gender and the adequacy of a sex-gender distinction well reveal dilemmas and increasing abstraction which feminist and queer theory has been forced into or to respond to them. These problems with a concept of gender have surfaced at least partly because gender aims to be a general category, but subjectivity is always particular. Moi's appropriation of the concept of the lived body offers more refined tools for theorizing sexed subjectivity and the experience of differently situated men and women, than does the more blunt category of gender. Agreeing with this means dispensing with gender altogether, however, only if the projects of feminist and queer theories consist in theorizing subjectivity. But I think they do not. The debates about gender and essentialism that Moi aims to bring to a close with her arguments have, I think, tended to narrow the interests of feminists and queer theorists to issues of experience, identity, and subjectivity. Her discussion clears the way for asking whether other aspects of a project for feminist and queer theory have been obscured by these debates, for which a resituated concept of gender might still be needed. In the remaining pages of this chapter I want to suggest that a concept of gender is important for theorizing social structures and their implications for the freedom and well-being of persons.

As I understand them, feminist and queer theories consist not only in giving account of the meaning of the lives of women and men in all their relational and sexual diversity. Nor is it only about analyzing how discourses construct subjects and the stereotypical or defamatory aspects of some of these discourses that contribute to the suffering of some men and women who fall on the wrong side of normalizing processes. Feminist and queer theories are also projects of social criticism. These are theoretical efforts to identify certain wrongful harms or injustices, locate and explain their sources in institutions and social relations, and propose directions for institutionally oriented action to change them. This latter set of tasks requires the theorist to have an account not only of individual experience, subjectivity, and identity, but also of social structures.

In other writings I have articulated a concept of social structure specifically directed at the project of giving an institutional account of sources of injustice and in response to the dilemmas that emerge from claiming that individuals share group identities.[5] Structures denote the confluence of institutional rules and interactive routines, mobilization of resources, and physical structures, which constitute the historical givens in relation to which individuals act and which are relatively stable over time. Structures also connote the wider social outcomes that result from the confluence of many individual actions within given institutional relations, whose collective consequences often do not bear the mark of any person or group's intention.

Alexander Wendt distinguishes two levels of structure—micro and macro levels. Microstructures refer to structural analysis of interaction. The patterning of practices and interactive routines, the rules actors implicitly and explicitly follow and the resources and instruments they mobilize in their interactions can all be regarded as structured. Gender structures are very important to interactions at this microlevel. In recommending that feminist social theory complement attention to subjectivity and identity with renewed attention to social structures, however, I am more concerned with what Wendt refers to as the macrolevel, which involves "multiply realizable outcomes."[6] That is to say, social theory that wishes to understand and criticize the constraints on individuals and groups that render them relatively unfree and limited in their opportunities in relation to others, need to have a picture of large-scale systemic outcomes of the operations of many institutions and practices that produce outcomes that constrain some people in specific ways at the same time that they enable others. Macrostructures depend on microlevel interactions for their production and reproduction, according to Wendt, but their form and the ways they constrain and enable cannot be reduced to effects of particular interactions.

Social structures position individuals in relations of labor and production, power and subordination, desire and sexuality, prestige and status. The way a person is positioned in structures is as much a function of how other people treat him or her within various institutional settings as is the attitude a person takes toward him- or herself. Any individual occupies multiple positions in structure, and these positionings become differently salient depending on the institutional setting and the position of others there.

From the point of view of critical social theory, the main reason to care about structures is to have an account of the constitution and causes of social inequality. Some people encounter relative constraints in their freedom and material well-being as the cumulative effect of the possibilities of their social positions, as compared with others who in their social positions have more options or easier access to benefits. Social groups defined by caste, class, race, age, ethnicity, and, of course, gender, name subjectivity identities less than axes of such structural inequality. They name structural positions whose occupants are privileged or disadvantaged in relation to one another due to the adherence of actors to institutional rules and norms and the pursuit of their interests and goals within institutions. A structural account offers a way of understanding inequality of opportunity, oppression, and domination that does not seek individualized perpetrators, but rather considers most actors complicit in its production, to a greater or lesser degree.

Nancy Folbre conceptualizes such issues of social inequality in terms she calls "structures of constraint."[7] Structures of constraint include sets of asset distributions, rules, norms, and preferences that afford more freedom and opportunity for benefits to some than others. Constraints define the range of options available to individuals, or the costs of pursuing some options rather than others. Time and money function as basic assets. Legal rules function as important constraints, but so do culture norms. They impose a "price" on nonconformity. Preferences can be constraints when they conflict with one another. A configuration of particular assets, rules, norms, and preferences creates the constraints that define what we call social groups based on gender, class, race, age, and so on. Thus membership in the group called "women" is the product of a loose configuration of different structural factors.

To describe and explain some of the structures and processes that effect differential opportunities and privileges in contemporary society, I suggest, we cannot do without a concept of gender. Feminist and queer theories need conceptual tools to describe the rules and practices of institutions that presume differing roles for men and women, or that presume that men and women are coupled with one another in intimate relations. We need tools for understanding how and why certain patterns in the allocation of tasks or status recognition remain persistent in ways that limit the options of many women and of most people whose sexual and intimate choices deviate from heterosexual norms. An important conceptual shift occurs, however, when we understand the concept of gender as a tool for theorizing structures more than subjects. We no longer need to ascribe a single or shared gender identity to men and women.

My own effort to respond to critiques of early feminist theories of gender turned in this direction of theorizing gender as an attribute of social structures more than of persons. In "Gender as Seriality: Thinking About Women as a Social Collective," I draw on a concept from Sartre's later philosophy, his idea of a series.[8] Gender, I suggest there, is best understood as a particular form of the social positioning of lived bodies in relation to one another within historically and socially specific institutions and processes that have material effects on the environment in which people act and reproduce relations of power and privilege among them. On this account, when it says that individual persons are "gendered" it means that we all *find ourselves* passively grouped according to these structural relations, in ways too impersonal to ground identity. I proposed that there are two basic axes of gender structures: a sexual division of labor and normative heterosexuality. Here I will take a lead from Bob Connell and add to these a third axis, gendered hierarchies of power.[9]

The structuring of work and occupations by gender is a basic aspect of all modern societies (and many premodern societies), with far reaching consequences for the lives of individuals, the constraints and opportunities they face. The core of a gendered division of labor in modern societies is the division between "private" and "public" work. An aspect of the basic structure of these societies is that the work of caring—for persons, their bodily needs, their emotional well-being, and the maintenance of their dwellings—takes place primarily in unpaid labor in private homes. While recent decades have seen some changes in the allocation of their work between men and women, it is still the case that this unpaid caring and household work falls primarily to women. The operations of the entire society depend on the regular performance of this work, yet it goes relatively unnoticed and little valued. The persons to whom this work is assigned have less time and energy to devote to other tasks and activities than do those who do less of it. This gendered division of labor persists apparently because people collectively do not wish to organize broadly funded public services that take more collective responsibility for care work. Despite many significant changes in gender ideas and ideology in contemporary societies, there has been little change in this basic division of labor. Indeed, neoliberal economic policies across the globe have had the effect of retrenching this division where it may have loosened.

Feminist social and political theory in the past twenty years has documented dozens of ways that this gendered structure constrains the opportunities of those persons doing unpaid care work, mostly women.[10] They work longer hours than others and are rendered dependent on other people for provision of their needs, which makes them vulnerable to poverty or abuse. Feminist researchers have also documented how this basic structure underlies occupational divisions in public paid work according to gender. When occupations involve caring they tend to become female gendered. Because many women arrange their public work lives in relation to caring responsibilities, only a relatively small number of occupations welcome them, which helps keep wages low in those occupations. The structuring of both private and public work along these lines exhibits gendered hierarchies of status and power, not to mention financial reward.

It might be thought that these structural consequences of a sexual division of labor describe Western industrial societies primarily. Theorized at the right level of categorical generality, however, similar structures describe much about many less developed countries, especially in urban life. As some feminist scholars of development have argued, for example, both government policy and the policies of international organizations such as the International Monetary Fund implicitly rely on the assumption that unpaid domestic labor is infinitely expandable, and that household caretakers are available to take up the slack in meeting the needs of their family members when food subsidies are slashed, school fees go up, or health clinics are closed.

A structural account of the sexual division of labor does not assume that this division of labor has the same content across societies. It is a theoretical framework that asks whether there are tasks and occupations usually performed by members of one sex or the other, and/or whether the social norms and cultural products of the society tend to represent certain tasks or occupations as more appropriately performed by members of one sex or the other. For any society, both today and in the past, the answer is usually yes, but there is nevertheless considerable variation among them in *which* occupations are sex associated, the ideologies often legitimating these associations, how many tasks are sex typed, and what implications this sexual division of labor has for the distribution of resources among persons, their relative status, and the constraints and opportunities that condition their lives.

A second axis of gender structuring in our society is normative hetero-sexuality. This structuring consists in the diverse institutional and ideological facts that privilege heterosexual coupling. These include the form and implications of many legal institutions, many rules and policies of private organizations in allocating positions and benefits, the structuring of schooling and mainstream media in accordance with these institutions, as well as the assumptions many people make in their everyday interactions with others. Together such social facts make structures with differential consequences on the lives of different men and women, which sometimes produce serious suffering or wrongful limitations on freedom. The system of normative heterosexuality significantly constrains the lives of men and women, with all their varying sexual and desiring inclinations, motivating some to adjust their lives in ways they believe will bring them material reward and acceptance, and others to carve out lives in the interstices of social relations where their desires and projects do not fit, or openly to rebel.

Cheshire Calhoun argues that lesbian and gay subordination is different in form from the structural constraints on the lives of women or people of color, for example. Whereas structures of female subordination or insti-tutionalized racism confine people perceived as belonging to certain cate-gories as having certain places or positions, Calhoun argues that persons who transgress heterosexual norms have no legitimized place at all in political citizenship, civil society, or private spheres. Structures of norma-tive heterosexuality constrain lesbians and gay men by enforcing their invisibility.[11]

An institutionalized valuation of particular associations of maleness or masculinity condition hierarchies of power in ways that constrain the pos-sible actions of many people and seem quite resistant to change. Positions and practices of institutionalized and organized violence are most impor-tant here—military and police forces, prison systems, and so forth. In gen-eral, the structuring of state institutions, corporations, and other bureaucracies according to hierarchies of decision-making authority and status afford some people significant privileges and freedom, and these are usually men, at the same time that they limit, constrain, and subordinate others, including most women and many men. Gendered hierarchies of power intersect with a sexual division of labor and normative hetero-sexuality in many ways to reproduce a sense of entitlement of men to women's service and an association of heterosexual masculinity with force and command.

When describing social structures as gendered it is neither necessary to make generalizations about men and women nor is it necessary to reduce varying gender structures to a common principle. A gendered occupa-tional division of labor may strongly code certain occupations as female and others as male, and these codings may have far-reaching implications for the power, prestige, and material reward incumbents of each enjoy. Nothing follows from this, however, about what most men or most women do for a living. Recognizing the structures of normative heterosex-uality may well result in theorizing plural understandings of gender, vary-ing rules and practices that make expectations on men and women regarding sexual interaction, relation of adults and children, social aes-thetics, relationship of persons to workplace roles, and so on, that do not share a common logic and in some respects may be in tension with one another. Structures of a gendered hierarchy of power differentiate men from one another according to social roles and dispositions and do not simply differentiate men and women. The most important thing about the analysis is to understand how the rules, relations, and their material con-sequences produce privileges for some people that underlie an interest in their maintenance, at the same time that they limit options of others, cause relative deprivations in their lives, or render them vulnerable to domination and exploitation.

In this chapter I have agreed with Toril Moi's proposal that the existen-tial phenomenological category of the lived body is a richer and more flexible concept than gender for theorizing the socially constituted experi-ence of women and men than either concepts of sex or gender. The lived body is particular in its morphology, material similarities, and differences from other bodies. I have argued, moreover, that this proposal should not mean dispensing with a category of gender, but rather confining its use to analysis of social structures for the purposes of understanding certain specific relations of power, opportunity, and resource distribution. An obvious question arises at this point, as to the relation of lived bodies to these structures.

Another reason that turning to a concept of lived body may be produc-tive for feminist and queer theory is precisely that it can offer a way of articulating how persons live out their positioning in social structures along with the opportunities and constraints they produce. I do not have the space here to develop the framework for such articulation, and I will offer only a few lines toward a sketch.

Gender structures, I said above, are historically given and condition the action and consciousness of individual persons. They precede or follow that action and consciousness. Each person experiences aspects of gender structures as facticity, as sociohistorical givens with which she or he must deal. Every person faces the question of what to wear, for example, and clothing options and conventions derive from multiple structures of profit seeking, class and occupational distinction, income distribution, hetero-sexual normativity, and spaces and expectations of occasions and activities and the possibilities of conformity and transgression they bring. However limited the choices or the resources to enact them, each person takes up the constrained possibilities that gender structures offer in their own way, forming their own habits as variations on those possibilities, or actively trying to resist or refigure them. Gender as structured is also lived through individual bodies, always as personal experiential response and not as a set of attributes that individuals have in common.

Pierre Bourdieu's concept of the *habitus* offers one interpretation of how generalized social structures are produced and reproduced in the movement and interaction of bodies. Especially in his understanding of gender structures, however, Bourdieu's understanding of the relation of social structures to actors and experience conceptualizes these structures too rigidly and ahistorically.[12] It may be more fruitful to draw on a theory of lived body like that of Maurice Merleau-Ponty, but connect it more explicitly than he does to how the body lives out its position in social structures of the division of labor, hierarchies of power, and norms of sex-uality.[13] Under the influence of such a theory of how bodies live out their structured positioning, moreover, one might find that a deconstructive gender theory such as Judith Butler's appears not as a theory of the deter-mination or constitution of gendered subjects, but as a theory of the vari-able movements of habituated bodies both reacting to, reproducing, and modifying structures.

NOTES

1. For one statement of the androgynous ideal, see Ann Ferguson, "Androg-yny as an Ideal for Human Development," in *Sexual Democracy: Women, Oppres-sion and Revolution* (Westview: Allen and Unwin, 1991).

2. Nancy Chodorow, *The Reproduction of Mothering* (Berkeley: University of California Press, 1999); Carol Gilligan, *In a Different Voice* (Cambridge: Harvard University Press, 1982); Nancy C. M. Hartsock, *Money, Sex and Power* (Northwest-ern University Press, 1983).

3. Linda Nicholson, "Interpreting Gender," *The Play of Reason: From the Modern to the Postmodern* (Ithaca: Cornell University Press, 1999), 53–76.

4. See Elizabeth Spelman, *Inessential Woman: Problems of Exclusion in Femi-nist Thought* (Boston: Beacon Press, 1988).

5. See *Inclusion and Democracy* (Oxford: Oxford University Press, 2000), especially Chapter 3; see also "Equality of Whom? Social Groups and Judgments of Injustice," *Journal of Political Philosophy* 9, no. 1 (March 2001): 1–18. There I build a definition of social structures by drawing primarily on ideas of Peter Blau, Anthony Giddens, and Jean Paul Sartre.

6. Alexander Wendt, *Social Theory and International Relations* (Cambridge: Cambridge University Press, 2000), Chapter 4.

7. Nancy Folbre, *Who Pays for the Kids?* (New York: Routledge, 1994), especially Chapter 2.

8. In I. M. Young, *Intersecting Voices: Dilemmas of Gender, Political Philosophy and Policy* (Princeton: Princeton University Press, 1997).

9. See Bob Connell, *Gender and Power* (Stanford: Stanford University Press, 1987).

10. Nancy Folbre's book, cited above, is an excellent analysis of the operations of these constraints in several countries in Europe, Asia, and Latin America as well as the United States.

11. Cheshire Calhoun, *Feminism, the Family, and the Politics of the Closet: Lesbian and Gay Displacement* (Oxford: Oxford University Press, 2000).

12. See for example, Pierre Bourdieu, *The Logic of Practice*, trans. Richard Nice, (Stanford: Stanford University Press, 1990), especially Chapters 3 and 4. Toril Moi herself explores the implications of Bourdieu's theory for feminist theory; see "Appropriating Bourdieu: Feminist Theory and Pierre Bourdieu's Sociology of Culture," Chapter 3 of *What Is a Woman?* (Oxford: Oxford University Press, 2001). Bourdieu's book, *La Domination Masculine* (Paris: Editions du Seuil, 1998) assumes that he can generalize about gender structures largely from his observations of Kabylic society in North Africa.

13. Nick Crossley argues that a reconstruction of Merleau-Ponty's theory of sociality and habit can better serve social theory than Bourdieu's concept of *habitus* because Merleau-Ponty's conceptualization gives more place to freedom and individual difference. See Crossley, "The Phenomenological Habitus and Its Construction," *Theory and Society* 30 (2001): 81–120; see also "Habitus, Agency and Change: Engaging with Bourdieu," paper presented at a conference on the Philosophy of the Social Science, Czech Academy of Sciences, Prague, May 2001.

2

Gendered Work and Individual Autonomy

Diana T. Meyers

A great deal of socially necessary labor is unwaged, undervalued, and coded feminine. Showing that caring for dependents is the main industry in this shadow economy numbers among the signal accomplishments of second wave feminism. Yet, after a quarter of a century of feminist critique and activism, little progress has been made in uncoupling caregiving from gender. Moreover, caregivers who are not impoverished remain economically insecure, and none are accorded the social status they deserve.

One of the many liabilities of caring for dependents is the threat it poses to individual autonomy. Mothers are culturally represented as self-sacrificial, unconditionally loving, and totally identified with their children—the prototype of a gladly nonautonomous being. This chapter argues that, as this maternal imagery suggests, coercive gender structures put dependency workers' autonomy in jeopardy and that these constraints are unjust.[1] Section 1 argues that default dependency work and autonomy are in principle compatible. Section 2 argues that gender and the family intersect to maintain the sexual division of labor, which prevents many default dependency workers from being as autonomous as they are entitled to be. In this section, I examine Diemut Bubeck's and Eva Kittay's accounts of dependency work and the policies they propose to free women from the coercion of the sexual division of labor. Although I think their suggestions are helpful, I urge that ensuring women's autonomy requires more profound social change. Thus, Section 3 outlines a number of changes in the structure of the family that I believe are necessary to eliminate the coercion that constrains default dependency workers' agency.

AUTONOMY AND WORK

For the purposes of this chapter, I shall understand *autonomy* to mean self-governance or self-determination. More specifically, to be autonomous is (1) to figure out what your personal values and goals are—what really matters to you as an individual and what you as an individual really want out of life; (2) to figure out how you can fulfill those self-chosen values and goals; and (3) to act in ways that are congruent with those self-chosen values and goals. Autonomous individuals have their own commitments, and these commitments are expressed in sizable and significant chunks of their conduct. For the most part, then, they do not suffer from chronic and acute alienation from themselves or their lives, for, within the limits set by social relations and human fallibility, they feel comfortable with spontaneity and in control of their lives.

With regard to the structuring of the paid as well as the unpaid work world, autonomy is at stake in three respects. First, one may be more or less autonomous in one's choice of work, for one may or may not have access to the resources necessary to qualify for it. An enthusiastic and talented teenage scientist who cannot afford to go to college has considerably less autonomy in her or his choice of work than another teenager whose parents can easily pay for college. Second, one may be more or less autonomous once one embarks on a particular type of work. Some workers (e.g., university professors) have a great deal of control over how their work is conducted; others (e.g., assembly line workers) do not. Some workers (e.g., servers in lucrative restaurants) have quite a bit of time to engage in outside pursuits; others (e.g., aides to important government officials) do not. Third, one may have more or less autonomy with respect to exiting one's work. Leaving some types of work requires no more than a few days' notice, but it is far more difficult to extricate oneself from the commitments and responsibilities that many other types of work entail. A soldier cannot desert her or his squadron; the star of a play cannot capriciously and suddenly leave the production; an obstetrician cannot abandon her or his medical practice without making arrangements for patients to receive care from someone else.

In each respect—choice of work, choice within work, choice to leave work—autonomy is a matter of degree. It depends on the range of occupations that are practically feasible and socially available to an individual. It depends on the extent to which the occupation provides opportunities for individualized decision-making and action and also on the extent to which it frees the individual to pursue other interests and projects. It depends on the limits that the occupation imposes on the individual's freedom to quit.

That an occupation gives workers latitude in which to make autonomous choices does not guarantee that they will do so. It is up to them to seize their work-related opportunities for autonomy. But they may not see that autonomy opportunities exist, or they may lack the skills necessary to take advantage of them. In addition, it is important to recognize that even if extensive constraints on autonomy are built in to the structure of a particular kind of work, some workers may nonetheless act autonomously. Some individuals may have values and goals that coincide with the stringent entrance requirements, the regimented day-to-day activity, or the onerous restrictions on quitting. They will experience no friction between their own sense of self and the way the work is structured. Hence, they will be able to autonomously comply with the established practices and aims of the work category and will need no additional options in order to act autonomously. Those who find the practices and the aims that define the work uncongenial may try to reform their work environment in order to bring it into better alignment with their own values and goals. Although they may fail to bring about all of the changes they desire, their attempt to effect change constitutes an autonomous act of dissent, for it enacts their own values and goals. It is important, then, to bear in mind that autonomy-discouraging practices and aims embedded in work structures do not rule out the possibility that some individuals will achieve autonomy within those contexts. However, I shall concentrate on the ways in which different kinds of work are structured and on how these structures promote or discourage autonomy with respect to entrance, participation, and exit.

Since the entrance requirements for dependency work are among the least restrictive, they impede autonomy far less than most kinds of work. Virtually anyone who wants to do dependency work can. But students of dependency work would reply that the relevant entrance issue is not whether there are ample opportunities to sign on, but rather whether the opportunities to refuse to do dependency work are sufficient for autonomy. Those who raise this issue base their skepticism on two claims: (1) Child- and elder care is socially necessary labor, and (2) dependency work is unchosen.[2]

It is undeniable that reproducing the species is socially necessary labor. It is not clear, however, that obligatory childcare is invariably unchosen in the United States and similar societies today. Admittedly, one can nonvoluntarily become responsible for children. For example, in order to spare their grandchildren the vagaries and hazards of the foster care system, mothers of drug-addicted women often feel they have no choice but to take responsibility for their daughters' children. Still, many obligations to do default dependency work, especially prolonged childcare, do not descend on individuals against their will or due to circumstances beyond their control, for they are direct consequences of voluntary action. Anyone who has access to contraception and abortion need not have children.[3] Of course, once one has children, taking care of them ceases to be optional. But since having children is not obligatory, childcare is not an unchosen obligation unless safe and reasonably affordable means to prevent or halt pregnancy are not available.

Elder care responsibilities initially seem to be less voluntary. Since no one can avoid having parents, and since many people's parents will eventually lose their ability to take care of themselves, it might seem that this kind of dependency work is thrust upon their offspring willy-nilly. In light of the fact that very old and helpless people are often distrustful of and embarrassed by stranger care and consequently feel betrayed if their children decline to take them in, it is arguable that becoming a dependency worker for an incapacitated parent is unchosen but mandatory. Yet, in our child-centered society, many would agree that two-income parents do nothing wrong if they refuse to take on elder care because both of them need to work for the sake of their children's future. Also, in contemporary middle-class America, elder care is increasingly considered optional thanks to long-term-care insurance and assisted living and nursing home facilities.[4] From this perspective, the family no longer seems to be the inevitable site of elder care.

I submit, then, that whether unchosen family relations in conjunction with the severe incapacity of a family member give rise to default dependency work obligations depends on social conventions that are presently in flux.[5] Moreover, I submit that widespread use of contraception and abortion shows that a commonly cited paradigm of a dependency relationship, namely, the mother-child relationship, is, for many women, not an unchosen relationship. If I am right, entering into a relationship that entails default dependency work or having a kinship relation to a person who becomes dependent does not necessarily interfere with autonomy.

The scope of choice within dependency work is considerably broader than the scope of choice in other types of work that are considered unskilled and menial.[6] The defining purposes of any type of work place limits on individual choice. As short-order cooks must produce meals, so must dependency workers meet the needs of their charges. But whereas short-order cooking procedures are standardized, caring responsibilities can be fulfilled in indefinitely many ways. Although the needs of the person being cared for dictate the scheduling of many of the dependency worker's tasks, providing nutrition, entertainment, and emotional support afford opportunities for dependency workers to be creative and express their own values. In fact, very few types of skilled labor grant workers as much discretion with respect to the way in which the work is performed as dependency work does. Compared to medical protocols, which rigidly circumscribe the day-to-day practices of physicians, standards of nutrition, hygiene, and safety specify a rudimentary baseline of care that leaves most of dependency work unregulated. There is no reason, then, to think that the activity of caring for dependents stifles autonomy.

In other respects, however, dependency work severely restricts individualized agency. Default dependency workers who cannot afford professional backup and who have no volunteer helpers are always on-call. Consequently, they have little opportunity to develop other talents and pursue other interests. Yet, a number of other types of work make similar demands on workers' time. Entrepreneurs, investment bankers, and attorneys are commonly expected to sacrifice leisure, which might be used to get involved in other projects, in exchange for the personal and financial rewards of unstinting dedication to their chosen profession. Unlike in other highly skilled types of work, however, it is exceedingly difficult to justify terminating a dependency relationship. Only very unusual, perhaps counterfactual circumstances could morally oblige other workers, even employers whom other workers depend on, never to disengage themselves. Conscience may oblige them to make more or less elaborate transition arrangements, but quitting for purely personal reasons is always an option. In contrast, moral reasons may forbid dependency workers to leave dependents, regardless of how disenchanted with their responsibilities the workers may be. Thus, the exit options of dependency workers, especially default dependency workers, are the narrowest of any work category.

In my view, dependency work is on the same continuum as other work categories. If other types of work are considered to be compatible with autonomy, there is good reason to consider dependency work compatible with autonomy too.[7] Every form of work, including dependency work, offers a distinctive combination of opportunities to meet one's own needs and gain personal fulfillment together with opportunities to shoulder social responsibilities and make a valued contribution. Yet, every form of work, including dependency work, places characteristic limits on individual choice, and, as Marx noted long ago, most kinds of workers are dependent on others to supply them with the resources they need to do their work. But no sensible person would value autonomy, nor would anyone ever be autonomous if autonomy precluded participation in modern economic institutions or deep commitments to values, persons, and projects. Moreover, since no credible account of autonomy requires that autonomous individuals be totally independent of other people or totally free to do as they please, people can be autonomous despite the constraints associated with work (Friedman 1997). I would urge, then, that the nature of dependency work does not prevent dependency workers from enacting their own values and goals. If I am right, dependency work is, in principle, compatible with autonomy.

DEPENDENCY WORK AND GENDER

That there is no necessary incompatibility between dependency work and autonomy does not entail that there is no contingent conflict between them. My defense of the compatibility of dependency work and autonomy glosses over a key feature of social reality, namely, that American culture currently embeds dependency work in a coercive gender system. Since gender norms propel women into marriage and childbearing, and since gender norms then propel mothers into dependency work, it is doubtful that women freely become mothers and dependency workers. If they do not, the availability of contraception and abortion does not ensure that procreation is voluntary. Moreover, women are unlikely to contest the expectation that they serve as default dependency workers, and they are likely to overidentify with their charges. Indeed, dependency workers appear to be living out a culturally ordained plotline rather than improvising lives that express self-chosen values. Diemut Bubeck and Eva Kittay agree that the feminization of dependency work interferes with women's autonomy and propose social programs that expand women's autonomy opportunities.

Bubeck argues that women's commitment to the ethic of care enrolls them in dependency work. She issues the standard liberal caveat that until women are equal to men and "really free to choose," one should refrain from judging whether their disposition to care is a consequence of their biological nature or a consequence of the social pressures brought to bear on them (Bubeck 1995, 170). But she holds that at present cultural representations of gender, gendered childrearing practices, gender segmented economic and family structures, and gender enforcing social sanctions foreclose women's freedom to choose (Bubeck 1995, 151, 160, 165, 172). Once they have been imbued with feminine norms, including the ethic of care, women find themselves trapped in the "circle of care" (Bubeck 1995, 171). Feminized women do dependency work both because they find it satisfying and because refusing to assume the responsibilities that convention assigns them would harm dependent persons (Bubeck 1995, 171, 246). Because the ethic of care proscribes harming others, it obliges women to continue as dependency workers, even when this work exploits them. Since exploitation may not harm them, their dependency duties take precedence. Thus, the circle of care degenerates into the "dilemma of exploitation" (Bubeck 1995, 246–247). For dependency workers who embrace the ethic of care, their obligation to meet the needs of people who would suffer harm without their assistance preempts their own freedom and interests.

Either Bubeck's analysis only applies to a minority of women, or it relies on an unfounded generalization about women's moral views. Many women who are default dependency workers are not single-minded devotees of the ethic of care. According to Carol Gilligan, only one-third of the women she studied focused exclusively on the care ethic. Another third focused exclusively on an ethic of rights and justice, and the remaining subjects used both approaches (Gilligan 1987, 25). Whether or not precisely these proportions hold true of the larger population, there is little doubt that women are a morally diverse lot. It is clear, then, that women's commitment to the ethic of care cannot explain the sexual division of labor, which is nearly universal. Nor can it explain why dependency workers are vulnerable to exploitation, for many of them do not subscribe to the ethic of care. Eva Kittay's account of coerced dependency work shifts the focus from individual women to the nature of dependency work and the institutional context that frames it.

Kittay anchors her analysis of dependency work in Robert Goodin's ethic of responsibility for the vulnerable. She agrees with Goodin that when one is related to a person in need in such a way that one is well situated to help, one is obligated to respond (Kittay 1999, 55). However, she qualifies Goodin's theory in order to accommodate a pair of seemingly irreconcilable intuitions: (1) A person can be obligated to come to the assistance of a needy person without any prior agreement to do so, and (2) no one is obligated to respond to every demand for help. According to Kittay, cultural norms distinguish needs from mere desires and specify the types of relationships within which individuals are obligated to meet others' needs (Kittay 1999, 56–57). Dependency relationships are an important class of obligation-imposing relations. They are relationships between a charge and a dependency worker—that is, between persons who are so seriously incapacitated that they would lack life-sustaining resources without someone's help and persons who are responsible for securing their well-being (Kittay 1999, 30–31, 38). Kinship and friendship are prime instances of culturally recognized settings that can give rise to a dependency relationship when a party to the relationship is vulnerable (Kittay 1999, 57). People do not always enter into these obligation-generating settings voluntarily. But because culture designates them as legitimate sites of valid dependency claims against others, the obligations to do dependency work that issue from them are not coercive (Kittay 1999, 61–62). For Kittay, then, it is possible for a person's commitment to dependency work to be nonvoluntary yet noncoerced, but it is also possible for a person's commitment to dependency work to be nonvoluntary and coerced.

To explain what is wrong with the patriarchal family and the sexual division of labor, Kittay cites the link between gender and dependency work and characterizes women's commitment to dependency work as nonvoluntary and *coerced*:

> Only by naturalizing dependency work (e.g., women are *naturally* better with children, the sick, the elderly) have ideologues made their constraints on freedom palatable to the modern sensibility. By so naturalizing the labor, the coercion required for the *modern* woman to engage in dependency work has been covered with sentimentality. (Kittay 1999, 95)

Because Kittay rejects voluntarist accounts of dependency obligations, she does not equate coerced dependency work with unchosen or nonconsensual dependency work. Instead, she equates coerced dependency work with unjustly imposed dependency work, and she defines unjustly imposed dependency work as dependency work mandated by a culturally accredited practice or institution that lacks a moral warrant (Kittay 1999, 59–61, 65). Nonvoluntary, noncoerced dependency work is dependency work that is required by a socially recognized, morally decent practice or institution. Nonvoluntary, coerced dependency work is dependency work that is required by a socially recognized, morally pernicious practice or institution.

Like Bubeck, Kittay contends that the customs and traditions that enforce the sexual division of labor in the heterosexual family mark this institution as unjust (Kittay 1999, 98–99). Thus, the dependency relations formed within it are coercive, and since Kittay holds that coercive dependency relations do not give rise to binding obligations, it would appear that women are caring for countless young or ailing people who are not entitled to their ministrations (Kittay 1999, 59–61, 65, 71–72). As a sexist institution, the modern family lacks the moral authority to extract care from women.

Despite her critique of the sexual division of labor, Kittay does not conclude that women have a right to repudiate default dependency work. In her view, the logic of dependency work rules out this option. She repeatedly affirms that adequate dependency work involves affective bonds between dependency workers and their charges and also that dependents regard their dependency workers as irreplaceable (Kittay 1999, 31, 53, 94, 112, 186). Although she acknowledges that dependency workers need not internalize the interests of their charges, she emphasizes that many do, and that doing so constrains their freedom and ties their self-respect to successfully meeting their charges' needs (Kittay 1999, 37, 42, 53, 94, 96–97, 112). Most importantly, she insists that dependency workers are *obligated* to put the rights and needs of their charges ahead of their own interests (Kittay 1999, 51–52, 65, 91, 96–97, 186). Evidently, the moral potency of dependents' needs overrides the injustice of the sexual division of labor and its unfair allocation of dependency work to women.

Here, Kittay's argument converges to some extent with Bubeck's. Both hold that the harm that dependents would suffer should women refuse to do dependency work leaves them no morally tenable choice other than continuing to do this work.[8] But whereas Bubeck attributes the coerciveness of women's dependency obligations to the gendered enculturation that impels them to embrace the ethic of care, Kittay attributes the coerciveness of women's dependency obligations to the injustice of the institution that foists dependency work upon them. Thus, unlike Bubeck's account, Kittay's does not rest on the empirically indefensible claim that there is a universal feminine predilection for dependency work or a universal feminine commitment to the ethic of care.

Despite these differences, Bubeck and Kittay propose essentially the same solution for women's diminished autonomy regarding dependency work. Both adapt a proposal of Susan Moller Okin's to compensate dependency workers and extend their freedom (Okin 1989, 180–181). Bubeck advocates establishing a publicly organized and funded "caring service" modeled on mandatory, gender-neutral military service—that is, drafting and training young people to do dependency work for a limited period of time (Bubeck 1995, 259–260). Kittay advocates socializing and universalizing compensation for dependency work—that is, using public funds to pay all default dependency workers a fair wage (Kittay 1999, 142). Both Bubeck's care corps and Kittay's maternal welfare agency are designed to make relief dependency workers available to default dependency workers at no cost. Bubeck's scheme creates a pool of publicly paid dependency workers that default workers can freely draw on. Kittay's scheme furnishes default dependency workers with money that they can use to hire back-up dependency workers if they want. For Bubeck and Kittay, the availability of supplementary dependency services neutralizes the coerciveness of women's dependency work and secures their liberty.

I shall set aside some obvious objections to these proposals: Bubeck's compels young people to sacrifice their freedom for the sake of others' freedom; Kittay's is prohibitively expensive;[9] both are politically unrealistic. I shall confine my discussion to whether these proposals eliminate the coercion that maintains the sexual division of labor in the family and that unjustly constrains women's autonomy.

Kittay's welfare plan would augment women's autonomy within default dependency work by increasing their delegation options. Since default dependency workers could use their income to hire helpers, Kittay's proposal would allow women to pursue interests and projects apart from dependency work. Also, some women might use their income to conduct their dependency work more autonomously (e.g., by hiring professionals to provide expert advice or by paying for specialized services for their charges). Still, state disbursed compensation would not solve the problem of women's coerced entrance into dependency work and their tendency to become overcommitted to dependency work. Since making gendered dependency work less economically disadvantageous would not degender and redistribute default dependency work, paying dependency workers would have little, if any, effect on the sentimentalization of feminine care that Kittay rightly deplores.[10]

As long as default dependency work is privatized and the sexual division of labor governs the distribution of default dependency work, women's autonomy will remain in jeopardy. Let us suppose, as Kittay seems to, that family members are one another's default dependency workers. Let us also suppose that Kittay's compensation program is in place and that default dependency workers are receiving wages commensurate with the worth of their work and sufficient to enable them to hire relief workers. Now suppose that a dependency professional does not show up for her or his shift. The default dependency worker must fill in, for she is ultimately responsible for her charge. Providing women who do not want to be dependency workers with funds to hire willing substitutes is at best a partial solution, for they remain the default dependency workers—the care providers of last resort. Consequently, their careers will be at risk of foundering, and their projects will be at risk of languishing, while their partners will remain exempt from these perils. Indeed, women who now rely on paid dependency workers are all too familiar with this predicament and its disproportionately adverse impact on their autonomy.

Kittay's proposal purports to rectify the injustice of family-based dependency relations and to bestow a moral warrant on family-based dependency obligations (Kittay 1999, 64, 65, 70, 72, 181). But it sidesteps the coerciveness of the conventional family—that is, the discriminatory allocation of default dependency work to women. I agree that it is unjust that dependency work is undervalued and un(under)compensated and that paying fair wages to all dependency workers would right this wrong. However, if the sexual division of labor, which compels women, but not men to do this work, is neither derived from this devaluation nor a less serious injustice than this devaluation, Kittay's maternal welfare system will not give the heterosexual, nuclear family the moral warrant it presently lacks. This family structure will remain unjust, and the dependency relations formed within it will remain coercive.

I have already argued that the injustice of the sexual division of labor is not a consequence of the economic devaluation of dependency work. Fairly remunerating dependency workers would leave a disparity between the scope of women's autonomy and the scope of men's autonomy because this compensation would not abolish the sexual division of labor. I would deny, moreover, that coercion is a less serious injustice than economic inequity. In my view, it is a grave injustice that the members of one social group—namely, women—are arbitrarily singled out and automatically assigned to dependency duty. Many of these women do not want this responsibility, and many men are equally able to assume it. The fact that some women gladly embrace this responsibility does not vindicate the coercive context in which they choose. Paying those who are forced to do default dependency work does not cancel out the injustice of their being forced to do it. Perhaps Kittay would agree that the persistence of this coercion is an equally serious injustice, for although her welfare proposal would not degender care, she endorses men's participation in dependency work (Kittay 1999, 183, 185).

With respect to its impact on women's autonomy vis-à-vis dependency work, Bubeck's proposal is quite similar to Kittay's. Like the maternal welfare agency, the care corps expands women's delegation options. Also, both of these institutions guarantee equality of opportunity. Kittay's compensation plan would grant male and female dependency workers the same rights. If a man chose to be a default dependency worker, he would be paid at the same rate as a woman. Bubeck's care corps is also gender-blind. Both men and women are to be drafted. By publicly affirming men's obligation to do dependency work and women's right not to care full time, this service symbolically affirms the desirability of restructuring family responsibilities. In addition, paying dependency workers would symbolically remove dependency work from the category of natural female functions, for in capitalist economies, wages serve as incentives to perform tasks that people would not otherwise choose to do or that they would not do conscientiously enough. Both of these schemes implicitly license women as well as men to defy gender norms.

Bubeck and Kittay agree that someone must care for dependents and that women should not be stuck with all of this work. They disagree about how aggressively feminists should pursue gender equity in the distribution of default dependency work. Bubeck's proposal is more radical than Kittay's, for it directly confronts the gender asymmetry that renders women's default dependency work coercive. Whereas Kittay's scheme makes men's participation in dependency work voluntary and leaves women's participation nonvoluntary, Bubeck's makes participation nonvoluntary for young men and women alike.[11] Unfortunately, it is uncertain whether care conscripts would transfer their degendered experience in the care corps to their family arrangements later in life.

DEGENDERING DEFAULT DEPENDENCY WORK

With respect to the opportunities for autonomy that work can afford, I have argued that dependency work is not so different from other types of work that it does not belong in the same category. However, as we have seen, dependency work impairs autonomy in three troubling ways: (1) pronatalist gender norms funnel women into procreation and stigmatize childlessness; (2) discriminatory gender norms slot women into the sexual division of labor; and (3) the needs of dependents oblige women to continue caring for their charges, even at great personal sacrifice. In other words, gender norms deprive default dependency workers who are women, which is to say the vast majority of default dependency workers, of entrance options, allocation options, and exit options. It is no wonder, then, that dependency work and autonomy are widely thought to be uniquely incompatible.

If my argument in Section 1 is correct, though, this incompatibility is socially constructed and socially remediable. Bubeck's and Kittay's proposals enlarge women's allocation options in one respect. They entitle default dependency workers to delegate some of their tasks to hired dependency workers. I welcome ameliorative initiatives of this sort, for many women desperately need supplemental dependency services right now, and these services will remain indispensable to default dependency workers after this work has been defeminized. However, because such reforms do not give today's default dependency workers leverage to negotiate increases in their male partners' share of this labor, I doubt that they are sufficient to free women from coercion and safeguard their autonomy. Only reforms that promise to abolish the sexual division of labor can fundamentally transform women's allocation options and equalize women's and men's entrance and exit options.

In my view, the normalization of motherhood and the normalization of family-based dependency relations are the chief culprits in the suppression of women's autonomy through dependency work. The former makes the very idea of deciding whether or not to become a mother sound weird, which effectively discredits the claim that women should be authorized to autonomously choose whether or not to give birth to dependents (Meyers 2002, 47–50). The latter identifies the heterosexual, nuclear family as the only reliable source of competent and dedicated dependency workers.[12] Since the family is imagined as a network of lifelong bonds, exit options for default dependency workers are unimaginable. Since the conventional family is an inveterately sexist institution, the cultural designation of the family as the presumptive site of dependency work all but seals women's fate. Adding a biologized conception of dependency work to the sexist family invests the woman/vessel/nurturer equation with all the sublime incontrovertibility of an axiomatic truth. The symbolism of payment for dependency work or a nonsexist corps of young dependency workers seems rhetorically puny in comparison with the aphoristic ring of a recent intro student's common sense pronouncement: "You made it; you take care of it. Not a hard concept."

The feminization of default dependency work is encoded in endlessly circulating stories and attention grabbing imagery. There are television characters fretting about their ticking "biological clocks" and fairytales depicting unmarried, childless women as scary witches. The image of the Madonna displaying her baby remains a powerful reminder of women's maternal "destiny," and the metaphor of sonographically assisted mother-child bonding greases the slide from childbearing into childrearing. These representations together with others like them supply the narrative templates and motifs for the life histories parents tell their children—life histories that tutor children in the syntax and semantics of culturally appropriate self-narration. Through these ubiquitous representations of women's "natural" life course, contemporary culture mythologizes the family and reproduction so masterfully and evangelizes the population so successfully that the ascription of default dependency work to women is sacrosanct.

Only degendering and redistributing default dependency work—that is, granting women a full range of allocation options—can contravene women's "natural" responsibilities and ensure their autonomy. Alas, there is no single policy reform that could effect these changes. Still, because I discern several incipient social trends that are denormalizing the sexual division of labor, and because I am convinced that cultural ratification often follows on the heels of social experimentation, I am not without hope. I shall conclude by briefly describing some of the experiments that could help denormalize the feminization of dependency work and the heterosexual, nuclear family's status as the locus of care par excellence.

Many dependency relations, I have urged, come about as a result of voluntary actions. Yet, because coercive gender norms militate against autonomous choice, relatively few women feel they have genuine entrance options. Nevertheless, Kath Weston's studies show that many lesbian couples carefully and open-mindedly think through their decisions to become mothers and then face off with the assisted reproduction industry or the adoption agencies, where prejudice against lesbian parenting is rife (Weston 1991, 190–191). Plainly, these women are creating their own entrance options and demonstrating the feasibility of autonomously choosing to take on dependency work. Their example is auspicious. But if it is to be generalized, destigmatizing the happily childless woman and the childless, heterosexual couple is imperative.[13]

With respect to allocation options as well as entrance options, I see gay men who decide to become parents through adoption or by contracting with birth mothers as the vanguard of freely chosen (indeed, chosen against all odds), gender-bending parent-child dependency work. Unlike the all-too-familiar, male dependency dodger, these men seek out dependency work and embrace it as a masculine value. In addition, some employers are now striving not only to reshape the interface between unpaid, default dependency work and paid work outside the home but also to undercut the presumption that women are default dependency workers. When male senior managers set an example by taking paternity leave or by opting for flexible work schedules or telecommuting, other male employees get the message that there is no penalty for taking advantage of these programs. Such nonsexist workplace climates free men to be default dependency workers or to share default dependency work with a partner, and small, but increasing numbers of men are embracing these possibilities (Abelson 1999, 33; Ligos 2000, 1). By modeling the compatibility of masculinity and default dependency work, gay men who become parents and male workers who avail themselves of their employers' family-friendly policies erode the sexual division of labor.

Although I believe that default dependency workers' exit options are necessarily more inhibited than those of other workers, secure entrance options and equal allocation options would mitigate the severe restrictions that dependency work imposes on exit options. Nevertheless, it is worth considering how exit options might be made morally defensible. Exit options for default dependency workers seem farfetched because abandoning a dependent is such a grievous wrong, because legitimating these options would require debiologizing dependency relations far more than many of us can comprehend, and because the nuclear family is the paradigmatic site of valid dependency relations. However, collective families would give children not one or two, but multiple parents. If more people formed such families and nonconsanguineous kinship relations became accepted, children whose birth mothers left the collective would still have the benefits of intact dependency relationships and a stable home environment. Since this would cause no worse disruption of children's lives than divorce does now, it seems that the same sorts of reasons that justify divorce would justify exiting a collective family.

Bubeck and Kittay envisage programs that would rescue women from unremitting dependency work. Perhaps this burden is the worst affront to women's autonomy that the sexual division of labor inflicts. Still, their subsidy programs would only carve out respites from coerced dependency work. Just as battered women's shelters do not stop domestic violence, neither a care corps nor a maternal welfare agency would expunge the coerciveness of the sexual division of labor. Both leave women's autonomy under siege. However, if a dependency worker relief policy were implemented, and if the reforms in family structure that I have sketched were achieved, women would enjoy a maximal array of culturally condoned options vis-à-vis dependency work. Such an autonomy-friendly cultural climate would surely embolden many more women to chart their own courses regarding dependency work, for it would gradually transform these options into live options—options that are not merely officially available, but that are subjectively available as well.

If I am right that denormalizing the heterosexual, nuclear family and denormalizing the dependency relations situated in the heterosexual, nuclear family are vital to defeminizing dependency work, feminists have many allies in their struggle. This convergence of opposition to sexism and heterosexism is a lucky coincidence because I can think of no feminist objective that seems more out of reach. For this reason (and many others), making common cause with these other progressive movements ought to be a feminist priority. If their combined forces succeed in displacing the heterosexual, nuclear family, *maternal autonomy* will cease to be an oxymoron, and dependency work will be reconciled with autonomy in women's real lives.

NOTES

1. I adopt Eva Kittay's expressions "dependency work" and "dependency worker" both to emphasize that care-giving is socially necessary work and to distinguish caring for dependents who could not function on their own from the less critical forms of emotional labor women commonly do. Also, I shall focus my discussion on default dependency workers—those who are presumed to be ultimately responsible for the care of different sorts of dependents, who are generally expected to do most of the dependency work, and whose services are not compensated. I shall use various expressions to refer to paid dependency workers, including "dependency professionals," "dependency employees," and so forth.

2. Feminist skeptics about the compatibility of dependency work and autonomy are specifically dubious about women's freedom to refuse default dependency work, for gender normalization predisposes women to accept disproportionate dependency responsibilities. I take up this issue in Section 2.

3. I realize that in many parts of the world these conditions are not met, and I believe that contraception and abortion should be more accessible to American women than they now are. However, in regard to the first point, I hasten to point out that feminist philosophers who work on dependency issues generally address them from the standpoint of affluent societies that have the means to fund programs to solve these problems (Okin 1989; Bubeck 1995; Kittay 1999). In regard to the second point, I would emphasize that I am not claiming that childbearing is voluntary for all American women. It is beyond the scope of this chapter, though, to establish when the difficulties of obtaining contraception or abortion become so onerous that childbearing ceases to be voluntary.

4. Forgiving middle-class American attitudes toward parents who institutionalize children born with cognitive disabilities establishes a precedent for middle-class American attitudes toward partner disability and elder care. For a long time, cultural mores have absolved parents of cognitively disabled children of dependency obligations. Sometimes judgments about peer disability replicate this leniency. Often when a middle-aged partner is incapacitated, the healthy partner cannot afford to stop working. Presumably, no one would criticize such an individual, irrespective of gender, for declining to become a full-time dependency worker. I suspect, however, that gender shapes many people's views about cases involving elderly heterosexual partners. My conjecture is that an elderly woman who could care for her partner at home but who chooses to move him to a nursing home is more likely to be deemed remiss in her dependency work duties than an elderly man who is in the same position and who makes the same decision.

5. For a related discussion of obligations to come to the aid of the vulnerable, see Walker 1998, 78–95.

6. I am not endorsing this assessment of dependency work. But both the minimal entrance requirements and the low pay of dependency workers suggest that, despite feminist protests, most people continue to regard dependency work as unskilled and menial.

7. This conclusion is, I believe, at odds with the implications of Eva Kittay's claim that dependency workers are not self-originators of valid claims (Kittay 1999, 94–95). Since dependency workers are obligated to press claims on behalf of their charges, they are not *self*-determining agents. But if work that requires one to speak on behalf of others whose claims one does not personally endorse is incompatible with autonomy, criminal lawyers who defend serial rapists (presumably) are never autonomous. If Kittay replies that these attorneys voluntarily agree to do this work but dependency workers do not, I would point out that, as I have argued, people have much more choice about taking on dependency work than Kittay acknowledges.

8. I suspect that Kittay's views about the ethics of dependency work leave her without a principled way of solving what she calls the "coercion problem," for it appears that one can have binding obligations within an unjust institution.

9. Notice that if the pay scale for default dependency work determines what hired dependency workers earn, their vulnerability to secondary dependency will not decrease unless the default workers are paid quite lavishly and required to pay their workers at the same rate that the government pays them.

10. As Kittay points out, publicly financed dependency work would also reduce dependency workers' vulnerability to exploitation and domination (Kittay 1999, 42). By improving dependency workers' exit options from marriages and similar partner relationships and empowering women to leave abusive partners, this program would expand women's autonomy in their love and sexual relationships. Although this is unquestionably a worthy goal, it is important to be clear that achieving it would not expand women's autonomy—that is, their entrance, allocation, or exit options—vis-à-vis default dependency work unless women took to threatening to leave their partners and their charges as a bargaining chip in negotiations over dependency responsibilities. If Bubeck and Kittay are right about the ethics of dependency work, this would not be a morally acceptable scenario.

11. No doubt, Kittay would point out that she supports early gender-neutral education in dependency work skills and also that her scheme offers all those who are good at dependency work and who want to do it the opportunity to do it under fair conditions, whereas some of Bubeck's conscripts will not be well-suited to dependency responsibilities. I suppose, however, that Bubeck would counter that the conscripts will receive training and that those who prove temperamentally unfit to serve would receive care exemptions and be sent to the military, where they belong.

12. For trenchant criticism of this privatization of dependency work, see Bubeck (1995, 225–229, 231–235) and Walker (1998, 87–89).

13. For some suggestions about refiguring womanhood in ways that would affirm women's autonomy with respect to decisions about motherhood, see Meyers (2002, 56–57).

3

The Role of Recognition in the Formation of Self-Understanding

Misha Strauss

It is tempting to think that an individual's self-understanding is simply a matter of assertion, of looking into one's heart and declaring oneself to be that which one finds there. But this heroic vision that has proved so captivating is misleading and obscures the many ways in which the successful construction and sustaining of an individual's self-understanding depends upon external factors, in particular, upon recognition received from other persons. The idea that recognition from others is in some way crucial for each individual's own project of creating and sustaining a self-understanding resonates strongly with a number of philosophers. According to these philosophers, recognition from others supposedly makes it possible for a person to "communicate the way she experiences herself and the world" (Bartky 1990, 17), "gain enough semantic authority to rearticulate herself" (Tirrell 1993, 3), "negotiate it [her own identity] through dialogue . . . with others" (Taylor 1994, 34), "construct independent self-definitions" (Collins 2000, 101), and "be acknowledged publicly as what [she] already [is]" (Appiah 1994, 149).

Others express this claim negatively that nonrecognition or misrecognition can "erase or deform moral kinship among human beings" by causing some to view others as "diminished subjects, or as disqualified (or peculiarly qualified) agents" (Walker 1998, 179, 178). What follows is that "sound principles regarding respect for persons, calculations of interpersonal utility, and habits of virtuous conduct towards persons will not avail" (192). Charles Taylor similarly writes, "nonrecognition or misrecognition can inflict harm, can be a form of oppression, imprisoning someone in a false, distorted, and reduced mode of being" (Taylor 1994, 25). These claims suggest that the stakes are very high if this condition for successful self-understanding is missing or withheld; what is less clear, however, is how these two versions of the recognition claim are linked. In other words, how is the positive claim that recognition contributes to an individual's self-understanding and the negative claim that an absence of recognition leads to unjust treatment linked? After all, to return to the heroic vision, shouldn't the individual, in the face of opposition, be able to withstand the slings and arrows of a cruel and uncomprehending world? Whatever the other damage, shouldn't a person who is not "publicly acknowledged" as herself still be able to arrive at some degree of self-understanding, no matter how beleaguered this self-understanding is?

Despite the intuitive appeal of the heroic vision, I support the recognition claim and further believe that only when we acknowledge the recognition claim can we begin to address the serious harms that result from nonrecognition or misrecognition. The claim about recognition reveals an important kind of dependency individuals have on others when it comes to the formation of self-understanding. As difficult as it sometimes is to acknowledge ways in which individuals are dependent upon others, there is a far more considerable cost in ignoring the role of recognition. Ultimately, I believe that when we cling to the heroic vision, we lose the ability to explain and, hopefully, correct the harms that result when recognition is missing or withheld. In this chapter, I will sketch a map of the recognition claim in order to differentiate the three senses in which recognition is used, motivate an acceptance of the recognition claim by describing the harms that result from lack of recognition, and finally suggest that we can only acknowledge these harms if we accept a relational account of the self that is in direct conflict with the heroic vision.[1]

THE RECOGNITION CLAIM

Recognition implies that something—in this context, someone—has been perceived correctly. The correct perceiving of a person carries a commitment to treating that person in a certain way, a way, I will argue, that is critical to a person's self-understanding. The first step in understanding the recognition claim is to get clear on precisely what is meant by recognition. The use of the term varies widely both according to what is the object of recognition and according to the kind of judgment that is rendered when someone is recognized by another. When recognition is invoked it is used in a number of different ways, which I have classified under three categories: recognition of personhood, agency, and personality. Sometimes understood as a form of respect based on universal criteria of personhood, sometimes as an acknowledgment of an individual's agency, and sometimes as a validation of an individual's skills of perception, recognition acknowledges an obligation to accord the recognized a certain status as a bearer of certain entitlements.

When understood as a form of respect based on universal criteria of personhood, recognition is an acknowledgment that an individual possesses certain features in virtue of which the individual is entitled to a set of rights and entitlements commensurate with others who share those features. Those features that command respect present themselves in two distinct forms: (1) respect can be owed to individuals in virtue of certain universal characteristics that they instantiate, such as rationality, or (2) respect can be owed to individuals in virtue of characteristics particular to members of a group. Recognition of groups motivates the "politics of difference" that demands respect for previously derogated peoples and cultures. Note the internal tension generated within this form of recognition between universal standards of equality and multicultural variation along a spectrum standard of equality. The granting of political rights based on universal equality makes it difficult, for example, for the Quebecois to secure the right to promote the language of their community within the broader Canadian community (Taylor 1994).

When understood as an acknowledgment of an individual's agency, recognition is a matter of seeing an individual as a subject, rather than as an object, who lives according to norms of her own making. Feminist psychoanalyst Jessica Benjamin, for example, claims that recognition is important for its power to affirm an individual's "sense of effective agency" (Benjamin 1988, 21). As Benjamin writes,

> A person comes to feel that "I am the doer who does, I am the author of my acts," by being with another person who recognizes her acts, her feelings, her intentions, her existence, her independence. Recognition is the essential response, the constant companion of assertion. The subject declares, "I am, I do," and then waits for the response, "You are, you have done." Recognition is thus reflexive; it includes not only the other's confirming response, but also how we find ourselves in that response.

In this sense, recognition acknowledges the separateness of other persons who are selves like us. In developmental terms, the parent does not simply comprise part of the external world the infant inhabits, an object who satisfies the infant's needs, nor is the infant merely an extension of itself. The infant comes into awareness of herself as an agent by coming to see the parent as a distinct individual, as a separate locus of activity.[2]

When understood as a validation of an individual's skills of perception, recognition is a matter of accepting an individual as she projects herself. It involves an acceptance or confirmation of a person's interpretation of herself and her surrounding environment. When this judgment is missing and the person receives messages that do not confirm her own understanding of how things are, the person's ability to "know how to classify things"—including her "own motivations, character traits, and impulses"—can be compromised (Bartky 1990, 18). This is precisely what is thwarted in Paul Benson's "gaslighting" example (Benson 1994). In this sense, recognition is a mirroring process whereby others confirm an individual's outward projection of herself. When this mirroring does not occur, the extent to which one's actions will not communicate one's intentions can reverberate, causing one to question whether, for example, a woman's suggestion at a business meeting is ignored because the suggestion is "intrinsically unintelligent" or because its maker is a woman (Bartky 1990, 18).

HARMS OF EXCLUSION AND
HARMS OF DEMORALIZATION

To briefly summarize, recognition is variously described as a judgment of respect, of validation, or—minus the evaluative component—as a willingness to see the person as she presents herself to others. Having reviewed what recognition is, I turn now to the various harms that are thought to result from lack of recognition or from misrecognition. These harms fall into two categories: harms of exclusion and harms of demoralization. Harms of exclusion are those that result from damaging exclusionary practices, and harms of demoralization are those that result from the undermining of skills of self-assessment and construction.[3]

There are a variety of exclusionary practices committed toward those who fail to be recognized that are thought to damage the possibility of successfully constructing and sustaining a thoroughgoing self-understanding. One form of exclusion is exclusion from moral consideration. Equal treatment requires a prior judgment of equality. Since equal treatment is a hallmark of due moral consideration in our culture, Margaret Urban Walker, for example, worries that failures of recognition lead to diminished moral standing within one's community. To paraphrase Walker, the use of universally applicable or impartially applied moral principles requires a prior judgment about who meets the relevant criteria of similarity and is thus admitted to the realm of due consideration. This prior judgment depends on the recognition that persons meet the appropriate criteria. So, one consequence of failure to recognize certain significant attributes in others is those persons' exclusion from being owed moral consideration (Walker 1998, 179). Lack of due moral consideration can be extremely damaging; it "can lead to disregard, ridicule, abuse, exclusion, subordination, subjugation, exploitation, violence, oppression, enslavement, and more than occasionally, extermination" (177).

A second exclusionary practice occurs when lack of recognition leads to the absence of iconic images in popular culture. Iconic images are those that appear in film, in literature, on television, in editorial cartoons—in short, they are the images that form our cultural mythology. These images "provide what we might call scripts: narratives that people can use in shaping their life plans and in telling their life stories" (Appiah 1994, 160). According to bell hooks, because positive images of Black women, for example, are largely invisible in popular culture, Black women filmgoers lose the opportunity to identify with cultural myths, with iconic images that represent normal or proper ways of being. Opportunities for identification are lost: "the capacity of black women to construct [themselves] as subjects in daily life" is lost. Individuals do not invent themselves in a vacuum; rather they construct a self-understanding by helping themselves to already existing symbols and exemplars that surround them. When a certain person is invisible to her larger community, she will not figure into the "collective identities" that are floating around. This will leave her without examples that represent ways of understanding herself and her community. Hilde Nelson makes a similar point with regard to master narratives. According to Nelson, master narratives are the

> stories found lying about in our culture that serve as summaries of socially shared understandings. . . . [They] are often archetypal, consisting of stock plots and readily recognizable character types, and we use them not only to make sense of our experience . . . but also to justify what we do. . . . As the repositories of common norms, master narratives exercise a certain authority over our moral imaginations. (Nelson 2001, 8)

Master narratives are used to organize our perceptions of others and to shape our reactions to them. When a master narrative not only lacks iconic imagery for certain groups of people but, furthermore, portrays a group as having negative or diminished capacities, members of that group will be further constrained by the way that others treat them.

A third exclusionary practice that results from nonrecognition or misrecognition is the loss of opportunities for participation in and creation of shared meanings. The possibility "of defining oneself, one's group, one's world" is contingent upon having semantic authority, and to gain semantic authority, a person must have permission from others to participate in the shared conceptual space created, must be seen and treated by others as "a full and active agent" (Tirrell 1993, 25). An important aspect of hav-

ing semantic authority is having the authority to influence "social interpretations and practices" (13). Just as the slave cannot make herself free
by declaration alone, neither can any individual make some aspect of herself mean something particular by assertion alone. What it means to be a
woman, a good father, to be courageous or pious will depend on social
agreements concerning the meanings of those terms. When an individual
is excluded from the conceptual space in which meanings are agreed
upon, two harms result. The first, as Lynne Tirrell observes, is the harm
of being reduced to the status of an object, as inevitably occurs when an
individual lives according to definitions entirely of others' making. bell
hooks notes,

> As subjects, people have the right to define their own reality, establish their
> own identities, name their own histories. . . . As objects, one's reality is
> defined by others, one's identity is created by others, one's history named
> only in ways that define one's relationship to those who are subject. (hooks
> 1992, 71)

bell hooks is not suggesting that individuals can unilaterally define themselves; instead she is saying that they should be able to participate in constructing the language with which they define themselves. The second
harm is that the expressive possibilities available to the excluded individual are likely to be derogatory, hateful, or harmful in more invidious ways.
Patricia Hill Collins catalogues the "controlling images" of Black women—
as mammies, matriarchs, welfare queens, ladies, and hoochie mamas—
and persuasively argues that even seemingly benign or laudatory images
are nonetheless controlling in the way that they impose upon Black
women externally defined roles that reflect serious biases against Black
women (Collins 2000, 72–84). Even the "Black lady," "the middle class
professional [woman] . . . who stayed in school, worked hard, and
achieved much" is too assertive and takes jobs away from Black men (81).
What makes an image controlling is that it is externally defined and represents the interests of the defining group.

A fourth exclusionary practice that results from the absence of recognition is the "deprivation of opportunity" to "occup[y] roles or enter . . .
into relationships that are identity-constituting" (Nelson 2001, 27). When
a failure of recognition results in the invisibility of certain features of a
person, that person might fail to appear qualified to enter into identity-
constituting roles or relationships. For example, law professor Patricia
Williams writes of the barriers to homeownership for African Americans
who are considered by banks to represent a greater financial risk than
their white counterparts. This makes middle-class aspirations more
expensive for Blacks than whites (Williams 1997, 38–43).[4] In *The Good*

Mother, the protagonist's friend suggests that the mother lost custody of her child in part because she herself never challenged the prevailing perception that a "good mother" is not sexual and does not take lovers outside the confines of marriage. Deprivation of opportunity may also occur when certain features are recognized, but judged to be disqualifying. Thus, a Catholic woman who feels called by God may not become a priest; a lesbian may not become a wife; a gay man may not become a four-star general; a transsexual may most assuredly not become a four-star general.

In addition to harms of exclusion, there are also harms of demoralization. When recognition is missing or is distorted, an individual is likely (1) to lose confidence in her abilities to arrive at an understanding of herself, (2) to experience a loss of control over the activity of construction, and even (3) to relinquish the activity of construction to others. These three possible consequences are harms of demoralization in the sense that they refer to ways in which nonrecognition or misrecognition can undermine an individual so thoroughly that her abilities to construct a self-understanding are underdeveloped or seriously weakened.

One consequence of recognition being absent is that an individual's confidence in her knowledge of herself is likely to be undermined. The absence of recognition "confutes self-possession: a firm grasp on one's individual identity and confidence that one's comportment is self-expressive in ways reasonably under one's control" (Walker 1998, 190). It is important, therefore, to an individual's confidence in her skills of observation and self-assessment that her beliefs are confirmed by others as being accurate or justified.

Another concern is that the individual will take on too completely the perceptions of others to the point that they wholly replace the individual's own efforts at self-assessment and self-construction. When the absence of recognition results in loss of status, this not only leads to constricted choices and likely a punitive system of reinforcing responses, but also to self-doubt. Individuals who are systematically exposed to nonrecognition or misrecognition could come to believe that these failures of recognition by others are justified. This would lead these individuals to substitute the judgment of others for their own.[5] In these instances, it is not unlikely that the individual will embrace a self-understanding of someone else's making or to construct a distorted self-understanding that incorporates derogated beliefs about himself.

WHY WE SHOULD ACCEPT A SOCIAL AND INTERPERSONAL CONCEPTION OF SELF-UNDERSTANDING

The catalogue of harms described thus far may clarify the claim that recognition is necessary for self-understanding and provide a compelling reason to accept the claim, but it does not by itself constitute a defense of this claim. Granted, the familiarity of the phenomena associated with non-recognition or the seeming utility of this notion as a tool of social critique might predispose one to be persuaded by the claim; nonetheless, a detailed list is not yet a reason to reject the heroic vision and all that it presupposes about the self. The claim that without recognition persons cannot construct for themselves an adequate self-understanding seems implausible to the extent that persons seem capable of forming beliefs about themselves within a hostile or isolated environment; however, I do not believe that what is at stake is the mere ability to form beliefs about oneself. The heart of the tension between the heroic vision and the recognition claim is a conflict between two contradictory claims, both of which we have reason to endorse: on the one hand, we want to believe that people are resilient and ultimately responsible for themselves, which is strongly reinforced by the heroic vision; yet, the heroic vision cannot make sense of the harms that result from the loss of recognition, which makes it impossible to talk about or take corrective measures to alleviate the conditions that cause these harms. What is really at stake is a commitment to a particular view of the self. Seemingly, a contradiction is generated because the heroic vision presents an atomistic self, whereas the recognition claim presents themes of shared language and coparticipation in a community that are consistent with a relational self. I want to suggest that Amy Gutmann got it right when she said that this is a false dichotomy:

> The unique self-creating and creative conception of human beings is not to be confused with a picture of "atomistic" individuals creating their identities *de novo* and pursuing their ends independently of each other. Part of the uniqueness of individuals results from the ways in which they integrate, reflect upon, and modify their own cultural heritage and that of other people with whom they come into contact. . . . The dichotomy posed by some political theorists between atomistic and socially constructed individuals is therefore a false one." (Gutman 1994, 7)

The dichotomy is false because the relational self of the recognition claim can accommodate personal resilience. In order to see how the recognition claim is underpinned by a relational self view, consider how two different versions of the recognition claim draw a connection between recognition and self-understanding.

Charles Taylor, who understands recognition as a judgment of respect, develops a version of the recognition claim that is based on the idea that a person's identity is culturally mediated. He writes:

> the discourse of recognition has become familiar to us . . . in the intimate sphere, where we understand the formation of identity . . . as taking place in

a continuing dialogue and struggle with significant others. And then, in the public sphere, where a politics of equal recognition has come to play a bigger and bigger role. (Taylor 1994, 37)

What the person discovers to be defining of himself will be the commitments, values, and long-term projects that he endorses: "To know who I am is to know where I stand" (Taylor 1994, 37). In the intimate sphere, these discoveries can only be made in the context of one's relationships with significant others, and in the social sphere, acknowledgment of these endorsements determines what rights are granted to individuals. Taylor argues that recognition has always played a significant role in the formation of self-understanding; however, fundamental shifts in the way self-understanding is understood have created, for the first time, "conditions in which the attempt to be recognized can fail" (35). Rather than deriving one's self-understanding from one's social position (which dictated a person's values and commitments), one now has to work out—in dialogue with others—that which one takes to be self-defining.[6]

Within a culture of "authenticity," identities will be constructed according to individual needs and preferences; yet they must be constructed in intelligible ways that are open to recognition. This opens up the possibility that differences between individual needs and publicly intelligible ways of being might generate sufficiently significant tensions that threaten the possibility of recognition for certain individuals.[7] Recognition both affects the quality of the personal relationships within which individuals discover those values, commitments, and projects they take to be self-defining, and it affects the degree to which one's community will support those values, commitments, and projects. So, Taylor would argue that individuals can only discover which values, commitments, and projects they endorse for themselves in the context of social relationships: these relationships provide the "raw material" that individuals ultimately endorse or reject as self-defining, and they provide access to tools of assessment. Peculiar to Taylor's view is the influence he attaches to what society mirrors back to individuals.

On Lynne Tirrell's view, recognition matters to identity because it confers the "semantic authority" necessary to the construction of one's self-understanding. According to Tirrell, semantic authority is the power to articulate one's own experiences, "a matter of having a say (about something) that others recognize and respect; it is an important, perhaps necessary element in constructing oneself as fully human" (Tirrell 1993, 16). There is a twofold reason why semantic authority plays a crucial role in the formation of one's self-understanding: one, "the 'conceptual space' established within a community by its linguistic and nonlinguistic practices governs the expressive possibilities available to its members" (3) and

two, "we depend on our communities to give our articulations 'uptake.'
. . . The slave can say she's not a slave all she wants; simply saying doesn't
make it so. For the saying to carry any weight, it must be respected by
others" (15). Semantic authority signifies both that we have been given
access to our community's "conceptual space" and that our articulations
of our self-understanding have credibility within our community. Tirrell
considers this important because she sees the activity of forming one's
self-understanding in part as a "project . . . of normative metaphysics";
this means that it is impossible to articulate beliefs about oneself "without
simultaneously defining, describing, and re-creating our social and material world" (2). If the reason why the community is given such importance
in this context is that "the norms and kinds of relationships possible [in a
particular community] . . . are the infrastructure of the different ways of
life made possible therein," then it might seem that in order to make the
construction of one's self-understanding possible that recognition need
only involve admittance to a community (9). This is important; however,
Tirrell's notion of recognition goes further. It also involves the granting
of opportunities to influence and shape "the linguistic and nonlinguistic
practices" that "govern . . . [one's] expressive possibilities." Since it is
from these possibilities that one constructs one's self-understanding, recognition means that an individual will participate in creating the "stuff"
out of which he shapes his understanding of himself. On Tirrell's view,
recognition performs a third function; the credibility it grants means that
an individual's assertions about herself will be taken seriously and given
appropriate "uptake" by her community, even if the assertions are novel
or surprising. To summarize Tirrell's version of the recognition claim,
then, recognition contributes to the formation of self-understanding in
three ways: it gives the individual access to a community which provides
possible forms of expression through which the individual constitutes her
self-understanding; it gives the individual authority to influence the meanings of the possible forms of expression; and it gives the individual's particular expressions credibility within the community.[8]

Regardless of which version of the recognition claim that one accepts,
and there are others as well as the two described above, acceptance of any
version of the recognition claim requires an acceptance of a relational self
as opposed to a view of the self as atomistic. I have already suggested that
the dichotomy between the relational self and the atomistic self is a false
one to the extent that the relational self of the recognition claim is compatible with the distinctness and separateness of individuals. Relational
autonomy is an "umbrella term" that holds at its core "the conviction that
persons are socially embedded and that agents' identities are formed
within the context of social relationships and shaped by a complex of

intersecting social determinants, such as race, class, gender, and ethnicity" (Mackenzie and Stoljar 2000, 4).[9]

In contrast, the beliefs associated with the individualistic self and the heroic vision of constructing one's self-understanding reject the social embeddedness of the self, contending instead "that agents' sense of themselves is independent of the family and community relationships in which they participate . . . [and] that agents' essential properties (that is, their natures, or metaphysical identities) are all intrinsic and not comprised, even in part, by their social relations in which they stand" (Mackenzie and Stoljar 2000, 7). If one rejects the heroic vision and the associated conception of the self, one does not thereby give up a belief in the independence of persons or the concept of autonomy (8). Rather, one only gives up a particular conception of autonomy in which selves must be completely free from the taint of influence in order to be properly constituted. And that kind of individualism seems so unlikely and unattractive that it doesn't seem like such a hard price to pay to trade such an extreme individualism for the more modest individualism of the recognition claim.

It is on this alternate view of self-understanding that recognition matters. On this alternate view, recognition matters because it affects the quality of the resources available to the individual that go into forming self-understanding, as well as the conditions for making belief and behavior coherent. Individuals can only discover which values, commitments, and projects they endorse for themselves in the context of social relationships: these relationships provide the "raw material" that individuals ultimately endorse or reject as self-defining, and they provide access to tools of assessment. Recognition contributes to the formation of self-understanding in the three ways Tirrell identifies: it gives the individual access to a community, which provides possible forms of self-expression; it gives the individual authority to influence the meanings of the possible forms of expression; and it gives the individual's particular expressions credibility within the community.

The recognition account of self-understanding is also better equipped than the heroic vision of self-understanding to accommodate the claim that individuals are not fully transparent to themselves. In circumstances of trying to understand one's own role in a particular situation or deliberating over a course of action, members of a person's community can help a person to reflect upon who she is and who she wants to be. Members of one's community do important emotional work that, as Hilde Nelson reminds us, both contributes to the construction of one's self-understanding and provides opportunities for transformation of one's self-understanding. Emotional work is "the work of managing another's feelings" (Nelson 2001, 14). It "names the management of *others'* emotions— soothing tempers, boosting confidence, fueling pride, preventing frictions, and mending egos" (Calhoun 1987, 118). In circumstances of trying to understand one's own role in a particular situation or deliberating over a course of action, members of a person's community can help a person to reflect upon who she is and who she wants to be. This is a critical activity because any individual's skills of observation and assessment are fallible and because persons are not always transparent to themselves. As Nelson writes, "[others] serve as a check on the deliberator's self-understanding by providing new interpretations of her interactions with others. . . . They help her to know her own thoughts" (Nelson 2001, 14–15). The naive undergraduate who has experienced harassment but does not "know how to accept the legitimacy of her anger" benefits from a friend who can "enabl[e] her to feel what, intellectually, she knows to be true" (Calhoun 1987, 120). This transformation is possible through the skilled ministrations of a friend who can help the undergraduate experience herself as someone who is entitled to anger in this circumstance. In this way, others contribute important assistance to individuals in helping to appropriately interpret situations and to accurately locate themselves in those situations. The quality of assistance individuals receive from others will depend on their being recognized by others—and being admitted to a community in which recognition is extended to its members. In the absence of recognition, individuals are likely to receive inappropriate management of their feelings from others or be deprived of assistance altogether.

But let me now turn to two suggestions that, despite the harms of misrecognition or nonrecognition, are ways in which individuals can construct a self-understanding in the absence of recognition. First, it might be said that the recognition claim overstates the power of a dominant meaning-giving group to withhold recognition. Even though the dominant culture creates conditions for nonrecognition or misrecognition, individuals can still seek out smaller subcommunities in which they can experience the benefits of recognition. Therefore, since individuals will be able to seek out the resources necessary to construct their sense of themselves, the perceived cost of the heroic vision is negligible and the harms identified by the recognition claim are overstated. My response to this objection is twofold: one, the objection actually reinforces the importance of recognition. Consider a woman in a small midwestern town who has sexual feelings for other women. As a member of her community, she knows only that her feelings are shameful, possibly sinful. She will find it very difficult to integrate these disparate elements of herself. But say she finds an alternative community in which she is able to associate with persons whom she respects and who also help her to see her feelings for other women positively. In this way, she receives from this group the kind of recognition that contributes in important and healthy ways to the construction and sustainment of her identity. However, this scenario requires the explanatory apparatus that the recognition claim provides. And two, even if our lesbian finds the benefits of a smaller community, she must still contend with the broader community in which she lives. The potential harms caused by lack of recognition from the broader community will still have the capacity to inflict damage, and therefore, the social critique argument for acknowledging the recognition claim remains.

Second, it might also be said that nonrecognition or misrecognition can contribute positively to the construction of self-identity insofar as conditions of resistance create a critical eye. As bell hooks writes, "The extent to which black women feel devalued, objectified, dehumanized in this society determines the scope and texture of looking relations. Those black women whose identities were constructed in resistance, by practices that oppose the dominant order, were most inclined to develop the oppositional gaze" (hooks 1992, 127). Despite the virtue of taking up a critical stance toward one's own community, even hooks would agree that there are less costly ways of achieving such virtues of character. Otherwise, we run the risk that we will "romanticize oppression by celebrating the character traits it breeds" (Scheman 1997, 126). I would also add that virtues born of adversity ought to be a matter of misfortune rather than injustice.

In this chapter, I have shown that recognition is a judgment that when conferred entitles the recognized person to certain treatment. When such acknowledgment is missing or withheld, certain harms arise: harms of exclusion and harms of demoralization. As I describe above, four harms of exclusion are: loss of moral consideration, loss of positive public images, loss of opportunities to shape shared meanings, and loss of opportunities for identity-constituting relationships. Harms of demoralization are: loss of confidence, loss of self-definition, and loss of judgment. These harms undermine an individual's ability to form a self-understanding because they prevent the development of or seriously weaken the skills of construction necessary for the cultivation of one's self-understanding. These harms have the further effect of constricting the availability of necessary resources.

Against the romantic appeal of the heroic vision, which prizes the ability of the rugged individual to single-handedly construct his own identity, I have argued that the construction of a person's self-understanding is inescapably embedded in social practice insofar as it relies on a shared language and a coparticipant attitude within a community. Recognition from others is necessary to the activity of constructing self-understanding because it confers semantic authority, grants access to the public space in which meaning is negotiated, and offers credibility. When a person loses these resources through lack of recognition, the damage done to the person's ability to construct a self-understanding exacts too high a price to believe that recognition plays anything but a critical role in the development of a person's identity—a role that should be acknowledged by any satisfactory account of identity.

NOTES

I am especially grateful to Susan Stark for being a patient listener and helpful critic during the writing of this chapter and to Hilde Nelson and Maggie Little for their careful reading of early drafts.

1. I do not mean to imply that loss of recognition is the only way that identities can be damaged. I am simply isolating a particular harm in order to better understand what constitutes a loss of recognition and the notion of the self that presupposes this form of damage.

2. P. F. Strawson can be seen as making a similar point in that the participant attitude is a recognition that one is a member of the moral community; the objective attitude withholds this recognition. Thanks to Hilde Nelson for suggesting this connection. At some point, I would like to explore the connections between this notion of recognition and the literature on Kantian respect. Kant might be surprised that his central notion of respect for the ability to set ends possessed by ourselves and others is critical to proper infant development and helps sustain our identity in adulthood.

3. These harms parallel the scheme that Hilde Nelson uses. She divides the harms of misrecognition into deprivation of opportunity and infiltrated consciousness.

4. See also Douglas S. Massey and Nancy A. Denton, *American Apartheid: Segregation and the Making of the Underclass* (Cambridge: Harvard University Press, 1993).

5. At its extreme this can lead to the phenomenon of "gaslighting" described by Paul Benson (1994). In this article, Benson describes a woman who "arrives at her sense of incompetence and estrangement from her conduct on the basis of reasons that are accepted by a scientific establishment which is socially validated and which she trusts" (Benson 1994, 656).

6. Historically, "the background that explained what people recognized as important to themselves was to a great extent determined by their place in society, and whatever roles or activities attached to this position" (Taylor 1994, 31). That view has been replaced by an ideal of authenticity, which gives great importance to the idea of "an *individualized* identity, one that is particular to me, and that I discover in myself" (28). It is up to me to be true to myself and to live my life according to what I find to be important: "Being true to myself means being true to my own originality, which is something only I can articulate and discover. In articulating it, I am defining myself. I am realizing a potentiality that is properly my own" (31).

7. There is a very interesting literature surrounding the "dilemma of difference" that explores the tension between universalist notions of equality and the inequalities that result from failures to recognize salient differences. See Martha

Minow, *Making All the Difference: Inclusion, Exclusion, and American Law* (Ithaca: Cornell University Press, 1990).

8. I recently came across Paul Benson's "Self-Worth and the Social Character of Responsibility" and was intrigued by the overlap between Tirrell's account of what recognition contributes to a person's self-understanding and Benson's account of the relational aspects that make individual responsibility possible. Benson lists three criteria: that an individual be regarded by others as someone who can be held accountable for her actions; that the norms "that regulate both moral appraisal of an agent's actions and the account of her conduct that she might give in response" be publicly shareable; and that the individual enjoys a position as participant in the moral dialogue of her community (Benson 2000, 81–83). Only when these criteria are met can attributions of moral responsibility be appropriately made. I believe that there is a potentially very interesting connection to be made between self-understanding and attributions of moral responsibility; however, I save that for another time. What I do want to call particular attention to here are the themes of shared language and coparticipation in a community that are thought to contribute to very individualistic aspects of a person such as responsibility or self-understanding.

9. Falling under this umbrella term is a rather broad range of claims about the social dependence of the self. Linda Barclay helpfully classifies these views as endorsements of a socially determined self, motivationally social self, and a constitutively social self. Within each of these, there are weaker and stronger versions (Barclay 2000). If I had to hazard a guess, the version of the recognition claim that can accommodate personal resilience and render visible the harms to identity caused by the absence of recognition would be associated with a weak version of a constitutively social self-view. According to this view, "even the most autonomous person's identity is always mediated to some extent by community" (Barclay 2000, 64).

4

Can There Be a Queer Politics of Recognition?

Cressida J. Heyes

The notion of "recognition" is a familiar one in contemporary political philosophy, most common in talk of multiculturalism and democratic accommodation of cultural diversity. The suggestion—given different inflections by philosophers such as Charles Taylor, Axel Honneth, and Iris Young—is that recognition discourse may help to reveal the political significance of damages caused by assimilation, cultural imperialism, systemic disrespect, or the stigmatization of nondominant identities. The politics of recognition emerges from a complex tangle of Hegelian, psychoanalytic, and existential inheritances, within which diverse models of subjectivity are at work. These traditions share, however, a belief that human flourishing, together with successful participation in community, depends on certain modes of intersubjectivity that embody acknowledgment of the Other, the attribution of value and mutual indebtedness to that Other, and shared respect. Our encounters with Others on the interpersonal, metaphorical, and public levels can be normatively evaluated by virtue of their success in cultivating these modes of intersubjectivity.

This chapter starts from the assumption that "misrecognition" describes forms of oppression that those with radical liberatory politics, including feminists, should struggle against. Nonetheless, I identify a number of difficulties with the language of recognition as it relates to politicized identities in general, and sexual identities in particular. Both through their intellectual history and in contemporary politics, demands for recognition have close links to understandings of subjects as having an

53

authentic or essential identity. But if feminist critiques of authenticity and essentialism are correct (e.g., Butler 1999; Heyes 2000), then the objects of recognition—the stable and enduring identities we might (re)claim as our own—are themselves politically suspect fictions. Whether "identity" is a concept we reluctantly deploy or enthusiastically embrace, I've argued elsewhere that the identities we acquire as women or lesbians, for example, are always works-in-progress rather than essential and static (Heyes 2000, 2003). Thus the central question of this chapter is whether a broadly "queer" (i.e., deconstructive, poststructural, historically embedded) sexual self can coherently demand to be recognized, or whether the tension between the account of identity inherited by a politics of recognition and antiessentialist impulses in feminist philosophy of sexuality is irresolvable. I suggest that a return to the intellectual roots of the politics of recognition in dialogical accounts of subject formation may provide an answer.

RECOGNITION AND SUBJECTIVITY

While all recognition theorists emphasize the importance of *intersubjectivity*, thus signaling a departure from atomistic understandings of the individual, it is by no means clear what exactly the object of recognition is or should be. Charles Taylor suggests:

> The demand for recognition is given urgency by the supposed links between recognition and identity, where this latter term designates something like a person's understanding of who they are, of their fundamental defining characteristics as a human being. The thesis is that our identity is partly shaped by recognition or its absence, often by the *mis*recognition of others, and so a person or group of people can suffer real damage, real distortion, if the people or society around them mirror back to them a confining or demeaning or contemptible picture of themselves. Nonrecognition or misrecognition can inflict harm, can be a form of oppression, imprisoning someone in a false, distorted, and reduced mode of being. (1994, 25)

Here Taylor links recognition to *identity*, and later in the essay to *authenticity*. Each of these terms merits lengthy analysis, but their imbrication in Taylor's germinal account already indicates that "recognition" may depend on controversial understandings of political subjects, perhaps especially when those subjects are being characterized as members of distinct social groups. Is the object worthy of recognition an essence? A capacity? Inwardly authentic or outwardly constructed? Particular to a group or universally shared?

Taylor is imagining conflicts within multicultural societies, but he might equally be describing a major preoccupation of feminist identity politics. Many feminist philosophers have used the language of recognition to convey the familiar claim that the negative representations "mirrored back" to women by patriarchal societies constitute real harms. And recent queer politics has often insisted on the importance of recognition of sexual difference as a part of liberation struggles. As Sonia Kruks points out, however, there's something historically and philosophically odd about the appropriation of a politics of recognition by a "politics of difference":

> What makes identity politics a significant departure from earlier, pre-identarian forms of the politics of recognition is its demand for recognition on the basis of the very grounds on which recognition has previously been denied: it is *qua* women, *qua* blacks, *qua* lesbians that groups demand recognition. . . . The demand is not for inclusion within the fold of "universal humankind," on the basis of shared human attributes; nor is it for respect "in spite of" one's differences. Rather, what is demanded is respect for oneself *as* different. (2001, 85)

These demands make sense in the context of the "degrading images" that continue to suggest what Anthony Appiah calls "negative life-scripts" for members of marginalized groups. As he says, "in order to construct a life with dignity, it seems natural to take the collective identity and construct positive life-scripts instead":

> [B]eing a Negro is recoded as being Black, and this requires, among other things, refusing to assimilate to white norms of speech and behavior. And if one is to be Black in a society that is racist then one has to deal constantly with assaults on one's dignity. In this context, insisting on the right to live a dignified life will not be enough. It will not even be enough to require being treated with equal dignity despite being Black, for that will require a concession that being Black counts naturally or to some degree against one's dignity. And so one will end up asking to be respected *as a Black.* (Appiah 1994, 161)

The problem with this philosophical move, as Appiah is quick to point out, is the risk of overgeneralizing the identity in question and attributing to it a new kind of essence that comes to represent its own tyranny. Affirming a way of being Black that is fully deserving of respect may mean exhorting members of Black communities to conform to an alternative "liberatory" ideal, often one that appeals to a previously suppressed history or to ways of life before or extra-oppression. Indeed, this is the kind of conflict we see being played out between U.S. proponents of Afrocentrism and their critics (Asante 1998; Mills 1998).

This chapter is part of a larger project, where in the context of queer theory I try to outline what recognition actually amounts to, what is politically valuable about demands for recognition, what such demands require, and to what extent a politics of recognition entails commitments to specific accounts of sexual subjectivity.[1] The admonitions of feminist theorists such as Nancy Fraser (1997) and Rosemary Hennessy (2000, esp. 111–142) that an excessive focus on cultural visibility may elide the material aspects of sex oppression are well taken; it is hard for any feminist to deny, however, that having one's identity qua member of a social group assimilated into another, stigmatized, misrepresented, or stereotyped are deeply significant political problems (ironically, even if one is skeptical about the very notion of "identity"). Misrecognition is painful, confusing, and can undermine self-esteem and one's sense of oneself as a politically engaged member of a community. I was drawn to the theoretical literature on recognition because it develops theories that predict exactly this kind of response on the part of subjects who are the victims of non- or misrecognition. Not being recognized is not the only form of oppression, but few would contest that it is real, consequential, and worthy of political attention. It works to exclude and marginalize individuals because of their social group membership in ways that have serious consequences for democratic community, political participation, and social justice.

For example, in her article "Passing for Black, Passing for White," Adrian Piper describes the failures of recognition that occur for her as a middle-class light-skinned African American moving in milieus segregated in complex ways by race and class. Her opening anecdote describes her experience at the new graduate student reception at her prestigious alma mater, where she nervously approaches the "eminent and honorable faculty, with names I knew from books I'd studied intensely and heard discussed with awe and reverence by my undergraduate teachers." "The most famous and highly respected member of the faculty observed me for awhile from a distance and then came forward. Without introduction or preamble he said to me with a triumphant smirk, 'Miss Piper, you're about as black as I am.'" For Piper, this moment of misrecognition (the erasure of her life experience as an African American, the assumption that she was more privileged than she had let on, the accusation of having lied about her identity) caused her to feel "numb . . . shocked and terrified, disoriented. . . . Later those feelings turned into wrenching grief and anger. . . . Finally, there was the groundless shame of the inadvertent imposter" (Piper 1996, 234–235).

We can imagine similar events in queer lives. I once attended a family wedding with my girlfriend of the time (a self-identified lesbian) where her father loudly announced, as the two of us came through the post-ceremony congratulatory line-up, "well, here's the only one I haven't married off yet!" His refusal to recognize her sexual identity and its complicated relationship to her feminist politics (she wasn't ever going to get *married*) was a moment of exquisite pain and rage. Conversely, queer writing is replete with anecdotes of the not-so-casual glance in the street between gay or lesbian strangers, the moment of recognition suffused with trepidation, desire, or amusement.

Thus in this chapter I assume that recognition—in the sense of being taken in account, acknowledged, and respected as the person one believes oneself to be—is desirable, and that failures of recognition are both damaging for individuals and politically consequential for relations among social groups. The demand for recognition is thus also necessarily an ethical demand, resisting the vilification of marginalized groups as unjustifiably damaging to their members' self-conceptions. This resistance must take place within a normative framework, where recognition is a comparative term (contrasting with that which will *not* be granted recognition). Otherwise the politics of difference would be indifferent with regard to the identities it endorsed—yet queer theorists obviously have good arguments against recognizing (in this ethical sense) neo-nazis or homophobic fundamentalists. Thus for me the politics of recognition worth considering emerges from a normative feminist framework.

RECOGNITION AND "GAY-IDENTITY POLITICS"

There is a distinctive affinity between what I'll call (following Nancy Fraser) "gay-identity politics," talk of recognition, and an account of subjectivity that relies on a *metaphysics of substance*—a humanist view of subjects that tends "to assume a substantive person who is the bearer of various essential and nonessential attributes" (Butler 1999, 14). Thus feminist critiques of this metaphysics and of identity politics in general seem, by implication, to preclude our endorsement of recognition talk. Let me give an example of these linkages and their positive connotations, since, at first pass, a politics of recognition seems to have a great deal to offer gay and lesbian theory. Recognition is explicitly linked to visibility, disclosure, and self-esteem—all key themes in gay politics. Much of the discourse around being closeted, coming out, being outed, or "pride" requires an understanding of the self as an object that has been invisible, and is now unveiled, for better or worse, in its authentic state. As Richard Mohr puts it in his discussion of outing—which he considered in 1992 to be "*the* problem in gay ethics" (showing perhaps how far this literature has moved in the past ten years)—outing "is making publicly acknowledged what most lesbians and gay men wish to be kept secret—their identity, what they are, possibly who they are." And later:

When I tell someone that someone else who does not want to be known as
a homosexual is a homosexual, I convey a secret. That which is hidden is
revealed. Metaphorically, I open the person's closet door to another, who
sees the person inside as homosexual. (Mohr 1992, 30, 11, 15)

Mohr's argument is centered around his rejection of privacy rights in
the context of outing, and he draws on the claim that working to stay closeted damages the self and limits possibilities for authenticity: "The life as
lie chiefly entails a devolution of the person as person, as moral agent.
The whiteness of the individual lies might be forgiven as self-defense, but
the dirtiness of the secret that the lies maintain cannot be. The dirt is the
loss of self, of personhood, the loss of that which makes human life peculiarly worth protecting to begin with." The alternative to this self-hatred is
"living in the truth"—openly acknowledging one's sexual orientation and
that of others (Mohr 1992, 32, 37).

This textual example could be bolstered by many others that take a similar tack: arguing (or assuming) that sexual identity is revelatory, and that
"gay ethics" should be deeply concerned with the extent to which individuals are non–self-deceiving or resist opportunities to "pass." Let me be
clear that I find much of value in this language, and I'm certainly not suggesting that self-deception is a good thing, or that refusing to pass cannot
constitute a courageous and politically useful form of resistance. I am
drawn to the language of recognition precisely because I believe that one
of the most destructive forces in heteronormative culture is the invisibility
of queer life. Visibility is not the only political good in my queer politics,
nor is it an unproblematic concept (see Oliver 2001, esp. 147–168), but it
certainly plays a significant role. However, Mohr's politics is definitively
located in a metaphysics of substance.[2] As Judith Butler argues, this view
must presume an interiority to the subject that represents, to echo Taylor,
"a person's understanding of who they are . . . their fundamental defining
characteristics as a human being." This discourse leads Mohr in familiar
ways into an account of the self as an authentic entity, which in "coming
out" reveals itself to the world and ensures its integrity. Thus recognition
talk, for proponents of gay-identity politics, has a philosophical affinity
with a particular account of subjectivity.

This affinity appears in more subtle form in Nancy Fraser's work, as an
attempt to separate off recognition as a remedy for "cultural" injustice
rather than structural (especially economic) oppression. Her analytic
approach works to associate a politics of recognition with a peculiarly
static and ossified account of political identity. For example, in "From
Redistribution to Recognition? Dilemmas of Justice in a 'Post-socialist'
Age," Fraser identifies two types of political demand in contemporary
Western democracies: on the one hand, demands for redistribution

understand the injustice done to a particular group of citizens as primarily economic, and the concomitant solution as "political-economic restructuring of some sort" (Fraser 1997, 15). The political paradigm underlying such demands, she argues, is distinctively different from claims based on a recognition model, where the injustice consists of "cultural" constructions of identity that the people to whom they are attributed want to reject: "The remedy for cultural injustice . . . is some sort of cultural or symbolic change" (15). These paradigms have contrasting understandings of group identity: "When we deal with collectivities that approach the ideal type of the exploited working class, we face distributive injustices requiring redistributive remedies. . . . The logic of the remedy is to put the group out of business as a group," whereas "when we deal with collectivities that approach the ideal type of the despised sexuality . . . we face injustices of misrecognition requiring remedies of recognition. . . . [The logic of the remedy] is to valorize the group's 'groupness' by recognizing its specificity" (19).

Fraser acknowledges that in practice a politics of redistribution often coexists and overlaps with a politics of recognition; however, in making her case she selects two examples of group-based politics that come closest to the ideal type in each case. Her example of a social collectivity that most neatly fits the redistribution model of justice is "the Marxian conception of the exploited class"; her example of a social collectivity that provokes claims to justice based on recognition is "a despised sexuality" (18). For Fraser, "gay and lesbian" demands for recognition are cultural claims par excellence, requiring an acknowledgment of the distinctive alterity of a defined minority group rather than an economic remedy:

> [Homosexuals'] mode of collectivity is that of a despised sexuality, rooted in the cultural-valuational structure of society. From this perspective, the injustice they suffer is quintessentially a matter of recognition. Gays and lesbians suffer from heterosexism: the authoritative construction of norms that privilege heterosexuality. Along with this goes homophobia: the cultural devaluation of homosexuality. Their sexuality thus disparaged, homosexuals are subject to shaming, harassment, discrimination, and violence, while being denied legal rights and equal protections—all fundamentally denials of recognition. (18)

Fraser's approach has been extensively criticized by those who see her characterization of the politics of sexuality as reducing heteronormativity to a "merely cultural" phenomenon, when in fact it is deeply imbricated with material and economic structures in ways that resist the false dichotomizing of recognition and redistribution (see e.g., Blum 1998; Butler 1997; Tully 2000; Young 1997). To achieve recognition for queers requires economic transformation as well as shifts in attitude. In my example above, the virtues of marrying off one's adult children operate at many levels: the psychological aspects of expecting sexual conformity are the more obviously "cultural," yet these are reinforced by expectations of economic success and bourgeois respectability (it is not a coincidence that my ex-girlfriend is considerably less financially secure than her married siblings, which in turn reinforces her marginality). As Judith Butler says:

> This is not simply a question of certain people suffering a lack of cultural recognition by others, but, rather, is a specific mode of sexual production and exchange that works to maintain the stability of gender, the heterosexuality of desire, and the naturalization of the family. (Butler 1997, 6)

I want to offer a related critique of Fraser's approach. Another consequence of dichotomizing recognition and redistribution and taking sexual politics to be the epitome of the former is that sexual selves tend to become reified, detached from the material processes that give them meaning. What needs to be recognized, on Fraser's analysis, is "a despised sexuality," "gay and lesbian sexual specificity" (Fraser 1997, 19). But unless this specificity is understood as materially produced, it tends to be understood as provoking an arbitrary cultural intolerance toward essentially different selves. This rendering not only skews and underestimates homophobia's imbrication with economic structures, but also tends to further marginalize any understanding of sexual selves as located in *processes*—especially of production, and not only economic but also historical and cultural.

In its ossifying of sexual subjects, Fraser's argument neglects to explore the limits of its own philosophical tradition: the politics of recognition has key origins, as I highlighted at the beginning of the chapter, in understandings of the self as having its own inner authenticity. While a politics of difference may set up tensions in this understanding, forcing us to ask whether the essential self we seek to be true to is the same kind of self as other members of our despised group or embodies some universal human quality (reason, or the capacity for moral reflection, perhaps), the appropriation of a politics of recognition by marginalized groups clearly draws on a history of authenticity. More critical awareness of this intellectual history causes other aspects of Fraser's argument to look profoundly contradictory.

For example, she offers a philosophically inconsistent reconciliation of her politics of recognition with the "transformative" remedies she prefers. Specifically, Fraser attempts to map redistribution and recognition to two alternative remedial strategies—affirmation and transformation. The former consists of "remedies aimed at correcting inequitable outcomes of social arrangements without disturbing the underlying framework that generates them"; the latter, of "remedies aimed at correcting inequitable outcomes precisely by restructuring the underlying generative framework" (Fraser 1997, 23). Affirmation in sexual politics is represented by "gay-identity politics," which seeks to "revalue gay and lesbian identity," while transformation is epitomized by "queer politics," which would "deconstruct the homo-hetero dichotomy" (24). The former strategy looks much like Mohr's gay ethics; the latter strategy, however, appears to diverge significantly from the very idea of recognition, and it is not clear how the two can coherently be combined (as Fraser's four-celled matrix mapping redistribution and recognition to affirmation and transformation suggests they can). For Fraser, recognition combines with transformative strategies to produce "deconstruction"—a "deep restructuring of relations of recognition" that "destabilizes group differentiation" (27).

If this is the strategy, however, it seems odd even to suggest any affinity with "recognition" as it is understood in identity politics. Put simply, how can one both *deconstruct* the meaning of particular identities while simultaneously *recognizing* them? If, as Fraser says, deconstruction requires "that all people be weaned from their attachment to current cultural constructions of their interests and identities" (31), then what could it have to do with recognition? Is the queer politics of recognition Fraser implicitly describes oxymoronic? Must recognition in fact be associated exclusively with gay-identity politics of the kind Mohr defends? Making sense of these questions is the central project of this chapter: how can we theorize the experiences of disrespect and the understanding of intersubjectivity so valuable in the literature on recognition, while acknowledging that the selves worthy of recognition are works-in-progress, liable to the deconstructive critique familiar from so-called queer theory?

THE LIMITS OF RECOGNITION

Attempts to describe a politics of recognition that goes beyond "gay-identity politics" seem troubled by deep tensions between opposing philosophical paradigms. Recognition, identity, and authenticity—along with the metaphysics of substance the trio imply—are interconnected and mutually reinforcing. Further, in their dominant presentation they are undergirded by demands that an *essentially different sexual self* be the object of recognition, again a contested and contingent premise, but one, as I've shown, embedded in the arguments of both Fraser and Mohr. The metaphysics of substance implied by positing an identifiable and distinctively different homosexual self has been extensively deconstructed and criticized in queer theory.

In particular, Foucauldian critics of the view of subjectivity it implies argue that the authenticity this sexed subject claims is in fact a product of the very juridical discourse that seeks to repress (or defend) it. Genealogical critique reveals the way norms of intelligibility are imposed on gendered and sexualized subjects, establishing conditions of possibility for them to claim identities as their own. Thus the very idea of "having" a "sexual orientation" may be the product of certain historical sexological discourses that congeal in the contemporary individual (Butler 1999; Foucault 1980a, 1980b). This position has been amply developed in the literature, and I won't attempt to present or defend it here. Whatever the particular history, genealogy, or constructionist argument invoked, many theorists of sexuality will object to a politics of recognition if this politics entails too casual reification of subjects that are historical artifacts (while some defenders of recognition via gay-identity politics will be suspicious of the self-reflexivity and contingency implied by genealogical critique).

Furthermore, a politics of recognition looks especially problematic—both metaphysically and politically—in light of the proliferation of "new" sex-gender identities such as transsexuality, transgender, intersexuality, and bisexuality. To the extent that the defining characteristics and practices of each of these identities have a history, of course, most aren't new at all. However, a number of theorists of sexuality have suggested that it is only during the late nineteenth and twentieth centuries that any of these labels began to be sedimented into "identities"; in this sense their provenance is relatively recent, and their genealogy and scope still actively contested (e.g., Hausman 1995; Dreger 1998). Philosophical moves between recognition, identity, and authenticity seem especially jumbled and fragile in these instances, not least because here the *legitimacy* of professed identities—and not only their accommodation—is clearly in question. Demands for recognition are harder to parse than in contexts where the oppressed identity is more firmly established, likely to be viewed as natural or essential to the self, or indisputably authentic. An emerging dynamic in queer politics, of which I am extremely wary, is to take this observation as grounds for excluding bisexual, transgendered, or intersexed persons from feminist and/or gay-lesbian space. These persons are somehow, critics suggest, less "real" or authentic—frauds, fakes, hypocrites or *poseurs*—and therefore unworthy of recognition on our own terms.

Thus the imbrication of identity, authenticity, and recognition leads all too easily to a quest for a unified phenomenon (whether a part of the body or the psyche), persisting through time, which can be identified as the sexual truth about an individual. I've been articulating phylogenetic critiques of this view, but there are also ontogenetic objections. Phenomenologically speaking, many people find it hard to accommodate their experience of themselves to a coherent identity of the kind required by dominant understandings of sexuality. Others are clearly drawn to the metaphysics of substance precisely because it neatly explains their own experience, but, as Eve Kosofsky Sedgwick points out, there are good reasons for working with a theory of sexuality that acknowledges that people are different from each other (Sedgwick 1990, 22–27); any metanarrative of sexual identity will work to discipline and exclude those who do not fit. Thus I think it is a tremendous mistake to see Foucauldian-inspired queer theory as entirely antithetical to lived experience when so many transgendered, intersexed, or bisexual narratives are rendered unintelligible by the very terms of gay-identity politics that are supposed to liberate us all.

THE ETHICS OF THE SELF AS A WORK-IN-PROGRESS

Everything in the preceding section suggests that in contemporary political philosophy recognition is linked to a kind of identity politics via a notion of authenticity that renders a queer politics of recognition oxymoronic. Yet, as my earlier examples showed, the experience of misrecognition—of being reduced or stereotyped or forced to pass—remains ethically significant. Proponents of gay-identity politics are liable to respond to my critique by suggesting that neither historicizing sexual identities nor highlighting the discourses that give them meaning is likely to erase these contemporary ethical questions, and I think they would be right. In conclusion, I want to briefly suggest that we can retain the notion of (mis)recognition that explains important justice claims without adopting wholesale the notion of a static, essential, or authentic self. We can do this by returning to a neglected strand in the intellectual history of the politics of recognition—instead of invoking its allegiance with the language of authenticity, we should recall its investment in dialogicality.

Many political theorists seem to have forgotten the intersubjective roots of recognition discourse, talking about recognizing alterity as if the Other were not always negotiating its identity. In its Hegelian and psychoanalytic origins, I would argue, recognition is always necessarily a dialogical process, in which the self recognizes and is in turn recognized by the Other, creating a mutually sustained dynamic (a fight to the death for orthodox Hegelians, or a less overtly conflictual interaction for others). The identity of the self being recognized is never independent of its relationship with the Other who recognizes or fails to recognize, nor does it find a definitive closure at any particular moment in its development. Rather, recognition is an ongoing component of a narrative process; thus, identities are always already formed and consolidated in relationships (Nelson 2001).

Psychoanalytic models give a keen sense of how this occurs in relationships between specific subjects. For example, according to Jessica Benjamin's account of human psychological development, a relationship of recognition in which the mother mirrors back to the infant his own emerging subjecthood, *and is in turn recognized* as a separate subject requiring accommodation in the play of the relationship is crucial to healthy psychological development. The infant whose every whim is met with capitulation will be recognized—in a truncated sense—but will not find the resistance to his will that defines his own subjecthood; on the other hand, the overly strict mother who constantly imposes her own desires onto her infant will risk crushing the fragile possibility of emotional independence.[3] Drawing on her clinical practice as a psychoanalyst, Benjamin describes in more detail than I can hope to capture the delicate balance of this negotiation, which to allow a successful balancing of separation and unity in this key relationship requires mutual recognition. "Domination and submission result from a breakdown of the necessary tension between self-assertion and mutual recognition that allows self and other to meet as sovereign equals" (Benjamin 1995, 12). Alienation from the Other is a psychopathology no less than incorporation (although for many object-relations theorists the former is distinctively masculine, while the latter is typically feminine).[4]

This model has application at the level of social groups, too. In the example at the beginning of this chapter we can see that there is a form of domination in a relationship that allows a white professor to assert his own racist misinterpretation of another's racial identity—to incorporate her into his own vision—while her opportunity for self-assertion or negotiation of that reading is severely curtailed. Understanding failures of recognition thus requires analysis of both the micro and macro operations of power that corrupt the possibilities for reciprocal relationships at both the intersubjective and social group levels (where these are mutually implicated). The conflation of the politics of recognition with identity politics that I've been tracing in this chapter is in many ways a travesty of the Hegelian and psychoanalytic traditions that inform recognition talk. Gender and sexuality, I am suggesting in ways I can't fully defend in this short space, are aspects of the self that can only be understood relationally, as always shifting and emerging features of "identity" that require the intersubjective reinforcement or challenge of others. Remembering this aspect of recognition, too easily forgotten by a politics that relies on a metaphysics of substance, helps recognition inform performativity theory, for example, in ways that have barely begun to be explored. There is a particular significance to this emphasis on intersubjectivity for sexuality: whatever sexual characteristics any individual may consolidate into an identity at any particular moment are always a developmentally achieved state; almost no one thinks, for example, that children have predispositional sexualities that will find definitive expression *entirely* independent and autonomous of their social context. Our ongoing sexual interactions and identifications are themselves what shape our so-called sexual identities, rather than merely expressing something that was always already there.

Therefore the next step, philosophically, is to stop thinking that recognition requires a static object: a self that has found its *telos* or achieved a permanent closure. With other feminist philosophers, I recommend a process metaphysics that understands identities as always in flux, involved in processes of becoming (e.g., Hacking 1986; Tuana 1995). We should be able to recognize others not only for *who they are*, but also for *what they do*. The least appealing aspect of demands for recognition is that they tend to assume that the object of recognition is both fixed and outside the ethical realm. What *is* ethical, on this view, is our intersubjective negotiation of these fixed objects, thus perpetuating an atomistic ontology of subjects who are not significantly formed by their necessary interaction. Of course, demands for change leveled by dominant group members at oppressed minorities ("you could stop being gay if you really tried") are often offensive, and many political strategies aim to short-circuit these interventions by insisting that such change is a priori impossible. However, feminists cannot afford to put the self outside the realm of criticism if we are to make sense of consciousness-raising and other forms of self-transformation that we expect of others and ourselves.

The most interesting ethico-political conflicts arise when we examine the possibilities for remaking ourselves. To adjudicate the ethical dilemmas raised by efforts at (and demands for) self-transformation will require a different way of thinking about recognition. It is not that we need to broaden the range of objects we think can be recognized (to include "bisexuals" as well as "gays and lesbians" for example), although that might be a useful intermediate position. Rather we need to broaden the language of recognition to include acknowledgment of our capacities and successes with regard to techniques of the self: "matrices of practical reason" that "permit individuals to effect by their own means, or with the help of others, a certain number of operations on their own bodies and souls, thoughts, conduct, and way of being, so as to transform themselves in order to attain a certain state of happiness, purity, wisdom, perfection, or immortality" (Foucault 1997, 225). Instead of recognizing an essentially different self we need to recognize an ethical attitude. This has significant implications for identity politics and concomitant notions of community—in particular in challenging approaches to political solidarity that appeal to experience as a ground for sameness.

CONCLUSION

In this chapter I have tried to show how contemporary political appropriations of demands for recognition have become allied with a view of the
self as static, essential, and authentic. This alliance makes any rapproche-
ment between the various understandings of sexuality labeled "queer theory" and the politics of recognition initially look unlikely. However, by
returning to the intellectual roots of recognition discourse we can see that
identity is generated through intersubjective negotiation, and that our
normative efforts are better directed to adjudicating a process within
which both subjects are ongoingly defined than to ruling on the legitimacy
of some identities over others. Thus incidents of recognition and misrecognition do define an ethical field, but one that raises very different questions from those of gay-identity politics. There can be a queer politics of
recognition, but we do not yet know what it would be like.

NOTES

1. For another piece of this project, see Heyes (2003).
2. That this is Mohr's intention is made even clearer by his dismissals of Butler's
position on closely related issues such as the materiality of the body and the
"social construction of sexuality" (not a phrase she would endorse, although
Mohr describes her as a social constructionist) (Mohr 1992, 142–145, 221–242).
3. I've used gender-specific pronouns here deliberately. In this literature the
archetypal relationship is between a male infant and the woman who mothers
him; part of Benjamin's feminist critique is, of course, that we need to see mothers
(who are usually, but not by definition, women) as subjects in their own right,
who cannot achieve the desired personhood for their children by being "selfless";
nor should boys be forced to separate psychologically (become masculine) in ways
that will cause alienation from the dialectic of recognition that characterizes all
human relationships.
4. For this reason, failures of recognition on the interpersonal level may be
experienced as particularly psychically wounding by women in this culture. I take
it that this observation connects to the work of feminist psychologists influenced
by object-relations psychoanalysis, who try to show how disconnection from the
"webs of relationship" that characterize human existence are pathological in distinctively gendered ways. See Heyes (1997) for a discussion of Gilligan.

5

Anorexia Nervosa and Our Unreasonable Perceptions

Kate Parsons

Approximately eight million people in the United States suffer from anorexia nervosa and 90 to 95 percent of them are female.[1] Between one and three out of every one hundred persons between the ages of ten and twenty purposefully starves herself, inducing health problems that range from permanent loss of bone mass, to severe kidney or liver damage and cardiac arrest. Recovery rates are disturbingly low: even among those undergoing treatment only about 60 percent of sufferers fully recover, and the remaining 40 percent only partially recover or do not improve at all. Among those who receive no treatment, 20 percent eventually die from malnourishment, assigning anorexia nervosa the highest mortality rate of any psychiatric disorder. A recent study by the Mayo Clinic reports that anorexia has been increasing by 36 percent every five years since the 1950s.[2]

It has been suggested that anorexia nervosa stems, in part, from a perceptual problem, and it is this alleged problem that I wish to explore in this chapter. I will ultimately defend a perceptual model of the anorectic's problem, but hope to shift the burden for this problematic perception away from the individual perceiver. I aim to challenge the assumption that anorexia stems from the anorectic's own perceptual failings, and to argue that responsibility for the development of the disorder extends onto the society in which she lives. To evaluate the anorectic's perception I will suggest three definitions of the term "reasonable" as it may apply to a perception. The *first* sense of "reasonable" is a subjective sense; it means that a perception is simply "reasonable to the perceiver." Reasonable here refers to the fact that the perceiver believes there are substantial reasons for her to see things as she does; the person who finds the perception reasonable is the perceiver her- or himself. The *second* I derive from the legal debates over the "reasonable person" standard; it requires that persons other than the perceiver would say that it is reasonable for the perceiver to have that perception. The "reasonable person" standard, as described by Martha Minow and Todd Rakoff, is a "standard that does not depend upon the subjective beliefs . . . of particular individuals" (1998, 40). This standard aims at a kind of objectivity, distinct from a "subjective perception" in that, as evaluators of the perception we recognize that *any other person in the same circumstances would see things in the same way* that the agent in question does. Objective is defined in contrast with the subjective here, but it does not suggest a criterion independent of all agents' beliefs.[3]

The *third* sense of reasonable I take from Allan Gibbard's definition of "rational" in *Wise Choices, Apt Feelings* (1990). The term reasonable may be substituted for rational without distortion of Gibbard's account, since Gibbard uses rational in an evaluative sense, as judging something rational. For Gibbard to call something rational means "to endorse it in some way" particularly to endorse it by "express[ing] one's acceptance of norms that permit it" (1990, 6–7). He classifies his definition as noncognitivist and "expressivistic" to indicate that when a person calls something "rational" that person is not articulating a proposition about the perception (which could be true or false), but is expressing his or her state of mind with regard to the perception. This will be the manner in which one might call a perception reasonable in the *third* sense—expressing one's acceptance and endorsement of those norms that permit it.

Ultimately I intend to show that we ought to judge the anorectic's perception as reasonable in the *second* sense and unreasonable in the *third* sense. Before we can properly say that the anorectic's perception is unreasonable in the *third* sense, however, it will be necessary to move through the first and second senses of reasonable described above.

To the general public—typically educated about anorexia nervosa only through popular media—anorectics suffer a perceptual failure: they see themselves as overweight when they are not, in fact, overweight. It is often suggested that the anorectic's inability to perceive correctly leads her to the bizarre conclusion that she must starve herself, that her distorted perception is responsible for the protrusion of her ribs, and for the soft, fuzzy hair that grows on her body to compensate for the absence of insulating fat. Magazines and television news programs emphasize the visual aspect of the issue; images of the anorectic portray thin young girls facing funhouse mirrors—ones that reflect a rounded, bulging body instead of the slight figure that is actually there. With no obvious answer to the question "Why can't she see that she's not fat?" most view her as having lost touch with reality; her distorted perception prevents her from seeing the truth of her circumstances.

Yet numerous independent research studies have been conducted on the visual perception skills of anorectics, and, perhaps surprisingly, these yield no clear evidence that there is anything uniquely wrong with an anorectic's visual perception skills. In fact, many researchers claim that anorectics do not visually overestimate the size of their bodies any more than control groups. We simply lack consistent indicators that anorexia stems from visual overestimation of the physical body.[4] Perhaps this is why so many television and magazine reports fail to support the "funhouse mirror" images with scientific evidence for the distortion; they tend to elaborate instead on factors that dispose a person toward eating disorders, such as low self-esteem or perfectionism, childhood trauma, and family dysfunction. While there is little reason to doubt the link established between these factors and a person's disposal toward anorexia, or to doubt the extent to which dealing with these may greatly aid in recovery, there is reason to continue exploration of the perceptual component and not to overlook its relevance to the disorder.

Focusing on the anorectic's self-worth, place in the family's dynamics, or history of trauma often entails exploring how she sees herself in terms of her more immediate relationships. This should not take the place of investigating how the anorectic sees herself in terms of the larger society in which she lives, however. Consider the approach captured in Steven Levenkron's novel *The Best Little Girl in the World* (1978), a fictional account of an anorectic, based on the research conducted in Levenkron's own practice. In the book the therapist, Sandy Sherman, counsels anorexic "Kessa" that the root of her problem lies not in what she sees but what is "in her head." He counsels: "I know your fear of gaining weight is real, or rather, I know you're really afraid of gaining weight, but that fear is coming from someplace else in your head. It's a question of reality, Kessa" (135).

Sherman explains to Kessa that although her fear is real to her, in terms of her experience of it, it has no basis in reality, since she is not actually fat, nor was she ever. Although the "fat" she sees on her body feels or seems real, it is in fact contrived in her mind as a manifestation of, and coping mechanism for, some deep-rooted problems within her family. On the therapist's approach Kessa's perception can only be deemed reasonable in the *first* sense I indicated above—it is reasonable to her, period. The counselor might be understood as saying that while it may seem reasonable *to* her, it is not reasonable *for* her to have such a perception.[5] Her manner of seeing is not traceable to anything that is actually there in the data before her, since her body is not in fact fat. Her manner of seeing becomes not really a perception at all, but a mere projection of what is "in her head" onto her body.

Feminist sociologists, psychologists, and philosophers have become rightly wary of attempts to locate women's problems "in the head," and the same suspicion should extend to the notion that anorexia is explicable as a projection rather than a perception. Taking my lead from Denise Russell's *Women, Madness and Medicine* (1995) and Susan Bordo's *Unbearable Weight* (1993), as works that argue for the relevance of social context in understanding psychiatric disorders, I want to turn to considering the position that anorexia is a group-based problem.[6] On a group-based model, anorexia is not merely the problem of certain troubled individuals, nor is it merely the problem of dysfunctional families; it is a larger social problem affecting women as a group, particularly those in modern, affluent societies. In making this shift I will not abandon the notion that anorexia is explicable in terms of perception; I will modify it. Anorexia can still be understood as a perceptual problem, but one of a different sort than that targeted by perceptual dysfunction researchers.

Consider the claim made by Susan Bordo in her book *Unbearable Weight* (1993): "The anorexic does not 'misperceive' her body; rather, she has learned all too well the dominant cultural standards of *how* to perceive" (57). Bordo's claim is that anorectics perceive their bodies in terms of the beauty and success standards (and the normative implications of these standards) enforced in their society. On this view, anorectics perceive themselves (and their bodies)[7] in terms of the norms that our society encourages; her actual size and weight are seen in terms of the size and weight she *ought* to be. What most informs her perception are social attitudes toward slenderness. Recognizing the normative importance of fitting into the category "thin," identifying the message that she is special and more appreciated when complying with the norms, the anorectic sees herself in the terms: "I am special if I am thin" (60).

Thinness is something that girls and women learn to desire early on (because it is deemed so desirable) and learn that their bodies will have a good deal to do with the extent to which they are viewed favorably by others. Their perceptions of their own bodies are heavily tied to their consciousness of how others might view them. Susie Orbach notes that "women are encouraged to see their bodies from the outside, as if they were commodities. Feminine perception is informed by a devastatingly fierce, visual acuity turned in on itself. It operates almost as a third eye" (1986, 36).

This "feminine perception," however, is not unique to anorectics. Widespread dissatisfaction with our bodies, the fear of "excess" weight and weight gain, and the prevalence of varying degrees of struggles with dieting are lamentably high and spreading to younger and younger sufferers. Bordo notes that young girls, as young as seven or eight, are beginning to diet and exercise rigorously. They have already adopted the fear of "gaining weight" and its equivalence to "losing attractiveness." These girls "jog daily, know how to count their calories obsessively, and risk vitamin deficiencies and delayed reproductive maturation" (1993, 61). The fact that this fear of weight gain is so prevalent has led Bordo and Orbach to suggest that we can establish a link between the general messages all women take in with regard to their bodies, to the specific way in which anorectics take in this message. Orbach claims that all women in our culture are to varying degrees vulnerable to being dissatisfied with their bodies and to the development of eating disorders. She writes that "while anorexia and other eating and body-image problems do not affect all women, there is a continuity in all women's experiences that makes them vulnerable to such problems" (48).

This vulnerability characterizes "the contemporary situation of women" (Bordo 1993, 47). Women are encouraged to buy countless products aimed at improving their bodies (to remove "unsightly" wrinkles, "embarrassing" cellulite, "unwanted" hair, "excess" flab), and spend innumerable hours worrying about the size and constitution of their meals and their exercise schedules. Anorectics may find themselves extremely vulnerable to such worries, representing the extreme end of a continuum upon which all women can be located.

The claim that anorectics are extremely vulnerable to these worries might be interpreted as a criticism of the anorectic's inability to assert sufficient agency in the face of social pressures. While Morag MacSween (1995) agrees with Bordo and Orbach that the pressure to be thin is real and experienced by almost all women, she worries that to represent the anorectic as extremely vulnerable accords her inadequate agency. MacSween prefers to say that the anorectic represents an extreme *transformation* of patriarchal pressures, rather than an extreme vulnerability to them.[8] She accords substantial explanatory power to the anorectic's typical claim that her refusal to eat is not about being thin, it is about control and power. Anorectics often cite food intake as the one thing they can control in their lives, and their refusal to eat as evidence of their independence and strength.

Yet the disagreement between MacSween's account and Bordo's and Orbach's—over whether the anorectic is better conceived as more vulnerable or more transformative than other women—is relatively insignificant compared to the point on which these theorists agree. They concur in their arguments that the anorectic's behavior is a response to the pressure of being a girl/woman. The difference between their accounts rests only on how to characterize the anorectic's response; Bordo and Orbach confirm that control and power are important goals of the anorectic, and Mac-Sween does not contend that the anorectic thereby gains the control she seeks, or that her transformative move is to be celebrated. All three theorists claim that the tragedy of the anorectic's circumstance is that she experiences such lack of control and power in the first place. The irony of the minor tension between these accounts, however, is that it has become the theoretical justification for promoting anorexic behavior among the more sophisticated Web sites and chat rooms that conceive of themselves as "pro-anorexia."[9]

The "pro-ana" sites and chat rooms provide a forum for anorectics to share tips, relate success stories, and provide support for their members. Though all are highly disturbing, as a group they are rather repetitive in their lists of foods with low calories, "inspirational" pictures of fashion models, diaries, and journals. One of the more sophisticated sites, however, lauds the anorectic particularly for her agency, decrying the claim that anorexia has anything to do with her vulnerability. Consider the passage that comes under the heading "Philosophy: There Are No Victims Here":

> Volitional, proactive anorexia is not a disease or a disorder. . . . It is a lifestyle choice that begins and ends with a particular faculty human beings seem in drastically short supply of today: the will. . . . In our victim-mentality saturated times, we seem to have forgotten the basic meaning of that classic statement by Eleanor Roosevelt, "No one can make you feel inferior without your consent." Likewise, no one and nothing can rule over you without your consent either.[10]

While feminists will likely shudder at the appeal to Eleanor Roosevelt, consider the author's twist on the notion of the oppressor. The anorectic struggles against a "society" of those who tell her she is ill, of those who might try to make her eat and thereby make her feel inferior.[11] The power of the culture that praises thinness is not oppressive; those who force food upon her are the oppressors, making the anorectic into a committed activist. This image of the "pro-ana" liberator (the "pro" refers not merely to advocacy but to the "proactive" anorectic) is to be contrasted with the "victim," the ED-anorectic (eating disordered anorectic):

> The ED-anorexic, or ED-anorectic, is one who perceives herself to be suffering from an affliction that causes compulsive thoughts and behaviors to which she must succumb or suffer. . . .

> Note carefully my use of the word "perceive." . . . because of our human tendency to place ourselves in denial of culpability, our willingness to believe ourselves subject to external controls rather than internal ones . . . we often

perceive ourselves as acting upon something other than the execution of our own volition. This phenomenon has been joked about with the phrase, "the devil made me do it!" Thus we can perceive ourselves to be subject to something other than our own choices, when strictly speaking, in reality, since we live inside ourselves and only our brains work our bodies, it is patently impossible for anything other than ourselves to be in control of ourselves. . . .

This flaw in our perception can be trained out, however. . . . There is no denying that circumstances, surroundings, emotional tides, desires, urges, conflicts, threats, ultimatums, and anticipated consequences and repercussion can and do influence our decisions. However these, in themselves, have no power to actually *make* those decisions for us.[12]

The tragedy of the message of this site is that followers are guided to their own demise, "liberated" only from the sustenance that allows them to exercise their will at all. The irony of the argument is that, like Bordo, Orbach, and MacSween, it recognizes an oppressive force against which the anorectic must struggle (the parallel is in structure, of course, not in content). The site's author characterizes the anorectic as one who must go against the norms of "society" and overcome pressures that are pervasive and go beyond one's immediate social group or family. This author even indicates that the anorectic's problem is perceptual, and her perception of herself must grapple unavoidably with the way in which others characterize her. In none of these accounts can the anorectic see herself apart from the way in which others see her.

I hope to have provided compelling evidence at this point that the category "thin" and its normative importance influence the self-perceptions of women in general—anorectics and others. The strength of this influence upon one's manner of seeing the self in terms of the norm that prescribes thinness, however, may vary depending upon the specific contexts and specific personality traits of the perceiver. The majority of those who develop anorexia nervosa live in affluent conditions, primarily in Western nations,[13] and are predominantly white—though anorexia should no longer be understood as a "rich, white girls' disorder."[14] Those who work in environments where attention to thinness is heavily emphasized (such as models, ice skaters, gymnasts, dancers); those who live with others who encourage thinness; those of a certain age group where attention to the body is heightened (teenagers, college students); those who have suffered through trauma, may be more susceptible to the development of anorexia to the extent that they live in an environment that pressures conformity with the cultural standard of thinness.[15]

On the accounts offered by Bordo, Orbach, and MacSween, we begin to see the mistake of locating the perceptual problems concerning the anorectic as problems "in the head"; to perceive in terms of the normative emphasis placed on thinness is to perceive in a manner significantly shaped by the conditions of one's social world. Indications of the importance of thinness are to be found nearly everywhere, from "suggestive" messages in the media to articulate reinforcements of its importance in various literatures and social groups. We live in an environment where images of thinness are paired with beauty and success standards on everything from billboards to cereal boxes. The message is pervasive, reinforced constantly, forming the living environment Sharlene Hesse-Biber (1996) calls "the cult of thinness." To perceive one's body in terms of the normative importance of thinness then is not to merely project a manner of seeing that comes from "inside the head." Seeing in such terms indicates that we see data outside of the head, that we take in data from the circumstances in which we live. Characterizing the anorectic's worries as a type of distortion, flight, or evasion of reality underestimates the power of that reality, and the extent to which her reality is that of women as a group.[16]

Where then does this take us in terms of evaluating the anorectic's perception as "reasonable" in the second sense? Reasonable in this second sense entails the recognition that any other person in the same circumstances would see things in the same manner as the agent in question. So what "circumstances" ought to count here? If we regard one of the relevant circumstances as the circumstance of being a woman, we are able to account for the fact that this disorder so disproportionably afflicts women over men, and for the fact that a clear majority of women in the United States are dissatisfied with their bodies and diet and/or exercise in order to be thinner. The desire to be thin is "normal" for women in the United States in both a normative and descriptive sense. While studies claiming that most women are dissatisfied with their bodies are published regularly (and ironically) in fashion magazines, ordinary language makes this point just as compellingly. In *People* magazine's special report, "A Body to Die For,"[17] Richard Jerome describes anorectic Merrick Ryan, a sufferer who "killed herself." He notes the turning point in the development of Ryan's disorder: "But at some point she was no longer the *normal* girl longing for a new figure. She grew psychologically obsessed with her weight and trapped in the self-loathing and despair of anorexia" [my emphasis]. Whether or not Jerome thinks the line between the "normal" and the "obsessed" is obvious, the fault here lies not merely in the unsubstantiated distinction, but in the way that "normal" is left unproblematized. In her autobiographical fiction, *Stick Figure: A Diary of My Former Self* (2000), Lori Gottlieb chronicles the development of her own anorexia nervosa through the observations of an astute eleven-year-old:

> Then Dr. Katz said to go to his office so we could talk about my "situation."
> "What situation?" I asked. I mean, everyone else is watching what they eat,

and *they're* not being sent to the pediatrician because of it. Dr. Katz didn't answer though. (82)

The line between "disordered" eating and "normal" eating is no doubt fuzzy, but skeptics may insist that we establish the line to account for the fact that most women would not qualify as "anorectics." Bordo and Orbach note that in response to their works, many theorists and physicians have posed the concern that, if we accept that the circumstances of the anorexic woman extend to those of nearly all women in our society, we end up diluting the seriousness of the illnesses of anorexia, explaining away more specific causal links to the development of the disorder.[18] After all, the majority of women in our society do not develop anorexia. There must be something significantly different about those who develop the illness, and our concentration should not be on what makes us all the same, but on what makes anorexic sufferers *different*.

Yet the claim that the circumstances of our social world make all women vulnerable (to varying degrees) to developing this eating disorder is not precluded by the fact that most women do not develop this eating disorder. Bordo responds that it is quite unlikely that we will find any direct causal links in the development of this disease (as we are unable to find in the development of many diseases). And although it can certainly be granted that the condition of being a woman in our society is not a sufficient cause for the development of anorexia, nor even a necessary cause for its development (since a small number of men have developed eating disorders—male dancers, jockeys, wrestlers, for example), this does not negate the relevance of gender and gendered social pressures. Given that the overwhelming majority of anorectics are women, and that those few men who do develop the disorders live in contexts in which they are subject to many of the same pressures of being a woman—where weight-management is more crucial to social and career successes, for example—we can certainly surmise that these pressures *dispose* women to the development of eating disorders more so than men.

To demand that a factor like gender be constitutive of the development of the disorder (rather than simply a contributing factor to it) in order to consider its causal relevance is to take a disturbingly narrow approach to the disorder. It is based, says Bordo, on a "misunderstanding (or misrepresentation) of the feminist position as involving the positing of an *identical* cultural situation for all *women* rather than the description of ideological and institutional parameters governing the construction of *gender* in our culture" (1993, 61). In fact there may even be reason to be suspicious of the demand for proof that gender constitutes the development of anorexia; Bordo likens the demand for such proof to those made by the tobacco industry. She writes:

Certainly, genetic and other factors will play a role in determining an *individual's* level of vulnerability to the disease. But when tobacco companies try to deny that smoking is the preeminent source of lung cancer among smokers *as a group*, diverting attention by pointing to all the other factors that may have entered in particular cases, we are likely to see this as a willful obfuscation in the service of their professional interests. (53)

While we need not conclude from this analogy that gender-skeptics are intentionally diverting our attention from the issue of gender, we should at the very least remain wary of their explanatory demands. The fact that "not all" subjects who smoke develop the disease certainly does not preclude their disposal toward it. In fact, as a society we are beginning to recognize social pressures as contributory to the development of smoking-related illness, without seeing these pressures as the only factor causing disease. As the recent proliferation of lawsuits would suggest, we are also less willing to tolerate the view that the smoker is one who forms her desire to smoke independently of her culture—the desire is developed partly on the basis of its being represented as "cool." The addictiveness of cigarettes is not precluded in this change in attitude; we are simply recognizing, and becoming less tolerant of, media images and role models that suggest that smoking is desirable. This change in public attitude indicates that we are certainly capable of recognizing the social dimension of the construction of desires, particularly the desire to engage in behavior hazardous to our health. Similarly, the desire for thinness is not a desire developed independently of culture but a desire based in the norms and pressures of our society. In fact, there is good reason to think that the pressure to be thin is stronger than that to smoke—in the words of eleven-year-old Gottlieb, "if you *don't* worry about being thin, everyone thinks you're a complete weirdo" (2000, 193).[19]

So let us return to considering whether the anorectic's perception can be called "reasonable" in the second sense. Reasonable in the second sense means that as evaluators of this perception, we recognize that any other person in the same circumstances would see things in the same way that the agent in question does. So far I have concentrated on the relevance of gender to how the anorectic perceives. In addition, consider the lack of a clear distinction between anorexic perceivers and control groups mentioned earlier (Van Deusen 1993; Dolan and Gitzinger 1994), and the experience shared between anorectics and "normal" women of feeling the overwhelming presence of thin-promoting imagery and the consequent desire to be thin (from Bordo and Orbach, to *People* magazine and Gottlieb's diary). To that add risk factors listed earlier, from the complicated intersections of class and race, to factors such as "weigh-ins" at gymnastics lessons every day, or living with a parent or friends who praise each pound lost. Considering these as "evidence," the imaginative leap one has to make to "see things in the same way" as the person in question (the anorectic perceiver) is starkly diminished. A jury working through the "reasonable person" standard, asked whether they can make the imaginative leap of seeing things in the same way as the agent in question, is a jury likely to find the perception of the person in question "reasonable."[20]

I would suggest that the anorexic perceiver is quite likely to be evaluated as reasonable in the second sense by such a jury, although I will not claim that it is inevitable that one would evaluate her as such. Regardless of whether we as evaluators or imaginative jurors are convinced of the anorexic perceiver's reasonableness, surely the conclusion that her perception is reasonable is undesirable. I suggest we turn next to the third sense of "reasonable" and then ultimately return to its relationship to the second.

Recall that in the third sense, drawn from Allan Gibbard's definition, to call something "reasonable" ("rational" in his terms) means "to endorse it in some way," particularly to endorse it by "express[ing] one's acceptance of norms that permit it" (1990, 6–7). Gibbard claims that when we call something "rational" we are not stating a proposition (which could be true or false) about the perception, but expressing our state of mind with regard to it. We are endorsing it—expressing our view that it makes sense, and that we accept those norms that permit it.

In defense of the term "rational," Gibbard considers the objection that the term might simply be another way of saying "coherent." But ultimately he claims that "rational" holds more epistemic weight than the term "coherent," and to support that claim he takes his reader through the case of what he calls an "idealized anorexic." Gibbard's "idealized anorexic" is an agent that would have entirely coherent preferences (idealized, he says, because anorectics in real life do not operate on entirely coherent preferences). She prefers death-by-starvation over living with "a figure plump enough to sustain life" (1990, 165) and this preference coheres with all her other views. He considers the idea that if there is truly such coherence, then her preferences may be something akin to "matters of taste"—not the sort of thing that can be properly evaluated or judged. Gibbard rejects this idea, however, first by appealing to our sense that to prefer life over starvation[21] "is not just a matter of taste" (165) but an issue on which one can be more or less rational. Hers is an "irrational" preference, he wants to maintain, even if we grant that it coheres with all of her views, and even if the anorectic is fully aware of her preferences and convinced that they are indeed "rationally required" (165). The irrationality of the preference is not to be found in its lack of coherence with others but in something else:

She is not, we think, simply acting rationally in the light of tastes we happen not to share. . . . We think her to be acting irrationally even if she accepts norms that prescribe what she is doing. We do not take a preference for life over starvation in these circumstances to be a matter of taste. (165–166)

We regard her view as irrational, Gibbard says, even when we grant that the dictates for her behavior follow directly from the norms that she accepts. Coherence merely in her own preferences and views is not enough to constitute our judging it "rational." We claim the authority to judge her irrational by virtue of our " 'seeing' something that she doesn't: that the fundamental norms she accepts just don't make sense" (1990, 175).

What am I doing . . . when I tell the coherent anorexic it makes no sense to starve herself to death? I am not trying to exert Socratic influence; that would only make sense if I thought her incoherent. Her problem, as I see it, is not that she fails to draw the right conclusions from premises she accepts, but that her premises are crazy. (175)

The problem with the anorectic is not that her logic skills need honing, says Gibbard, but that the initial premises from which she begins to reason are flawed. The initial set of norms, from which she derives the dictate that she ought to drastically reduce her caloric intake, are suspect and less trustworthy: in challenging her behavior, Gibbard says, "I am claiming that her norms are crazy, so that my own are, in a fundamental way, more to be trusted than hers" (1990, 175).

When Gibbard deems the anorectic's norms "crazy," however, he appears to blur any distinction between a norm that prescribes thinness and one that prescribes starvation. He overlooks the fact that in a case like this the latter is a derivative of the former, it comes from recognizing the importance of thinness. Although in the initial language of his example Gibbard does describe the anorectic's behavior as aiming at the goal of a trim figure, he soon stops qualifying her behavior in terms of this larger goal and describes her as preferring "starvation" itself to life with a suffi-ciently plump figure. In abandoning this qualification, Gibbard presents a convincing case for one whose norms are, indeed, "crazy." While both norms—one that emphasizes thinness and the other that emphasizes star-vation—would prescribe the cessation, or at least drastic reduction, of food intake, the one which prescribes starvation in itself, apart from the primary goal of achieving thinness, provides a stronger candidate for Gib-bard's "craziness." The problem here is that he has abandoned the more difficult norm, the less obviously "crazy" norm that prescribes thinness.

One may take note, again, that Gibbard does qualify his example as a "fanciful" one only, insisting that the "idealized" anorectic is distinct from real anorectics, in that "[r]eal anorexia nervosa does not consist in acting on coherent preferences" (1990, 165, n. 10). The fanciful example can be understood as operating from a coherent system of norms in which preference for starvation outranks life with a figure plump enough to sustain health. But it is crucial to recognize that the explanatory power and persuasiveness of his example lies partly in our familiarity with anorexia, in the similarity of this case to our limited knowledge of real-life cases of anorexia. The anorectic, prima facie, appears to hold to the hierarchy he outlines. The appeal of the example lies in the fact that we consider this to be a real epistemic problem with moral implications, and not merely the hypothetical difficulty of dealing with a life form whose norms are utterly unfamiliar to us. The power of his example draws its strength from the expectation that we will consider this a real problem, in the fact that we recognize, even if we cannot relate to entirely, such a being and the moral difficulties captured by her stance.

The norms of a real anorectic do present us with a difficulty in judging her perceptions, yet in a manner distinct from Gibbard's take on the problem. Gibbard's claim that we can judge the anorectic "irrational" fails on a slippage in his reference to the norms she presumably holds. In real cases of anorexia, the norm that can be identified as initially guiding anorexic behavior is one that prescribes thinness, not one that esteems starvation in its own right. It is crucial to understand part of the motivation of the anorectic in early stages; she starves herself as a *means* to thinness and does not, initially, esteem starvation in its own right. Consider the declaration found on one of the pro-anorexia sites:

> I for one, do not want to die. That is not the purpose of Ana! I am losing weight and taking control of my own body. I'm making it healthier by losing weight. There are dangers to being overweight just as much as there are when you are underweight.[22]

Only in more advanced stages, when the starvation becomes closely entwined with the ideal of maintaining control, would starvation be esteemed itself, if at all. At this point, her behavior becomes "aberrant" (having gone too far from more respectable dieting) and her norms appear to us more "crazy," since thinness has long been achieved, and she appears to be starving herself for no readily recognizable purpose. But this "craziness," of course, is more a product of the advanced nature of the disorder and the obsessive components that develop in relation to it. At this point food is an overwhelming presence in the life of the anorectic; it is transformed into the ultimate opponent that is to be controlled at all costs. Starvation could even actually *become* that which the anorectic prefers to life with a figure plump enough to sustain life, but in a real case of anorexia, starvation is likely to be preferred to life only when the disease has taken over the anorectic's way of life.

So to draw this distinction more carefully, we note that the norm the anorectic operates under is not one prescribing starvation but one prescribing thinness (the norm that seems less "crazy"). Now, however, it becomes harder to judge the anorectic "irrational" on the basis of adhering to crazy norms. Her norm does not appear to be "crazy" in the sense that we cannot recognize or relate to this norm at all; quite the contrary. We seem to be back to the difficulty of judging anything wrong at all with the anorectic's perception.

Yet Gibbard's view, even when this slippage is corrected, can still be useful for evaluating the perception of the anorectic. Let us clarify what Gibbard means when he says that to judge something "rational" is to endorse it, particularly by "express[ing] one's acceptance of norms that permit it." We need still to clarify what "norms" are and what it means to "accept" them. A norm on Gibbard's account is "a rule or prescription, expressible by an imperative" (1990, 46). The norm in question in my account pertaining to anorexia is: "One should or ought to be thin," expressible by the imperative "Be thin!" The existence of a norm is not dependent upon anyone stating, making, or even accepting it, nor is its influence on us dependent upon these things. To "accept" a norm is not, Gibbard says, something that can be defined precisely, but it is best understood on a model of language and discussion. "Accepting a norm is something that we do primarily in the context of normative discussion, actual and imaginary" (75). When you "accept" a norm you would be prepared to state (or can imagine avowing) that the norm in question ought to outweigh others in a given situation (60). "We take positions, and thereby expose ourselves to demands for consistency," having worked out what we think, as we do in a community or as we would in a community, attempting to coordinate our thoughts. "Accepting" a norm can be contrasted with "being in the grip of" or "internalizing" a norm, kinds of obedience to the norm that do not hinge upon accepting it. One can be motivated, influenced, or guided by a norm without actually "accepting" it.

In evaluating the case of the anorexic perceiver, if one is to view her perception as reasonable, that means accepting the norms that permit her perception; if one is to view her perception as unreasonable that means failing to accept the norms that permit her perception. To accept these norms is to be prepared to state (or imagine avowing) that the norm in question ought to outweigh others in a given situation; given that the norm prescribing thinness can be linked to behavior that threatens physical health (not just in those with eating disorders, but in those who engage in fad dieting, take dangerous diet pills, reduce fat intake to unhealthy levels, cut important nutrients out of their diets), most of us—even those with disordered eating patterns—would in fact not "accept" that the norm prescribing thinness ought to outweigh that of physical health. If we would not accept this norm in the full sense of "accept" that Gibbard gives, then we do not accept the norms that permit the perception of the anorectic. We thereby have grounds on which to call her perception "unreasonable."

So at this point we can breathe a sigh of relief; it is, after all, much more comforting to be able to call the anorectic "unreasonable" and match our intuitions that there is something quite problematic about her perception. But if relief were my goal, I would certainly have wasted the reader's time arguing that we can also find her reasonable according to the second standard. While the second sense of reasonable leads us to an unsatisfying judgment about the anorectic's perception (in that it leans toward the notion that her perception is reasonable), it is a critical step toward fully understanding the unreasonableness of the anorectic's perception in the third sense. Without many of the details provided in analysis of the second sense of reasonable most would still be likely to see these as *her* norms, rather than norms that can be located in our larger culture, and to claim that what are "unreasonable" are *her* isolated norms rather than ones that are part of cultural practices and pressures. Now the unreasonableness of the perception is not based on *how the perceiver* takes in the norms but on *what we think* of the norms that shape her perception. What we come away with, from the discussion of reasonable in the second sense, is a recognition that the anorectic's perception does not come out of nowhere, that it is traceable to the norms of our society and to the circumstances in which she lives, including the circumstance of being a woman.

This shifts the burden of the problem from the anorexic perceiver onto the larger culture and the norms that shape her perception. Ultimately this widens the scope of responsibility for her problematic perception—if her perception is to be altered it will take work not only on her part but also on the part of a society that so heavily enforces norms idealizing thinness in women. Our intuition that there is something problematic and thereby unreasonable about the anorectic's perception is confirmed, but the scope and responsibility for the problematic perception is appropriately widened.

NOTES

1. In this piece my references to anorexia nervosa are not meant to exclude related eating disorders such as bulimia nervosa. While there are important dis-

tinctions to be made between anorexic behavior and bulimic behavior, the perceptual issue I hope to elucidate here does not rest on such distinctions.

2. The Mayo Clinic study is referred to in Nova's production of "Dying to Be
Thin" detailed at www.pbs.org. U.S. statistics are updated regularly on the Web
sites of ANRED (Anorexia Nervosa and Related Eating Disorders) at www.
anred.com, and ANAD (National Association of Anorexia Nervosa and Associated
Disorders) at www.anad.org.

3. I note that this aims at a "kind" of objectivity because, as evaluators of the
perception, we would not be claiming that the perception "really" is reasonable,
independent of whether that agent or anyone else believes it to be so. The definition is objective in the sense that Elizabeth Lloyd describes as "public or in principle publicly accessible." Lloyd distinguishes this type of objectivity from three
others: (1) "objective means detached, disinterested, unbiased, impersonal,
invested in no particular point of view"; (2) "objective means existing independently or separately from us"; (3) "objective means really existing, Really Real, the
way things really are" (1995, 355).

Cases involving sexual harassment articulate the sense of objectivity employed
here. The reasonable person standard is an "objective standard" as described in
the EEOC *Compliance Manual on Sexual Harassment* and is distinguished from
a "subjective perception" in *Harris v. Forklift Systems, Inc.* 510 U.S. 17 (1993). As
stated in *Highlander v. K.F.C. National Management Co.*, 805 F.2d 644, 650, 41
EPD ¶ 36,675 (6th Cir. 1986) one must "adopt the perspective of a reasonable
person's reaction to a similar environment under similar or like circumstances."

4. This is true of bulimics as well. For extended discussion of these studies,
see Van Deusen (1993) and Dolan and Gitzinger (1994).

5. Of course, as a skilled therapist, one aims to correct this perception primarily because it contributes to dangerous, life-threatening behavior; the therapist is
not typically motivated to reveal the truth just for its own sake. I am grateful to
Linda Parsons-Sewell for this point.

6. Russell criticizes the DSM-III-R (presumably the latest version at the time of
publication) for its focus on "particular individuals rather than problematic features of a particular social context" (1995, 40).

7. I set aside here the question of whether, and to what extent, the self should
be regarded as distinct from the body, although it is a rich and highly relevant
discussion.

8. MacSween presents a psychoanalytic read on the response of the anorectic.
The anorectic, she says, forges an individual, tragic "solution" to the problem of
having been born female in our society, of having a body that is valued merely as
a passive object for consumption. The anorectic rejects this social meaning
ascribed to her body, in which the only "desire" a woman can have is to be open
to intrusion from objects outside her body. By refusing to eat, she asserts herself;
she refuses to give into the social construction of her desire. MacSween writes:
"In anorexia the experience of feminine bodily openness is centered on the
mouth. Not eating forms a barrier between the anorexic self and the threatening
world against which the open feminine body has no defences. Not eating decon-
structs feminine responsiveness" (1995, 249).

MacSween's argument should not be interpreted as any type of praise for this assertion of agency. She sees this aspect of her work simply as an explanation of the anorectic's desire for control. As a philosopher untrained in the psychoanalytic tradition, I found her explication at first to be overstated, but then more compelling once I considered it in conjunction with Rosalind Coward's work on the construction of desire (1985). Coward claims that the construction of women's desire is played out on the look of the contemporary fashion model: her arched body, coy eyes under half-lowered lids, and ready, half-open lips convey the messages simultaneously "I want you" and "Come and get me."

9. I find myself gravely troubled over whether to include discussion of these sites here. Organizations working to prevent and treat eating disorders have been fighting admirably to get servers to shut the sites down. My worry is twofold: one is that the sites are "triggering"; a person who is in recovery from disordered eating, or one who is developing a disorder, puts recovery in serious jeopardy simply by reading the tips and discussion. In addition, Webmasters may gain confidence in the importance of their sites by counting the number of visitors. I would strongly urge readers to abstain from accessing the sites. For discussion of their contents, see instead articles available on the Web: "Web sites offer 'blueprint' for anorexia" by Judith Graham searchable at seattletimes.nwsource.com; "Proanorexia forums pop up on the Web" by Alfred Lubrano searchable at the Web site for *The Inquirer* (Philadelphia); "Nurturing and Anorexia Obsession" by Lynell George searchable at www.latimes.com.

10. From the Web site at pages.ivillage.com/slenderfungus/.

11. At one point on the site the oppressive figure becomes "the government." The author writes in bold, "Reality Check: The government is NOT your friend. The government is NOT your protector. . . . If the majority believes it, it is probably wrong." Below this text appears the image of the food pyramid (typically distributed in elementary schools) that separates foods into the major food groups.

12. From the Web site at pages.ivillage.com/slenderfungus/.

13. Upsetting the notion that anorexia is a Western problem is the steady rise of sufferers in Japan.

14. The notion that anorexia is a white girls' disorder is problematic. In "Minority Women: The Untold Story" (published at www.pbs.org) Marian Fitzgibbon and Melinda Stolley state: "A primary reason why eating disorders appeared to be restricted to white women seems to be that white women were the only people with these problems who underwent study. Specialists conducted most of the early research in this area on college campuses or in hospital clinics. For reasons related to economics, access to care, and cultural attitudes toward psychological treatment, middle-class white females were the ones seeking treatment and thus the ones who became the subjects of research."

I should add that such evidence should not be the only motivation for critiquing the notion that anorexia is a white girls' disorder. Doris Witt's article "What (N)ever Happened to Aunt Jemima: Eating Disorders, Fetal Rights, and Black Female Appetite in Contemporary American Culture" (1998) compellingly argues that the work of Chernin, Orbach, and Bordo merits criticism for the following: "in the process of linking upward class mobility to compulsory starvation for African-American women, Bordo inadvertently naturalizes lower-class black female appetite." Noting the prevalence of imagery that equates black women with food and appetite, and juxtaposing this with eating disorders literature that suggests black women are exempt from this pressure, Witt claims: "Black women are not just . . . an absence in eating disorders but a constitutive absence, and this is an important distinction." The comparative lack of pressure on African American women to be exceedingly thin may itself be evidence of racism. For further discussion of this point see Becky Thompson's "Food, Bodies, and Growing Up Female: Childhood Lessons about Culture, Race, and Class" in Fallon, Katzman, and Wooley, eds. *Feminist Perspectives on Eating Disorders* (1994).

15. This pressure to conform is played out particularly on the bodies of women of American minority groups and of immigrant women. Marian Fitzgibbon and Melinda Stolley (cited in the note above) report that among African American, Latina, and Native American women "eating disorders . . . may be related to acculturation." They claim: "It seems that eating disorders may relate to the degree to which African-American women [and Latina and Native American, they note later] have assimilated into the dominant American social milieu," the dominant milieu being white not just demographically, but in terms of standards of beauty. A recent article in the *Washington Post* cites a study by Fari Chelin, who makes similar claims in her studies of immigrant women; those that are isolated from their own cultures and have to assimilate into white cultures quickly, often develop eating disorders. See Emily Wax's article "Immigrant Girls Are Starving to Be American, Studies Find," in the *Washington Post* (March 6, 2000).

16. For a longer discussion of this claim see Bordo's chapter "Whose Body Is This?" (1993, 45–69).

17. Richard Jerome, "A Body to Die For," *People* (October 30, 2000).

18. At the 1983 "Eating Disorders and the Psychology of Women" conference participants objected to Orbach's suggestion that anorexia is at the extreme end of the continuum on which all women in our society are located (Bordo 1993, 47–49).

19. Jean Kilbourne adds a moral imperative to this equivalence: "We need to be as outspoken about this issue as the pro-health activists are about alcohol and tobacco advertising" (396) in "Still Killing Us Softly: Advertising and the Obsession with Thinness" in Fallon, Katzman, and Wooley, eds. *Feminist Perspectives on Eating Disorders* (1994). If one should object still to the equivalence on the basis that smoking is physically addictive, new research on "activity anorexia" suggests that there is an addictive component to calorie deprivation, perpetuated by exercise (see Epling and Pierce 1996). If one is still not persuaded of the equivalence on the basis that anorexia is a mental disorder, consider the argument of Denise Russell: "The consistent lack of a broader perspective is likely to encourage diagnoses of 'mental disorder' when there is far more disturbance in the social environment than in the mind of the diagnosed person, and where the 'treatment programme' should be directed towards fixing up that environment rather than continually trying to make the disturbed individual fit in with the disturbing environment" (1995, 40).

20. Once again, this judgment is to be based on the anorectic's perception, not

on her behavior. If one should still object at this point that the anorexic perceiver can be separated from other perceivers on the basis that she perceives thinness as more important than any other group of perceivers does, consider whether she differs, as a perceiver, from the woman who exercises obsessively for hours on end to lose weight, or the woman who ingests only diet drinks for weeks. These *behaviors* are surely different from the behavior of depriving oneself of food, but this does not constitute a clear counterexample of a distinct type of perceiving. For research on the ways in which excessive exercise and anorexia are mutually reinforcing, see emerging research on the topic of "activity anorexia" (Epling and Pierce 1996).

21. Gibbard makes what I believe to be an illegitimate equivalence here: he first describes the case as one of preferring a trim figure over a figure plump enough to sustain life, to one of preferring starvation over life. I will discuss what is wrong with this move in subsequent paragraphs, but I indicate my objection here in order to signal that the change in descriptive terminology is Gibbard's, not my own.

22. From the Web site at myonlyhopeisana.cjb.net/.

II

RESPONSIBILITY

6

The Impurities of Epistemic Responsibility: Developing a Practice-Oriented Epistemology

Heidi E. Grasswick

As early as 1987, Lorraine Code wondered in her book *Epistemic Responsibility* "just what will be entailed in putting epistemic responsibility in a central place in theory of knowledge" (Code 1987, 50). Though this early work was not explicitly feminist, Code herself has later acknowledged that these early investigations opened up the possibility for her "that there could be feminist interventions, both critical and revisionist in the discourse of epistemology" (Code 1995, 10). In this chapter I argue that it is very important for feminists to develop an epistemology within which the concept of epistemic responsibility holds a central place. Developing a responsibility-centered epistemology focuses our normative epistemological questions on the agents of actual knowing practices, resisting the temptation of excessive abstraction and idealization. But feminists do not yet have available a fully developed and adequate concept of epistemic responsibility; the concept needs work, in part because it does not come with an innocent philosophical history. Feminists need to continue to develop ideas of responsibility that will be consistent with their insights and concerns. Fortunately, many feminist ethicists have done significant work developing feminist conceptions of moral responsibility, and here I investigate the work of Claudia Card and Margaret Urban Walker with an eye toward applying and adapting it to the case of a responsibility-centered epistemology. In following these feminist ethicists, I argue that a viable concept of epistemic responsibility must be consistent with the *impurities* of epistemic agency. Not only is epistemic agency impure in terms of the limited degree of choice we face as individuals when exercising this agency, but it is also impure in the sense of always being integrated with other ethical concerns as we make decisions regarding how to know.

THE IMPORTANCE OF EPISTEMIC RESPONSIBILITY

As a discourse focused on the need for social and political transformation, feminist theory is clearly a normative enterprise. Feminist *epistemology*, then, can be viewed as doubly normative: it is committed both to making ethico-political normative distinctions (i.e., oppression-free societies are better than those with extensive systems of oppression), and to making epistemically normative distinctions (i.e., some knowledge claims and practices are epistemically better than others). One of the major motivations for doing work in feminist epistemology is to try to articulate the connection between these two normative dimensions: how does good knowing encourage social transformation in positive directions, and how do various elements of oppressive societies influence the quality of knowing that can occur within them?

When feminist philosophers turned their attention to the field of epistemology in the early 1980s, it did not take long for them to realize that the standardly available epistemological analyses were ill equipped to handle their feminist concerns. For example, it was not unusual for analytic philosophers to locate the normative nature of epistemology in an analysis of the "justifiedness" of beliefs (see for example Castañeda 1988, 211; Kim 1994, 35). But this standard hypersanitized epistemological task of identifying conditions of justified (true) belief struck feminists as either completely wrongheaded in its abstraction, or simply irrelevant to assessing the gender bias evident in the messy social world of knowledge practices. Feminists have insisted on the need to attend to the actual (social) practices of knowledge-seeking, an insistence that has put them in good company with other naturalists and social epistemologists.

In many cases, this split between the highly normative task of outlining (ideal) conditions of justified belief, and the analysis of the actual activities and practices of knowledge-seeking has been understood as a split between the normative and the descriptive tasks of epistemologists.[1] Consequently, feminist epistemologists who attend to our social practices of knowing are sometimes criticized for producing no more than description, or for being engaged in "mere sociology." But to equate the realm of the normative with idealized analyses of justified belief, and similarly to equate the realm of the descriptive with attention to the actual practices and activities of knowledge-seeking is itself a mistake that inevitably results in a misreading of feminist epistemology. As Code has noted, "feminists examine *practices* of knowledge construction to produce critical retellings of what historically and materially 'situated' knowers actually do" (Code 1995, 176). Feminists are just as interested in how we ought to engage in the activities and practices of knowledge-seeking as they are in describing those practices. Normative epistemological assessment need not be restricted to judgments of whether particular claims or beliefs are good or bad, epistemically speaking. Normative epistemological assessment can also take the form of developing models of how to *practice* good inquiry. As Lisa Heldke and Stephen Kellert write, "Making, evaluating, and communicating knowledge is a human activity which invites questions of 'how are we to act?'" (1995, 366).

Being interested in how we can practice good inquiry implies a corresponding interest in the agents of this inquiry. What are these agents to do, and who are they? Developing an epistemological framework around the idea of epistemically responsible agents is a good way of ensuring that the epistemology remains focused on practices and actual activities of knowledge-seeking, without escaping into the idealized world of justified true belief. Additionally, a responsibility-centered epistemology, by focusing on the agents of knowledge, encompasses the transformative nature of a feminist epistemology. Feminist epistemologists believe that our knowledge-seeking practices can be changed and improved; they can be transformed, by responsible epistemic agents, into practices that do a better job of constructing knowledge for us. Without a viable conception of responsible epistemic agency, this transformative potential of feminist epistemology is threatened.

FEMINIST CONCERNS ABOUT (EPISTEMIC) RESPONSIBILITY

But as we investigate the idea of epistemic responsibility further, it is not immediately obvious that it will help feminist epistemologists achieve their goal of a normative theory that focuses on the actual practices of knowing, and certainly some problematic conceptions of epistemic responsibility need to be ruled out. To begin with, some epistemologists have merely used the term epistemic responsibility as a code word for the justification of beliefs, the very kind of normative analysis that I have suggested feminists want to move away from. For example, we find Jaegwon Kim writing, "If a belief is justified for us, then it is *permissible* and *reasonable*, from the epistemic point of view, for us to hold it, and it would be *epistemically irresponsible* to hold beliefs that contradict it" (Kim 1994, 35). If what I have said above is correct, feminists will not be interested in focusing on this particular use of "epistemic responsibility" that simply applies the ethical term of responsibility to epistemology by way of a loose analogy, judging whether or not one should or shouldn't hold a particular belief.

Other epistemologists, however, have clearly taken epistemic responsibility to involve reference to the actions of agents, not just the status of their beliefs. Hilary Kornblith, for example, defines an epistemically responsible agent as one who "desires to have true beliefs, and thus desires to have his beliefs produced by processes which lead to true beliefs; his actions are guided by these desires" (1983, 34). For such theorists, action and inquiry are central to the concept of an epistemically responsible agent. Being epistemically responsible means that you are willing to investigate the world, to go and gather evidence, and not just be satisfied with the evidence you have at your disposal. Kornblith's conception, which appeals to the actions required to follow one's desire for the truth, has similarities to Code's early discussions of epistemic responsibility, in which she negotiates the dual recognition of the "considerable choice" agents exercise in coming to know the world, and a "normative realism" that demands knowers be responsible to how the world is, and the evidence they find for this (Code 1987). My arguments for the importance of a responsibility-centered epistemology clearly depend on a conception of epistemic responsibility that is closely tied to the action of human agents and their participation in knowledge practices. While I will have more to say shortly about whether or not feminists should understand epistemic responsibility as simply derivable from one's desire for true beliefs, we first need to address some more general concerns about the language and framework of responsibility that feminist ethicists have expressed.

As their discussions of moral responsibility demonstrate, feminists have not been uniformly enamored with the concept. In particular, many feminists have been uncomfortable with the judgmental language of responsibility that follows when praise and blame are taken to be its primary features. Many have worried about the dangers of a preoccupation with judging people as good or bad, praiseworthy or blameworthy. And some, such as Marilyn Frye, have worried about the cultural specificity of the ethical framework of responsibility and the authority it grants particular agents to dominate others of different groups. Employing the words of Minnie Bruce Pratt, Frye describes the ethical orientation of her own upbringing as a member of a white upwardly mobile Christian family: "I was taught to be a *judge*, of moral responsibility and of punishment only in relation to my ethical system" (quoted in Frye 1992, 140). As Frye continues, this time in her own words:

> I was being taught that because one knows what is right, it is morally appropriate to have and exercise what I now would call race privilege and class privilege . . . to dominate others. . . . Knowing right from wrong is what constitutes one as a certain sort of agent in the world. One understands one's agency as that of the judge, teacher/preacher, director, administrator, manager, and in this mode, as a decision maker, planner, policy maker, organizer. (1992, 140)

But perhaps the most sustained feminist critique of responsibility as a moral concept has come from Sarah Hoagland, who has argued that "moral accountability as we understand it—centrally focused on 'praise' and 'blame'—does not present us with a viable concept of choice under oppression" (1988, 215). For Hoagland, it is of utmost importance that we be able to understand women as moral agents who are able to act within a context of oppression without demoralization. To focus on praise and blame, or the extremes of victimization and contrarily blaming the victim, fails to do justice to the complexity of women's lives within the context of limited choices (217).[2]

I think these concerns stem from a common view among these feminists that the language of responsibility, particularly when it is focused on praise and blame, reflects a preoccupation with *purity*. People want to see the world and its agents in clear terms, and a traditional ethics of responsibility represents a kind of ethics of purity, judging people and using the concept of responsibility to place people in the categories of praiseworthy, blameworthy, and innocent. Feminists such as Frye and Hoagland are concerned with the problems of placing a normative framework of purity on an impure world. For Hoagland, persons living under conditions of oppression do not have the luxury of purity, and to analyze their lives within such a purified framework is not only inaccurate, but it can do damage and cause harm.[3] For Frye, a framework of judgmental ethics can result in an arrogance that fails to perceive the domination it participates in. Given these critiques, which I have only sketched very briefly here, it is clear that if responsibility is to remain useful for feminist ethicists or epistemologists, it must be capable of being adapted to an impure world.

CARD AND FORWARD-LOOKING RESPONSIBILITY IN AN IMPURE WORLD

One theorist who has made significant progress developing the concept of responsibility for use in an impure world is Claudia Card with her work on the relationship between responsibility and moral luck. Rather than focus on the praise and blame aspects of responsibility, Card notes that this "credit" sense of responsibility is primarily "backward-looking" and captures only one of several senses of responsibility in operation. In contrast, Card focuses her attention on the forward-looking sense of responsibility—what it means for one to *take* responsibility either for one's character or actions. In backward-looking analyses of responsibility, one of the primary determinations of whether one was responsible for an action depends on whether that action was under the control of the moral agent. Thus, the presence of moral luck seems to threaten these backward-looking attributions of moral responsibility, where moral luck is defined as "factors beyond the control of the affected agent, good or bad," and relevant to "our choices (or failures to choose) to do what is morally right or wrong or with our having a moral character—virtues, vices, integrity" (Card 1996, 22). The presence of moral luck is, of course, one of the many features of an impure world that must be handled by an adequate conception of moral responsibility. To many, it has seemed that moral luck directly impedes moral responsibility.[4] Card, however, investigates what it would mean to take responsibility in the forward-looking sense while recognizing the existence of moral luck, particularly in the case of characters formed through experiences of oppression. She is interested in "the implications for taking responsibility for oneself of a history of bad moral luck, such as comes with a history of child abuse or a heritage of oppression" (Card 1996, 24). Card is not simply ignoring the problems of the "backward-looking" praise/blame sense of responsibility. Rather, she argues these backward-looking attributions of responsibility are in fact derived from the assumption that one is a responsible agent in the forward-looking sense. As Card writes, "The forward-looking senses of 'taking responsibility' are more basic not because praise or blame are due only depending on whether we follow through on voluntary undertakings but because we presuppose at least a minimal capacity in others to take responsibility in the forward-looking sense when we praise or blame them" (1996, 29). Card here has captured the important link between ideas of responsibility and agency, and she recognizes the importance of recovering the agency of women who act within the context of oppression.

The upshot of Card's analysis that the prerequisite for becoming a responsible agent in the forward-looking sense, as one who can take responsibility for one's history, character, and actions, lies not so much in the development of autonomy and voluntary control, but rather in the development of integrity. According to Card, as long as autonomy is conceptualized in terms of "considerations of dependence and independence" and is taken to be the key to responsibility, responsibility and moral luck are irreconcilable. However, Card suggests that the ability to take responsibility for one's actions, history, and character comes from the development of integrity, a concept that "involves considerations of consistency, coherence, and commitment" (1996, 32) and thus is able to coexist with moral luck. By developing integrity, one develops such capacities as "reliability and the bases for self-esteem" (Card 1996, 24). When one has integrity, one is capable of taking responsibility, standing behind the person one has become and the conduct one engages in, shaped as they are by moral luck.[5] Thus, she provides us with a forward-looking sense of responsibility that can accommodate the impurities of the world and the lives we live.[6] Analyses of praise and blame then become secondary discussions of whether or not the person could be expected to take responsibility for such a situation.[7]

It is important to note that Card's framework here, and her motivation for turning toward integrity, depends very much on understanding autonomy purely in terms of voluntary control and independence. More recently, many feminist theorists have attempted to reconceptualize the idea of autonomy, making it a more relational concept that is not clearly focused on the dependency/independency contrast.[8] If one develops a relational sense of autonomy, Card's dismissal of autonomy as integral to a viable concept of responsibility would be more difficult to maintain.[9] But whether we move to either an analysis of integrity, or a more relational understanding of autonomy, her point remains that any concept of autonomy that is taken to be primarily about independence from others will not be reconcilable with moral luck, or choices made within contexts of oppression. Any concept of responsibility that is tied to this sense of autonomy as independence will not adapt well to an impure environment. Pure voluntary control is not required to act in an impure world and is rarely found. But Card's analysis does not imply that issues of control become irrelevant to discussions of responsibility, only that pure voluntary control and independence are not prerequisites for responsibility.

Card's framework and her focus on integrity, and her insights concerning the importance of a forward-looking sense of responsibility, can be readily adapted to the concerns of feminist epistemologists. Increasing attention to the social nature of knowing has made it clear that there is a lot that individual knowers do not have control over as they investigate the world, and feminist epistemologists have questioned the ideal of autonomy and autonomous knowing (built on the contrast between dependent and independent knowing) that epistemologists have commonly worked with. As feminists and other social epistemologists have pointed out, the quality of an individual's knowledge-seeking depends very much on the trustworthiness and epistemic skills of those around her. One's knowing is subject to a great deal of epistemic luck, which does not bode well for any concept of epistemic responsibility that relies on autonomy and self-reliance as a prerequisite in knowing. Without reworking epistemic responsibility in a way that rejects autonomy (understood as independence) as a prerequisite, I doubt epistemic responsibility could play a very useful role in feminist epistemologies that describe epistemic life as rife with social intersections and interactions. Furthermore, Card's focus on integrity identifies precisely what knowers will look for in others upon whom they depend. When we trust the testimony of others, it is not because we think of them as being independent or autonomous, but rather because we take them to have epistemic integrity, that is, we take them to be *reliable*, and we understand them to value goals of knowledge-seeking. Reliability doesn't imply that they are always right, but rather they are likely to be appropriately cautious when their testimony is unsure. What we need for successful knowing is communities of responsible knowers, in the sense of knowers who have integrity. We need networks of reliable and trustworthy knowers. By connecting responsibility with integrity rather than a nonrelational sense of autonomy, Card makes responsibility a much more usable concept for feminist epistemologists and ethicists alike.

Additionally, the primacy Card places on the forward-looking sense of responsibility has implications for the epistemic realm. For example, many feminist accounts of knowing have stressed the role of the community in setting out epistemic standards. Individuals in a certain sense "inherit" the rules and standards of their communities' knowledge-seeking practices. Thus, we might conclude that individuals are not, and cannot, be held responsible for their role in the continuation of these practices. Yet when we focus on the forward-looking sense of responsibility that Card articulates, we can understand how an individual agent might *take* responsibility for her participation in a particular way of knowing. That is to say, she may be willing to stand behind the practice, play by its rules, and commit to it, not because she has inherited the practice, but because she finds it acceptable. As part of her taking responsibility, she may also intervene in the practice, just as feminists have intervened in other epistemic practices, engaging in them partially while finding parts of the practices unacceptable, again, being willing to stand behind these engagements. And she may take responsibility for her participation in these practices even in circumstances where we would not hold her accountable for her participation or intervention.[10]

A good example of the value of Card's analysis can be found in feminist critiques of androcentric science. It has been difficult to reconcile feminist critiques of androcentric science with the sense that individual (male) scientists should not be *blamed* for their adherence to the community epistemic standards, which include androcentric values, when those standards are understood as the contemporary standards of "good science."[11] Yet Card's attention to the *taking* of responsibility, coupled with her claim that one can take responsibility in cases where we would not hold individuals accountable, explains how we can criticize existing practices, and take responsibility for our interventions and engagements with practices, without necessarily resorting to blaming individuals for the existence of these problematic practices. I find Card's analysis helpful because it identifies exactly what a critical epistemology would hope for—a recognition that individuals are agents who can stand behind and intervene in social knowing practices, though they do not individually create those practices. Her account draws attention to an important way in which epistemic practices can change—by individuals being willing to stand behind certain practices, interventions, beliefs, and characters.

WALKER AND PRACTICES OF RESPONSIBILITY: THE IMPURITY OF TRUTH-SEEKING

Card's focus on integrity, and the secondary role she assigns to practices of praise and blame within discussions of responsibility, allows feminist ethicists and epistemologists alike to understand how responsibility can be reconciled with the impurities of the world within which our individual agency is exercised. By creating a certain leeway between forward-looking and backward-looking senses of responsibility, and granting primacy to the forward-looking sense, Card alleviates some of the concerns of feminists skeptical of the viability of responsibility given its close association with the heavy-handed practices of praise and blame. But of course, even as Card gives us this leeway, emphasizing how human agents can outrun expectations and take responsibility for their characters, histories, practices and actions, we will eventually be drawn back to questions concerning the appropriateness of particular community standards and practices of accountability. If the normative task of feminist epistemology involves concerns about how to practice good inquiry, it will include discussions of how to assess the appropriateness of holding someone responsible for their contributions to inquiry. Here I use Margaret Urban Walker's attempt to outline the normative framework of a practice-oriented ethics to explore how feminists might assess our practices of epistemic responsibility. One of my conclusions will be that feminists committed to a practice-oriented epistemology will find that a viable concept of epistemic responsibility is impure in yet another sense from that discussed above: contrary to Kornblith and his understanding of epistemic responsibility as forming your beliefs *purely* in accordance with your desire for the truth, a viable feminist conception of epistemic responsibility cannot be so purified.

Making responsible decisions about what kind of epistemic inquiry we are committed to pursuing will always reach beyond Kornblith's abstract concern with truth. Epistemic responsible action is always necessarily "contaminated" with moral and political concerns.

In her book *Moral Understandings*, Walker develops what she calls an *expressive-collaborative* conception of morality that focuses on moral responsibilities and their distributions.[12] In proposing her expressive-collaborative conception, Walker hopes to offer an alternative to the dominant *theoretical-juridical* model of morality and moral theory, which she takes to be mistaken in its "representation of morality as a compact, propositionally codifiable, impersonally action-guiding code within an agent, or as a compact set of law-like propositions that 'explain' the moral behavior of a well-formed moral agent" (1998, 7–8). In contrast, she argues that her expressive-collaborative conception better captures the evident features of morality "as a socially embodied medium of understanding and adjustment in which people account to each other for the identities, relationships, and values that define their responsibilities" (61). According to this conception, morality is "interpersonal and constructive" (60). Whereas Walker believes ethicists have mistakenly represented morality as a body of theoretical knowledge, her account represents morality as social practices of responsibility by which we hold ourselves accountable to one another. Examining responsibilities and their distributions becomes the primary method of understanding given practices of morality. Walker calls for a "geography of responsibilities" that would map "the structure of standing assumptions that guides the distribution of responsibilities— how they are assigned, negotiated, deflected—in particular forms of moral life" (99). Thus, on her expressive-collaborative model, ideas of responsibility and accountability take on a central role.

Walker not only describes morality as social practice, but also seeks to explain what the normative task of ethics would look like according to her expressive-collaborative model. Moral theorists committed to her expressive-collaborative model will be unable to appeal to any absolute or transcendent moral standards according to which they could evaluate particular moral practices. But Walker argues that we can look for justifications *through* practices rather than outside of them. Normative moral assessment will be necessarily comparative; in the absence of absolute standards, the most we can do is compare various practices, and only a better practice would suffice to justify the rejection of an existing practice.[13] As Walker puts it, "The only thing that corrects or refutes a morality on moral grounds is another, better justified, morality that shows the first one is wrong. What is involved in justifying a morality, however, is no one thing and no simple ones" (1998, 204). Furthermore, the focus of assessment will be on the construction and distribution of responsibilities. As

Walker claims, "An 'ethics of responsibility' as a normative moral view would try to put people and responsibilities in the right places with respect to each other" (78). By focusing her attention on responsibilities and their distributions, Walker is able to create a framework where the normative questions of moral philosophy turn on whether we find these constructions and distributions of responsibility acceptable. We critically assess "the *habitability* of a particular form of moral-social life" (214). Walker provides us with a kind of justification and normative framework appropriate to an impure world of activities and practices.

Walker suggests certain questions and tests to which we could subject our practices in an attempt to critically evaluate their acceptability. One important test is the test of "transparency," which demands that our practices be able to survive our clear understanding of what is going on. Transparency "is the state in which we can 'see through' intervening media to what is really there," so it consists in "seeing how we live, both through and in spite of our moral understandings and practices of responsibility" (Walker 1998, 216). If a practice relies for its continuance on our inability to understand it for what it really is, so much the worse for the practice.

Walker's sketch of this kind of critical moral assessment suggests that her model of the normative task of ethics has much in common with naturalized epistemology:

> It's not different from the realization that there aren't "foundations" of knowledge; it is another, and distinctively complicated, case of it. This is not to give up on questions of justification but to take a different view of it, one that is consistent with a naturalized, but reflexively and socially critical, epistemology. If naturalized epistemologies have advice to offer, any "we" must begin with some of what it believes are its best-entrenched, most durable, powerful, and fruitful insights, and see where they lead and what may be learned from them. It is possible that one will learn that some of them were less durable, powerful, and fruitful than one hoped, or useful in different or more disturbing ways than one believed. (Walker 1998, 212)

Here, Walker casts the case of morality and moral knowledge as a subset of (naturalized) epistemological investigations. In what follows, I investigate what it would mean to generalize her moral epistemology to other fields of knowing, staying focused as she does on the issue of responsibilities.[14] What would the guiding questions of a normative epistemology be if knowledge-seeking was taken to consist of social practices of epistemic responsibilities? Walker understands ethics as answering the question of how to live. I suggest that epistemological concerns, correspondingly, answer the question of how to live *if we want to know*, and of course, knowing captures a very important part of our lives. But as I shall indicate shortly, we must also concern ourselves with *how* we want to know.

One of Walker's points is that "a lot of what we need in order to under-stand specifically moral judgments or principles goes beyond specifically moral matters. We need to understand a *social world*" (1998, 203). Simi-larly, feminist epistemologists have argued that we cannot understand knowers and their epistemic activities without grasping the social prac-tices in which they are engaged and the social contexts in which they are embedded. Normative epistemic assessment then, will become a matter of assessing social practices *in an epistemic light*, rather than trying to clearly mark off what is or is not part of an epistemic practice. There will be no "pure" epistemic practices. Along the lines of Walker's suggestions, we would ask ourselves how well particular social practices do at allowing us to know, and more importantly, who is the "us"? By attending to the distribution of epistemic responsibilities—who has cognitive authority and what is expected of them in virtue of that authority—we can both understand the workings of our epistemic practices better and assess whether we are satisfied with such distributions and practices. We can examine why particular positions are invested with cognitive authority (such as the authority of experts) and we can critically assess whether such cognitive authority is deserved, given how knowledge is being gener-ated—that is, given how the actual practice is being played out. We can ask whether one *should* be more willing to believe some more than others in particular contexts. And these answers might differ depending on whom we are talking about. For example, given the history of racial bias in the construction of scientific knowledge, bias that has in many cases worked against the interests of non-Caucasians, one might argue that members of these groups have less reason to trust in the expertise of sci-entists than do Caucasians.[15] By attending to distributions of responsibili-ties, we not only investigate whether others are living up to our expectations of their particular cognitive roles in social life, but we also investigate why we construct these expectations and whether these expec-tations are functioning well, given our epistemic goals.

In such analyses, Walker's transparency test will be key. Applying the transparency test, we can ask whether or not a given practice would sur-vive the participants' recognition of what is really going on. For example, feminist critiques of science have exposed the androcentrism at work in psychological development studies that use all male subjects and yet pur-port to generalize about human development. As Lynn Hankinson Nelson notes, it is only once feminists have made connections between gender and knowledge that the unacceptability of the practice becomes clear, and psychologists then uniformly claim what wasn't obvious before—that *"anyone can see* that you can't build a theory about psychological devel-opment from studies limited to males" (1994, 295). Once exposed, andro-centric practices fail the transparency test, for they claimed to construct knowledge in a gender-neutral way, when they did not. Failing the transparency test gives us reason to change our practices.

But of course whereas Walker's analysis is designed for understanding the realm of ethics, in which questions of how we relate and interact with one another are primary, applying her analysis to the epistemic realm raises the question of possible disanalogies between ethics and epistemology. For example, is Walker's concern with "habitability" an obvious ethical value, inappropriately understood as an epistemic concern? Shouldn't our epistemic responsibilities be purely governed by our desire to seek the truth, as Kornblith suggests? How does the normative pull of realism apply to this practice-oriented and responsibility-centered epistemology?

When assessing practices in an epistemic light, we will obviously be acutely interested in the reliability of these practices—how well they do at helping us construct reliable representations of the world. But within the realm of epistemic practice and inquiry, truth is never self-announcing. And as many epistemologists have pointed out, both feminist and nonfeminist, the "search for truth" does not adequately capture the considerations we use to assess and construct our epistemic practices: epistemic concerns are more multiple and complex than that, involving the search for *significant* truths and the avoidance of error.[16] Furthermore, if we view inquiry as practices constructed of distributions of epistemic responsibility, involving reliance on others' cognitive authority, it becomes clear that epistemic assessment will never be *simply* a matter of assessing reliability, nor will reliability be simple to ascertain. Though our epistemic practices do help us know the world, our assessments must be framed in terms of choices regarding *how* we come to know the world and whether we are satisfied with the methods, costs, and value of the results of a given epistemic practice. The focus is on our activities within the practices and whether we find reasons to adjust *how* we know, since there is no single correct way. As Code writes, "There are genuine choices about how to know the world and its inhabitants: choices that become apparent only in more complex epistemic circumstances" (1995, 3). According to Code, attention to issues of epistemic responsibility inevitably blurs the boundaries of ethics and epistemology (12).[17]

So Walker's consideration of the habitability of our practices is, I think, also appropriate to take up within the epistemic realm. Its ethical relevance does not exclude it from being understood as having epistemological relevance. If we are focusing our epistemological investigations on the practices of inquiry, decisions concerning the appropriate distribution of epistemic responsibilities will include decisions regarding whether we are satisfied with the particular ways in which our concerns of truth and knowledge are playing out in our practices. How committed are we to discerning the world around us? In what ways, and at what cost? Given the variety of ways in which we can know, judging our practices will never be simply a matter of assessing whether they do or don't allow us to know. Rather, it will be a matter of asking: in what ways do they allow us to know, and are we willing to commit to those ways, keeping in mind the associated costs? What kind of knowledge do they permit us to construct, who attains it, and is it the kind *we* want, keeping in mind the need to clarify who that *we* is? Decisions based on the answers to such questions are epistemic decisions. They concern our knowledge practices. But more specifically, they also concern the relation of epistemic interests to other parts of our lives; in deciding *how* we want to know, we are regulating our various epistemic desires and commitments in relation to our other concerns. As such, both our critical assessments of epistemic practices and the epistemic responsibilities that ensue are best viewed as impure, epistemically speaking.

CONCLUSION

I began this chapter arguing for the important place of the concept of epistemic responsibility within a feminist epistemology committed to attending to the practices and activities of inquiry. Yet a viable conception of epistemic responsibility needs to take account of, and be adaptable to, the impurities of our epistemic lives that feminists have so aptly noted. Our epistemic agency is exercised within a social world of dependence on others, through the development of networks of trust and reliability that demand complex analysis. I have found resources in the work of two feminist ethicists and have argued for the applicability of their analyses to the epistemic realm. Claudia Card's work on the importance of integrity and forward-looking senses of responsibility helps us understand how one's individual epistemic agency can be exercised within an impure world of limited choices and tremendous social influences; Walker's analysis of morality, as constituted by practices of responsibility, provides us with a model for a normative epistemology that guides us in the critical assessment of our epistemic practices and distributions of epistemic responsibility. I have argued though that this epistemological assessment too is always impure, epistemically speaking.

Although a Walker-style assessment of the expectations and distributions of epistemic responsibility may seem a far cry from the kind of normative assessment mainstream epistemologists had in mind when they tried to outline conditions of knowledge and rational belief, there is an important sense in which these projects are deeply connected. Placing questions of responsibility at the center of a normative epistemology reminds us that the point of asking the oftentimes difficult epistemological questions that mainstream epistemologists have focused on—How do we know? What counts as justification? What counts as knowledge?—are in fact questions ultimately designed to help us, as people, figure out how to know well. Card and Walker have both given us an indication of how feminist epistemologists can proceed in this direction, while taking account of the impurities of epistemic agency that are so integral to our lives.

NOTES

An earlier version of this chapter was presented at the Society for Analytical Feminism, May 2000, Chicago. The chapter has benefited from the thoughtful comments of Lisa Bergin, Carolyn McLeod, and Claudia Card. Part of the project was completed at the Calgary Institute for the Humanities where I was a Visiting Research Fellow during my 2000–2001 leave from Middlebury College, and I would like to acknowledge the assistance of both these institutions.

1. Debates about whether or not a naturalized epistemology can be sufficiently normative sometimes focus on whether or not this is a legitimate interpretation of the split between the normative and the descriptive.

2. In contrast to Frye and Hoagland, some feminists have argued that praise and blame do serve important purposes. Barbara Houston, for example, argues that to eschew moral blame would hinder attempts to increase our sense of moral agency (Houston 1992). Cheshire Calhoun has pointed out the important function of blame as an educator and a motivator, even in moral contexts, where agents could not be expected to be aware of their wrong-doing (Calhoun 1989). I omit an extended discussion of such "positive" feminist literature on blame, because I am primarily interested in understanding the concerns of feminists who take the concept of responsibility to be too focused on praise and blame, and then developing a viable sense of responsibility that will not be *solely* focused on praise and blame. I do not see the issue as focused on whether or not praise and blame should be eliminated altogether.

3. As Hoagland describes the worries, when we praise someone, we tend to worship, and with our unreasonable expectations, end up bitterly disappointed in her; when we blame someone, we hold her up as the epitome of evil. Relatedly, we obsess over making sure we cannot be blamed for any bad behavior, and we fail to move forward as a result (Hoagland 1988, 217).

4. Perhaps most famous are the discussions of Bernard Williams and Thomas Nagel on the significance of moral luck for morality.

5. There will be cases where the oppression and moral luck are so severe that one may be unable to develop integrity, Card's prerequisite for responsible agency. Card notes that when we return to determinations of "whether it makes sense to hold an agent responsible, we need to know whether that agent's luck made the development or maintenance of integrity impossible or impossibly difficult" (1996, 33). But this is very different from focusing on issues of autonomy, understood as independence, as a prerequisite for responsible agency.

6. Margaret Urban Walker has also discussed moral luck in terms of impure agency in "Moral Luck and the Virtues of Impure Agency" (1991). Walker's discussion also identifies integrity as fundamental to impure agency, but she doesn't focus specifically on issues of agency within a context of oppression.

7. Card's distinction between the forward- and backward-looking senses of responsibility is in part intended to distinguish different standards of responsibility. There are situations where, as an agent, one might *take* responsibility, even though we would not *expect* her to do so (and therefore we would not *hold her* responsible).

8. See for example *Relational Autonomy*, the recent anthology edited by Mackenzie and Stoljar (2000).

9. Such a relational view of autonomy may well include integrity as part of it (Card, personal communication).

10. In many cases the taking of responsibility that an agent demonstrates "outruns" the expectations we have of agents.

11. I am here specifically discussing only cases where androcentric investigations did live up to the current scientific standards, not cases where the individuals' research failed to live up to the community standards (thus constituting cases of "bad science"). Feminists have critiqued both these kinds of cases.

12. Walker does not consider this expressive-collaborative conception to offer a full-fledged moral theory, but instead a "template and interpretive grid for moral inquiry" (1998, 9).

13. I think Walker's insistence on the comparative nature of normative assessment is an important one, and one that has been made in contemporary philosophy of science with respect to scientific theories. As many post-Kuhnians have pointed out, scientific theories are justified in large part comparatively; theory A is selected because it does a *better* job at explaining the phenomena than the other currently available theories B, C, and D. In the case of moral practices, the relevant questions will be different: What good comes of the practice? Is it habitable? Can it survive the test of transparency in making visible its actual operations? The comparative nature of the assessment remains the same though.

14. One might think that the above quote from Walker shows my project—examining how Walker's ethical model can be applied to the epistemic realm—to be ill-conceived. After all, if Walker is herself appealing to naturalized epistemology to make sense of her ethical project, applying her project to epistemology merely seems to take us back to where we started. What I want to stress though, is that it is not just her naturalized attempt at justification that I am interested in examining, but rather that naturalized attempt within her model of ethics as practices of responsibility. What can we learn by thinking of the normative task of epistemological investigations as an investigation into practices of epistemic responsibility?

15. For a survey of the literature pertaining to racial bias in science see Sandra Harding's *The "Racial" Economy of Science* (1993).

16. See for example Elizabeth Anderson's "Knowledge, Human Interests, and Objectivity in Feminist Epistemology" (1995).

17. Another example of this intentional blurring of the boundaries of the moral and the epistemological can be found in Katherine Pyne Addelson's discussions of the "moral and intellectual responsibilities" of professional academics and knowledge makers (1991, 1994).

7

Memoirs of the Sick and the Queer: Genre and the Possibility of Oppositional Subjectivity

Abby Wilkerson

On the face of it, it may seem peculiar to identify narratives of coming out and those of illness as kindred stories. One of the earliest organized collective actions of the lesbian and gay liberation movement, after all, was the successful attempt to remove the official medical pathologization of homosexuality from the American Psychiatric Association's *Diagnostics and Statistics Manual*. Writers such as James Baldwin (1978), Barbara Deming (1985), and Martin Duberman (1991) have eloquently depicted the pivotal struggle of consciousness, especially before Stonewall and before lesbian-feminist visibility, as precisely that of learning to see oneself and one's desires as in some way healthy rather than sick. And in the case of the illness narrative (whose most recognized authors—surprise!—tend to be heterosexual), it seems that sickness is burden enough, a status its authors tend to display with every hope and intention of ultimately eluding, by whatever means possible, regardless of any gains in the form of greater wisdom, simpler living, or deeper understanding of other people's burdens. Perhaps it is not surprising, then, that writers and readers of both kinds of narratives, taken as distinct genres, might overlook any substantive connections between them. Yet what I want to suggest is that considering these genres together can teach us about (1) the possibilities of and conditions for oppositional subjectivity, and (2) the role of genre in shaping stories, their uses, and ultimately their readers.

Scholars have created a rich body of work on narrative ethics.[1] My interest in this chapter is to begin to examine how certain genres can contribute to the project of critiquing and transforming unjust power relations in society, and how genre categories may present obstacles to achieving this goal. If identities are both learned and constituted through stories, what kinds of stories can help to deconstruct oppressive identities that have been created by oppressive master narratives, and begin to build more advantageous identities individually and collectively?[2] How can stories promote the moral agency that variously situated actors may harness in making change? To address these questions, I will first survey commonalities of illness narratives and coming-out stories that make them particularly useful for this purpose; go on to consider certain challenges to these genres that may limit their oppositional value; then conclude by reflecting how, in the face of these challenges, personal narratives may contribute to more inclusive social relations, highlighting the role of genre and of the subjective and emotive aspects of narrative.

QUEERING THE NORMAL,
DE-CENTERING THE EXPERT

Both coming-out stories and illness narratives challenge oppressive social norms by offering alternatives to "master narratives" that depict certain features of the social world as inevitable, such as normative heterosexuality, or the social authority of doctors over patients, or of medical knowledge over experiential knowledge.[3] While many master narratives lend tacit support to an unjust status quo through upholding a vision of what counts as normal, alternative stories have the potential to unsettle it.

On the most basic level, authors of both coming-out stories and illness narratives offer similarly situated readers the comforting, even sanity-preserving message that they are not alone in a world at best indifferent, at worst openly hostile, to their interests, needs, too often their very existence. This function of both genres has been frequently noted in academic literature and in the popular press as well. The ways in which both also attend in important ways to issues of social justice has been underappreciated, however, especially in the case of illness narratives, perhaps because they are based on individual experience. (Thirty years of feminists chanting "the personal is the political" has not done the job.) The first coming-out anthologies of the 1970s and early 1980s can be taken as records of personal psychological growth, individual journeys to greater self-esteem and self-acceptance, and by extension, self-help tools for readers. A closer reading, however, indicates a profoundly political dimension involving two crucial elements. These stories document both the larger climate of societal heterosexism as it affects individual lives through the institution-alized discourses of medicine, law, religion, work, school, and family, as well as the emerging counter-discourse of the lesbian and gay liberation movement, revealing both societal oppression and collective resistance through the lens of personal experiences of the coming-out process, as it attacks heterosexist notions of "normal sexuality" that pathologize those who are queer-identified. Biddy Martin writes of lesbian autobiographies as "emptying traditional representations of their content, of contesting the only apparent self-evidence of 'normal' (read heterosexual) life course" (1993, 279).

A similar political dimension is also central to illness narratives. This genre represents an extremely broad range of experience that is useful to situate in the context of disability studies. Disability is most commonly understood in terms of motor or sensory impairments. But the framework of disability studies is now moving our attention beyond this limited para-digm to include other chronic, terminal, or temporary but severe condi-tions, because they, like motor impairment, are taken to be similarly representative of the ordinary human condition, rather than a departure from it or aberration. This move prompts us to consider how human social arrangements provide for embodied human life with its vast array of particular limitations, needs, and joys; how self-determination is facili-tated or denied in a thousand ways small and large; and how collective responses to human suffering are hindered or facilitated by and within particular social arrangements. To be disabled or to be ill in this society is to be stigmatized, considered a less than ideal version of one's "real" self. It is to become subject in every way to medical discourse, which has the social authority to define the truth of the body and ultimately of selfhood, undermining the social authority of the sick or disabled, significantly com-pounding the physical and psychological harms that may result from spe-cific conditions themselves (to the extent that they can be abstracted from their social milieu). Ultimately, it is to be considered fundamentally abnor-mal, a direct assault to identity, especially in the case of severe, chronic, or long-term illness.

Sociologist Arthur Frank (1995) has argued that the "sick role" imposes "narrative surrender" in which medical discourse defines reality at the expense of persons and life-meanings; thus, creating and attending to ill-ness stories constitutes resistance to the medical colonization of human life and its power to define the normal person. A disability perspective draws attention to the ways in which notions of normalcy are structured by an illusory ideal body of physical constancy and perfection—an ideal often contested in narratives of disability and illness.[4]

Both coming-out stories and illness narratives represent a fundamental crisis of selfhood: an identity structured according to a particular set of organizing principles, or one still searching for some such order, is then threatened by the crisis of illness (and disability is often constructed as illness, though they are by no means synonymous) or the apparent sexual/ social anomaly of the initial stages of coming out. This destabilized self must ultimately be reconstructed, a process that becomes the central impetus of the narrative, even—perhaps especially—in illness stories that do not result in a cure or in the restoration of all things as they were before. Both genres are also centrally preoccupied with knowing, discovering, realizing, weighing evidence, making or finding meaning, making sense, interpreting. Both present a socially grounded rather than an individualistic epistemology (whether interpersonal or based in larger social movements) and use personal experience to challenge professional or institutional authority and knowledge.

These two genres share a central concern with the complicated relationships between experience, identity, politics, and knowledge. Too often "the personal is political" has been taken to mean that experience is somehow in and of itself the ground of a transcendently authentic politics. In particular, embodied experience is often perceived as fundamentally "real," speaking its own truths on its own terms. Yet while embodied experience is certainly central to both genres, I take each to be fundamentally structured by a struggle for language and concepts amounting to a preoccupation with the discursive mediation of experience. This is particularly striking since both illness/disability and coming out are experiences whose groundedness in the body is quite apparent, yet in these stories bodies often require the mediation of discourse in order to speak their own truths: again and again we see that unmediated experiences do not necessarily speak for themselves in any self-evident ways, particularly in a social context that undermines their legitimacy, or more precisely the legitimacy of certain groups as subjects of knowledge.

As the 1980 collection *The Coming Out Stories* was being prepared for publication, Adrienne Rich wrote to the editors, "Living in the void of namelessness, as so many lesbians do, living in the silence, we must all have had intense experiences of immense significance which became unavailable to us because we had no names for them. When I think of the 'coming out process' I think of it as the beginning of naming, of memory, of making the connections between past and present and future that enable human beings to have an identity" (Stanley and Wolfe 1980, xviii). As Julia Penelope Stanley and Susan J. Wolfe note in their introduction to the volume, "Because the relationship between naming oneself and the processes involved in 'coming out' is so clear, we have organized the stories in the anthology (very roughly) on the basis of whether or not the woman had a name for her feelings" (xvix). For example, early in the volume, Janet Cooper writes of the gap between sensation and cognition she experienced as a teenager in the 1950s:

> I thrilled creating the strategy to brush against another girl's [skin] or to arrange to sit so close to her that some part of our bodies touched, or to exchange sparkling glances longer than we had any reason to look. I did not know how to name these sensations coming out. I was still unable to conceptualize what being a Lesbian meant and I thought the context in which I heard people whisper the words bull dagger, dyke, lesbian, and homosexual was slanderous. (Stanley and Wolfe 1980, 54)

Later, however, Patricia E. Hand recounts the evolution in her understanding of herself from "gay" to "lesbian" to "dyke" as a progression not only of greater self-acceptance, but of increasing "strength, solidarity and community with other Lesbians" who made these terms available to her as positive self-declarations (Stanley and Wolfe 1980, 180). Writers such as Julia Penelope Stanley, Miriam Keiffer, and Barbara Grier also note the profound impact of learning language such as "homosexual" or "lesbian" for the first time, and the shifts in perspective eventually made available to them through their participation in the "wimmin's movement" (205). Thus, there is an important sense in which coming *out* is coming *into* a language for one's own desire. And this language, with its positive valences, can only be created collectively.

The relationship between discourse and experience is also emphasized in accounts of illness or disability. Understandings of what is occurring are mediated by medical discourse as well as other discourses as they are taken up by individuals. Frank, after his own experiences with heart disease and cancer, wrote, "Too many ill persons are deprived of conversation. Too many believe they cannot talk about their illness. Talk is not the only way to elevate illness beyond pain and loss, but for most people it may be the most reliable way" (1991, 4–5). Frank and his physician made an implicit "deal" to speak of his illness with the same detachment with which a mechanic would discuss problems with his car—a "deal" essentially imposed on Frank as the price of being treated with some degree of respect. Yet, writes Frank, "My body is the means and medium of my life; I live not only in my body but also through it. No one should be asked to detach his mind from his body and then talk about this body as a thing, out there. No one should have to stay cool and professional while being told his or her body is breaking down, though medical patients always have to do just that" (10–11). Frank continues: "I needed some recognition of what was happening to me" (11). Here Frank is not merely repeating standard complaints of physician insensitivity, but rather indicating the problematic ways in which medical discourse shapes experiences of

110 Abby Wilkerson

and responses to illness, and the deep need for discursive alternatives for conceptualizing these embodied experiences in the contexts of our lives. "Conversation" thus signifies the struggle of persons to define our own reality in the face of hegemonic medical discourse.

"APOSITIONALITY" AND THE CHALLENGE TO "(OP)POSITIONALITY"

While these genres reflect and constitute oppositional subjectivities in the ways I have suggested, they also face certain challenges to their oppositional values. Chief among them is a tendency to reflect mainly the experiences of the most privileged. The canonical coming-out story tends to present coming out as the primary crisis and turning point of a life. The authors represented in Stanley and Wolfe's collection tend to construct lesbianism not so much as a biologically innate desire (as mainstream liberal discourse continues to do), but rather as a conscious, emotionally and physically felt response to a social context in which the institution of heterosexuality is a means for the patriarchal control of women. Thus, coming out is simultaneously an assertion of sexual identity and an act of feminist political solidarity.

Yet many critics by now have noted that identifying sexuality as the center of one's identity and politics clearly reflects a position of relative racial and economic privilege, and able-bodied, able-minded privilege must be acknowledged here as well. Robert McRuer has shown how some white, gay male coming-out novels such as Edmund White's display what McRuer terms "white apositionality," presenting experiences of the most privileged as the representative gay experience, an aspect of the canonical coming-out novel that McRuer argues undermines the possibility of "queer (op)positionality," which requires taking account of privilege as an essential first step in seeking a truly inclusive queer movement (McRuer 1997, 46). A similar if not identical critique can certainly be applied to The Coming Out Stories. "Apositionality," especially in terms of race, is the norm here, so much so that "La Guera" by Cherríe Moraga (writing then as Cherríe Moraga Lawrence) presents a radical departure from the rest of the volume, constructing her own lesbianism as the source of a complex politics opposing multiple forms of domination:

It wasn't until I acknowledged and confronted my own lesbianism in the flesh, that my heartfelt identification with and empathy for my mother's oppression—due to being poor, uneducated, and Chicana—was realized. My lesbianism is the avenue through which I have learned the most about silence and oppression, and it continues to be the most tactile reminder to me that we are not free human beings. (Stanley and Wolfe 1980, 189).

For Moraga, however, neither the women's movement nor lesbian feminism in particular is wholly and purely liberatory for her. Instead, Moraga writes of the harms imposed on her by the middle-class white norms embedded in the language of white feminists and in other contexts. On one level, this piece unsettles the collection's tendency to present lesbian identity as monolithic, and represents an important first step toward the critique of racial and class bias in the women's movement, which Moraga, together with Gloria Anzaldúa and their contributors, significantly advanced in the following year with *This Bridge Called My Back* (1981). Yet because it is the only piece of forty-one in *The Coming Out Stories* to address racism among feminists or lesbians, Moraga's concerns in "La Guera" are rendered wildly unrepresentative of lesbian identity.[5]

Similar critical conversations are only beginning in the realm of illness narrative and need to be extended much further. Scholars of illness narratives have indeed acknowledged that people dealing with both serious illness and poverty may well be forced to expend whatever energy is available to them in struggling to survive rather than pursuing publication. Moreover, for all but the most wealthy, severe illness or disability often imposes tremendous financial strains, so that even those who were not impoverished before their illness may eventually become so as a result. Yet the problem goes deeper than a dearth of published narratives by those experiencing multiple forms of oppression, to some of the most influential critical frameworks in this literature, where "apositionality" may result in a potentially exclusionary focus, or in readings that undermine the force of overtly political narratives.

The typical illness narrative, within the loose body of works taken up by theorists, is structured around illness as a threat to one's well-being and even one's continued existence, destabilizing personhood and identity to a degree that many or even most authors seem never to have encountered before. A stable and orderly prior life is typically evoked, even if these qualities are apparent to the author only in retrospect. Anne Hunsaker Hawkins, in her study of what she calls "pathography" or illness narrative, argues that these narratives are organized by "myths and metaphors that give meaning to the illness, organizing and interpreting it, but also [function] as dynamic constructs that actually shape and 'in form' the experience. [P]athography restores the mythic dimension that our scientific, technological culture ignores or disallows" (2000, 230–231). Scholars of illness narratives repeatedly point to the organizing metaphor of the journey as one of the most common. Hawkins argues that this is so because it "is the way [some people] actually experience their illness: It suggests the various progressive stages in an illness, it means leaving the familiar and the known to embark on an unpredictable experience involving risk, danger, and fear, and it has a goal, which can simply be returning to health or learning from their illness in such a way as to redefine the priorities and values in their lives" (230).

Frank divides the genre into three major types: the restitution narrative, celebrating the power of medicine to restore the individual to health and the self to its former equilibrium; the chaos narrative, in which illness is perceived as lack of control and incoherence (which strictly speaking is an aspect of certain narratives rather than a type of narrative, since the structured nature of narrative stands in contrast to chaos); and the quest narrative, in which "illness is the occasion of a journey that becomes a quest" (1995, 115). In Frank's view only the third type fully "affords the ill person a voice as teller of her own story, because only in quest stories does the *teller* have a story to tell" (115). Typically, the author of these stories discovers in illness a means of self-transformation. Frank places most published illness stories in this category.

This myth of the journey to the strange land, the quest for self-transformation, indeed has profound significance, offering to people who are sick or disabled an opportunity for becoming subjects of their own lives rather than objects of medical discourse, and for entering into a larger cultural community in which individual suffering becomes the ground of compassionate human connectedness. Nonetheless, this myth is far from universal to the extent that it reflects a position of social privilege not shared by everyone. Such a narrative can only be written by authors for whom a sudden illness or disability presents the greatest threat to their autonomy, well-being, and sense of self, a position that entails having avoided other major traumas such as ongoing racial or sexual harassment, hate crimes, sexual abuse, poverty, severe racial or sexual discrimination, and so on. Those facing such patterns of socially based harms would be far less likely to find the suffering imposed by illness to be a total and radical departure from a life in which a basic measure of comfort and autonomy, as well as a basic sense of safety in the world, could be taken for granted. Journalist John Hockenberry, who uses a wheelchair, makes this point clear in his accounts of his travels in Iraqi Kurdistan, where "day-to-day life was [for most people] close to the experience of living in a wheelchair. It was to go through life with the presumption that things were not going to go your way, an experience relatively rare in America and the industrialized world, but extremely common almost anywhere else. The presumption of physical adversity was widespread" (quoted in Couser 1997, 204).

In a different narrative form, which nonetheless shares many features of first-person illness narratives, psychologist Steven Schwartzberg interviewed nineteen gay men with AIDS, studying their "meaning-making" efforts in response to their illnesses. His chapter titles identify four distinct "styles of adaptation" emerging from the interviews, with striking similarities to Frank's typology: "Transformation: A Journey of Growth"; "Rupture: The Shattering of Meaning"; "Camouflage: The Fine Line of Self-Deception"; and "Impassivity: Minimizing the Trauma." While some of the men whose stories are organized by the theme of transformation construct their "quest" in spiritual terms distinct from politics, most of them reach this sense of transformation through a new or renewed sense of solidarity with other gay men and people with AIDS and through strengthened commitments to gay advocacy. It is noteworthy that almost all of the men in the study were white and all were economically stable, well-educated, and living in cities with large gay communities (1996, 237)—positions of relative social and cultural privilege; thus living with AIDS may well have been the greatest threat they had experienced despite being subject to the strictures of a hetero-normative society as gay men. For those facing multiple vectors of oppression, it seems far less likely that serious illness would be constructed primarily in terms of an opportunity for transformation.

Thus both the coming-out story and the illness narrative exhibit exclusionary tendencies that seriously limit their counter-discursive potential, since prioritizing the single dimension of illness/disability or sexual identity may be logical or useful only to those who can generally expect things to "go their way" in other aspects of life. How, then, can personal narrative help us to imagine and enact liberatory social arrangements, as respectful of pleasure as they are responsive to suffering?

GENRE, SUBJECTIVITY, AND SOCIAL TRANSFORMATION

An important first step is to seek the multiple dimensions in and of stories. This activity should be considered integral to telling stories as well as to receiving and interpreting them. Audre Lorde exemplifies such an approach in *The Cancer Journals* (1980). This work attests to the ways in which the mainstream discourse of recovery from breast cancer influences women who have had mastectomies to experience their changed bodies as shameful and indecent, shaping their life crises and ultimately their reconstructions of a destabilized self primarily in terms of preserving an attractive appearance for the sake of others. Lorde's identity and experiences, as framed by her political consciousness, provide the means for critiquing the social relations of breast cancer. She is the lesbian told that a breast prosthesis will enable her to get a man, the Black woman given a prosthesis that looks sickly pale against her skin, the feminist scolded because she makes others uncomfortable with her unashamedly asymmetrical chest. Lorde's work and that of other feminist cancer survivors helped women not only to learn to love their changed bodies but also to establish discursive contexts that facilitated political analyses of and activist responses to cancer as both personal diagnosis and social epidemic. Cancer is thereby reclaimed as a position from which to diagnose and treat a "malignant society," malignant, that is, in its hierarchies of sexuality, race, and gender, among other vectors of oppression.

I do not mean to suggest by this example that the best or most useful narratives are automatically those demonstrating the greatest number of distinct forms of oppression. What I do want to recommend is that we make the analysis of power imbalances central to our inquiries and explorations of narrative, that we begin with a central concern for detecting and dismantling unjust social hierarchies, and examine social group difference as it structures consciousness and material reality (Young 1990). Narrative identity, Paul John Eakin (1999) argues, is constructed through "social accountability," which disciplines us to talk of and experience ourselves in particular ways, and punishes us when we fail to do so. Yet for members of oppressed groups, some of the narrative constructions defined as essential to social participation must be undone in order to legitimize the self on the individual and collective levels. As Carol Thomas notes in her analysis of narratives by women with disabilities, "Without the counter-narratives of others who challenge social 'norms' we, as isolated individuals, are trapped within the story-lines of the prevailing narratives" (1999, 54). Hilde Lindemann Nelson provides a conceptually powerful model for this process in her work on "counterstories," which she defines as any "story that resists an oppressive identity and attempts to replace it with one that commands respect" (2001, 6). This work also provides a rich array of examples attending to a variety of differences.

Nelson and I are in agreement on an oppositional approach to narrative (that is, employing narrative in opposing unjust social norms), but I advocate a significant role for the *subjective* aspect of narrative as well. First, oppositional subjectivity involves an experiential dimension that is a necessary condition for speaking as a witness. In their work on survivor discourse, Linda Martín Alcoff and Laura Gray-Rosendale identify a witness as "someone who knows the truth and has the courage to tell it" (1996, 220). Although social relations construct authority in terms of expertise, there is nonetheless a culturally recognized form of authority that resides in the witness as well, due to her direct experience. Only the witness can tell us *what it was like* to live through her experience, a powerful form of testimony that has perhaps a unique capacity for fostering empathy in her listeners.

Another critical component of subjectivity for both tellers and hearers of stories is emotion. While many philosophers have been suspicious of emotion as the enemy of reason, others have argued that rationality and emotion are complementary. David B. Morris advocates a kind of engagement he calls "thinking *with* stories" (after Arthur Frank), rather than thinking *about* them—"a process in which we as thinkers do not so much work on narrative as take the radical step back, almost a return to childhood experience, of allowing narrative to work on us" (2001, 55). Emotion is critical to this process; for Morris, narrative, emotion, and pain are all intertwined in ethics in important ways. His image of looking into the eyes of someone in pain is a metaphor for narrative's ability to foster a direct and immediate recognition of the personhood of the other, a moral recognition that registers on a deep emotional level: "The face, like narrative, exerts a kind of 'call.' It connects us to the other in an ethics that precedes reason, thought, and principle, an ethics born of immediate contact" (68). Morris presents "an ethics of right moments, when emotion inspires an inexorable drive toward right conduct that principles alone cannot provoke" (69). He is not arguing for a nonrational ethics, however, but instead "suggest[ing] that reason and emotion may share integrated, complementary roles in the creation of moral knowledge and ethical action" (71), as he believes a narrative ethics exemplifies.

Sydney Callahan (2000) appeals to neurobiology and developmental psychology to ground her account of the complex intertwining of cognitive and emotional processes in ethical reflection. She concludes that ethical decision making is an "art" (32), whose "goal is an emotively grounded reflective equilibrium [of reason and emotion] in which all systems are integrated, all tests are satisfied, and a wholehearted decision can be made" (33). As Morris suggests, these complementary workings of cognition and emotion are especially evident in narrative ethics: "The ambiguities, complexities, ironies, and plural meanings so valued by scholars of narrative are more than invitations to intellectual analysis. Especially in moments of dire conflict and inescapable choice . . . they make a crucial contribution to engaging the emotions of characters and audiences" (2001, 67).

I find these arguments valuable because I have seen emotion—the outrage, for example, of some students learning of oppressive social conditions of which they were previously unaware—serve as a powerful resource in transforming consciousness, a necessary precondition for action. Indeed, Mary Pellauer (1985) has argued persuasively that the *suppression* of emotions is a major contributor to social injustice, when, for example, we develop "moral callousness," an emotional insensitivity, to the suffering of others, or our own, an attitude she argues society has maintained toward violence against women in particular. Thus, we should explore emotion as an important ethical resource, a partner with reason as a resource for overturning unjust social hierarchies and motivating people (especially the socially privileged) to attend to the experiences of those different from themselves. Attending to the multiple dimensions of stories and other aspects of their oppositional value, then, goes hand in hand with attending to and valorizing their subjective dimensions; these strategies can channel moral reflection in productive directions for social change. Fostering awareness of the subjective reality of the Other may well be necessary to promote the solidarity upon which inclusiveness is based.

The value of such strategies, however, will be severely constrained unless we also pay attention to the ways in which conventions of genres and the boundaries between them are shaped and maintained. Disability activists have demonstrated how both public and domestic spaces are structured in ways that facilitate access for some users while hindering it for others. Similarly, genres are structured to accommodate some writers and readers while barring others. Daily practices of the publishing industry, for example—from manuscript decisions to bookstore shelf categories to marketing lists—shape and reinforce genre boundaries. So does the work of libraries, popular press reviewers, and scholars. Too often genres are treated as reflecting a fundamental natural reality, rather than reflecting and reinforcing a socially created phenomenon. Designating a work an illness narrative or a coming-out story is a gate-keeping function. We should consider in particular how these categories sometimes function to exclude some works while drawing attention to others.

For example, Daphne Scholinski's *The Last Time I Wore a Dress* (1997), her memoir of involuntary commitment and diagnosis with gender identity disorder, is not addressed in either the scholarly literature on illness narratives, or in courses on them. Perhaps this is because Scholinski rejects the idea that her unconventional gender expression is "sick" or in any way problematic except through others' responses to it. In a Web search, this work appears occasionally in courses on transgender, on women and madness, and in several composition courses with themes such as "finding a voice" (facilitated by its being excerpted in a composition anthology). It does not, as far as I can tell, appear on syllabi for courses on illness narrative (other than my own), at least none posted on the Web. In fact, the genre of illness narratives precludes consideration of stories that reject their protagonists' pathologization. If genre boundaries prevent us from considering such stories, we lose an important resource for understanding and transforming the social relations of illness and the power of professional and institutional discourse over individuals. Our conception of a genre can also direct our attention to some aspects of a work at the expense of others, or render a work and its concerns exceptional or a special case, as when gay men's AIDS stories are considered unrepresentative of illness narratives insofar as they focus on sexual identity and larger political issues. Disciplinary borders could be usefully expanded beyond the conventional literary narrative, to include, for example, participatory action research or ethnographic studies with an ethos of responsiveness and responsibility toward the communities being studied, or anthologies such as Evelyn White's *The Black Women's Health Book* (1994).

In short, I advocate making oppositional subjectivity central to our conceptualization and uses of illness narratives, coming-out stories, and other genre frameworks. It should also influence our critical analysis of genre itself, which affects how narratives are taken up, in what contexts, and by whom, as well as which narratives are considered relevant for which purposes. Stories of the sick and the queer are indeed kindred stories in challenging oppressive notions of normality, and they should be considered together with others that also unsettle unjust norms in provocative and productive ways.

NOTES

I would like to thank Pam Presser for her insightful discussion with me of a number of issues addressed in this chapter. Thanks also to Ami Bar On, Bob McRuer, Iris Young, and other audience members of the 2001 Narrative International Conference and the 2001 Feminist Ethics and Social Theory Conference for helpful comments on earlier versions of this chapter.

1. See Hilde Lindemann Nelson (2001) for a useful review of major approaches to narrative ethics. Thomas Couser (1997), Arthur Frank (1991, 1995), Anne Hunsaker Hawkins (1993, 1998), Arthur Kleinman (1988), and Hilde Lindemann Nelson (1997) are key works on illness narratives.

2. See Paul John Eakin (1999) and Hilde Lindemann Nelson (2001) on the narrative construction and constitution of identity.

3. See Nelson (2001) for a useful discussion of master narratives and the features needed by alternative stories in order to mount a successful challenge to them. I will take up Nelson's notion of counterstories shortly.

4. See Lennard J. Davis (1995) and Rosemarie Garland Thomson (1997) for particularly astute critiques of the idealized social law of normalcy.

5. Lisa C. Moore's collection of Black lesbian coming out stories broadens the racial representation of coming out. She addresses the need for such an anthology in her introduction: "I came out in college in a community of white lesbians. In the early 1980s, coming out literature was all the rage, and I'd read it all. . . . Sure, I looked for black images in gay literature, but the lack of them didn't phase me much. . . . After moving to Atlanta, though, I found myself completely surrounded by beautiful black women; it altered my perceptions of reality. . . . Suddenly, I longed for black images in gay literature; I found it incredibly lacking" (1997, ii).

8

Integrity and Vulnerability

Cheryl L. Hughes

Over the past twenty-five years, medical care has gradually shifted from a traditional, paternalistic model of care based on the knowledge and authority of the physician, to a patient-centered model based on the principles of beneficence and respect for autonomy. Consider, for example, the American Hospital Association's *Patient Bill of Rights*, first presented in 1972 and revised in 1992 (Beauchamp and Walters 1999, 69–70). Respect for autonomy is rooted in the liberal political tradition that places primary value on individual freedom and self-governance. The autonomous agent must be free from interference or external constraint and must have the critical mental capacities to make informed choices based on his or her values, beliefs, and individual interests. The principle of beneficence is closely linked with respect for autonomy and involves action that aims at the welfare and well-being of the individual. Whereas respect for autonomy primarily involves a negative duty of noninterference, beneficence includes the negative duty to avoid harm or injury to others as well as the positive duty to assist others in fulfilling their legitimate and important individual goals. Thus for example, clinical therapies aim at promotion of health and restoration of function (beneficence) and require the informed consent of the patient (respect for autonomy).

When there is a potential conflict between beneficent concern for the health of a patient and respect for autonomy, autonomy is given priority. We respect the right of competent adults to make decisions and define their own lives for themselves, even when others might argue that their decisions are not in their best interests. We respect the decision of a competent adult to refuse medical treatment, for example, even when treatment is necessary to save the person's life. Thus according to one recent formulation of this view: "To respect the autonomy of self-determining agents is to recognize them as *entitled* to determine their own destiny, with due regard to their considered evaluations and view of the world" (Beauchamp and Walters 1999, 19).

Ronald Dworkin has suggested that this way of formulating respect for autonomy is ultimately based in the value we attach to the integrity of the individual, where integrity is understood as "the capacity to express one's own character—values, commitments, convictions, and critical as well as experiential interests—in the life one leads" (1993, 224). According to Dworkin, recognizing a right of autonomy in bioethics involves promoting the personal integrity that makes "self-creation" possible:

> It allows us to lead our own lives rather than be led along them, so that each of us can be, to the extent a scheme of rights can make this possible, what we have made of ourselves. We allow someone to choose death over radical amputation or a blood transfusion, if that is his informed wish, because we acknowledge his right to a life structured by his own values. (224)

This principled emphasis on autonomy and the integrity of self-determination becomes problematic, however, when we consider the experiences of persons suffering from chronic diseases, especially those that involve physical and mental deterioration and the gradual loss of independence. Consider the following case:

> Mrs. B is an eighty-six-year-old widow who lives in a retirement home. She has one very good friend but no family nearby. She suffers from chronic kidney failure and has been on dialysis for about eighteen months. Over the past eight months, Mrs. B has told her doctors, her nurses, and her friend that she wants to stop dialysis. She understands that her life depends on receiving dialysis, but she hates the process and says that she does not want to live this way. Yet she continues to board the van that takes her to the dialysis center three times each week. She claims that every time she tells her nephrologist she wants to stop, he describes the risks of falls, fractures, and a miserable death. Even with the dialysis, Mrs. B has been hospitalized three times after falls or for pneumonia. With each hospital stay, her statements about discontinuing dialysis are stronger, although when her nephrologist comes by on his rounds, she is quiet and appears to accede to treatment. She says that her wishes are clear and her instructions ignored, but she also admits that she is confused about whether it is truly right to discontinue the treatments. A consulting psychiatrist concludes that she is oriented, competent, and severely depressed, as evidenced by her wish to discontinue treatment. He prescribes Prozac.[1]

Mrs. B does not seem to demonstrate the personal integrity that Dworkin describes. In fact, she seems to offer us a clear example of someone who lacks integrity. She seems to be easily swayed by others, preferring to accommodate herself to the wishes of her caregivers and compromise her own values. Perhaps she is weak-willed, lacking the courage to act consistently on her own convictions; or perhaps she is simply a hypocrite, insisting on her right to end dialysis when she is among friends and complaining that her wishes are ignored, but never actively insisting on her rights when she is with her doctor. All of these behaviors mark her as someone who seems to be deficient in integrity under Dworkin's definition.

But we should pay attention to the vulnerability of this patient. Severe chronic illness forces an individual to revise her hopes and expectations, alter her daily life, and accept an increased and often unwelcome dependence on family and other caregivers. Chronic illness can disrupt the integrity and identity of the person who must learn to live with new needs and limitations. Chronic disease and disability may also disrupt important social relationships because of others' fear and misunderstanding or humiliating sympathy. Vulnerability increases with conditions that are life threatening, such as heart disease, cancer, and renal disease; and many chronic diseases such as Parkinson's disease and Alzheimer's disease are progressively debilitating and will gradually lead to nearly complete dependence on others. With an aging population, the prevalence of chronic and degenerative illnesses of old age will increase. How can we meet the needs of people suffering from chronic illness and treat them with dignity as full members of the moral community? How can we continue to respect agency and integrity as individual control diminishes and the ability to actively maintain a meaningful life declines?

In what follows, I will first explore Dworkin's answer to these questions based on his analysis of integrity. I will then consider alternative views of integrity drawn from recent feminist work and Ricoeur's theory of narrative identity. I will argue that Dworkin's view of integrity as self-creation is too narrow and too individualistic to adequately guide our moral responses to the vulnerable. A revised view of integrity as an important social and relational virtue will offer better resources for treating vulnerable persons with the respect that honors the dignity and integrity of their lives.

INTEGRITY AND SELF-CREATION

In his analysis of the relation between patient autonomy and integrity, Dworkin (1993) focuses on the rights of people in the late stages of Alzheimer's disease. His concern is for the special cases of individuals who were once competent but who become demented, and he asks whether such patients retain a right to autonomy. Consider an example that Dworkin uses:

> Margo is a 54 year-old Alzheimer's victim who is a shadow of her former self. An attendant cares for her in her apartment, which is carefully locked to prevent her from wandering out at night in her nightgown. Margo says she is reading mysteries but she seems to open a book at random and to be happy just sitting, humming to herself, rocking back and forth slowly, napping, and occasionally turning a page in the book. Margo attends an art class for Alzheimer's patients and paints the same picture every time. To the medical student who visits her, she appears to be "one of the happiest people he has ever known," taking simple but real pleasure in things like eating peanut-butter sandwiches. Yet the student asks, "When a person can no longer accumulate new memories as the old rapidly fade, what remains? Who is Margo?" (220–221)

Do people like Margo retain any sense of personal integrity or a right to autonomy? As Dworkin asks, should we care about the dignity of a dementia patient if she herself has no sense of it? The case of Margo seems to be a difficult case for any talk of integrity or autonomy. According to Dworkin's analysis, respect for autonomy protects a person's capacity for "self-creation," the capacity to shape one's life according to the individual's distinctive sense of character and values or a distinctive sense of self (Dworkin 1993, 224). But the seriously and permanently demented person loses this capacity for integrity in shaping his or her own life and therefore also loses the right to autonomy. Of course the incompetent and demented Alzheimer's patient still has the right to beneficence, the right that decisions should be made based on his best interests and well-being. But, according to Dworkin, the patient no longer has the right to make choices about a guardian, use of his property, or his medical treatment because he lacks the competence to act with integrity: "the ability to act out of genuine preference or character or conviction or a sense of self" (225).

At this point, Dworkin introduces the notion of "precedent autonomy." He argues that if integrity as self-creation is the basis for a right to autonomy, then we must respect the *past* wishes of an individual. Thus a competent person might make a living will that would stipulate how he should be treated if he suffers the serious dementia and decline of Alzheimer's disease. As with other advance decisions about treatment at the end of life, Dworkin argues that we should respect the individual's right to control the shape of her life, to avoid treatment at the end of life as an Alzheimer's victim that would compromise the character of her life as a whole. The demented person lacks the necessary capacity for a fresh exercise of autonomy; but the former decision about her own life remains in force.

This would mean, for example, that we would respect an advance directive to withhold routine medical care for pneumonia or other life-threatening conditions in an Alzheimer's patient. If certain forms of voluntary euthanasia become permissible, we might be obliged to respect an advance directive requesting that an individual be helped to die as soon as possible in the event she develops the serious dementia of Alzheimer's disease.

Patients like Margo seem to enjoy the simple pleasures of their lives, the pleasures of good food or the loving touch of another person, and we might think that beneficent concern for these continuing pleasures would outweigh any advance directive. However, according to Dworkin, such "experiential interests" may contribute to a good life, but they are given much less weight than our "critical interests." Critical interests are those projects, plans, and defining choices that give meaning and coherence to our lives, make our lives more successful or more valuable on the whole, and link past, present, and future. Since the demented person no longer has the capacity for shaping critical interests, he must retain the critical interests that he defined for himself when he was competent. And thus, once again we are obliged to determine the best interests of the patient in terms of integrity where this is understood to mean fidelity to the narrative coherence of the individual's life *before* dementia. This comes out clearly when Dworkin reports that half the people he surveyed were "repelled by the idea of living demented, totally dependent lives, speaking gibberish, incapable of understanding that there is a world beyond them. . . . They think a life ending like that is seriously marred" (1993, 231). According to Dworkin, it is compassion "toward the whole person" that underlies beneficence.

In my view, this way of describing autonomy and beneficence leads to intuitively troubling consequences. Dworkin gives no weight to the apparently comfortable existence of patients like Margo; he gives no weight to their relationships with family and friends. He gives no weight to the relationships of caregivers or the wider community to these vulnerable patients. His argument assumes that valuable and meaningful life ends with the onset of dementia, that degenerative disease and disability inevitably mar the life created by an individual. But I think that Dworkin is mistaken in his analysis of integrity in terms of "self-creation." In what follows, I want to explore the ways in which integrity is not simply a personal virtue, not simply a static notion of personal unity, or fidelity to character, or even narrative unity where one is viewed as the sole author and arbiter of one's narrative identity. Using insights from recent feminist work and from Ricoeur's theory of narrative identity, I want to challenge Dworkin's conclusions by challenging his concept of integrity.

RETHINKING INTEGRITY FROM
A FEMINIST PERSPECTIVE

Cheshire Calhoun (1995) has argued that integrity is not only a personal virtue but also a social virtue. Standing firm on one's basic moral principles, protecting the boundaries of the self by remaining true to one's projects, insisting that there are some things one will not do regardless of the consequences—all of these involve "standing for something" in relation to other members of the community. Standing for something means representing and endorsing a socially recognized position (Calhoun 1995, 254). Thus integrity is both personal and social, involving proper regard for one's own moral status as well as proper regard for one's place among other moral beings—integrity is tied to viewing oneself as a member of an evaluating community and caring about what that community endorses.

Perhaps more importantly, according to Calhoun, one does not simply exercise the virtue of integrity by asserting and defending oneself and "sticking to one's guns"(Calhoun 1995, 259). Integrity is a social virtue in the further sense that one is expressing one's best judgment about what is worth doing. One takes one's stand before others who share the goal of determining what is worth doing. One must acknowledge the singularity of one's own best judgment and acknowledge others as deliberators who must also abide by their best judgments (259–260). We are involved with others in the ongoing project of defining what is worth doing, and we must take seriously the doubts and best judgments of our co-deliberators. Integrity is therefore not exclusively a personal and individual virtue, but a social virtue—"the virtue of having a proper regard for one's own judgment as a deliberator among deliberators" (259).

Victoria Davion (1991) has also criticized the usual notions of integrity as being incompatible with change and development across a human life. She points out that many feminists have experienced radical changes in their fundamental values and commitments. If integrity depends exclusively on some core of "unconditional commitments" or critical interests, then it would seem that radical change in a person's life would always involve a loss of integrity. Against this view, Davion argues that integrity includes a minimum of truly unconditional commitments and a process of working on the self, caring about the self, and reflectively assessing particular commitments as part of the process through which an individual grows and changes. Integrity is not just a static defense of oneself or one's critical interests; we should also understand integrity as "being willing to explore commitments and change them when necessary" (183). Davion notes that one can maintain the wholeness and harmony of a life of integrity by monitoring the process of change and development—one can weave together events and experiences and changing roles by reflecting on deeper values and understanding how one's beliefs fit together. Thus Davion concludes that we can best understand integrity as "an unconditional commitment to monitor who we are becoming" (186). One can still maintain core commitments and develop a coherent wholeness if one is committed to this work of self-knowledge and reflection through changes over time.

Margaret Urban Walker has also developed a concept of integrity that is "true to the changing, deeply relational character of human lives" (1997, 63). Walker describes integrity as reliable accountability—the willingness to maintain, or reestablish, our reliability in matters involving important commitments and goods (64). Her view emphasizes local dependability, flexibility, and responsiveness to the moral costs of error and change. Walker appeals to a narrative understanding of the moral construction of lives. We give our lives a distinctive individual character through narratives of identity, relationship, and value; but both one's identity and one's values are bound up with specific relationships to others. We develop "a history of our shared understandings of what kinds of things, relationships, and commitments really *are* important, and what their relative importance is" (69).

Like Davion's work, Walker's view makes room for growth and change over time. As we accumulate new experiences, we will bring our values under scrutiny. We will sometimes reaffirm values, but we may also reinterpret, refine, revise, or even replace values over time. Walker goes beyond Davion's call for self-monitoring to preserve integrity through change. Maintaining integrity involves making sense of what reasons one has for acting and then submitting those reasons to others. We do not act with integrity unless we take account of our responsibilities and relationships to others and offer a moral justification that is always interpersonal.

Walker also goes beyond Cheshire Calhoun's work on the social aspects of integrity. She places more emphasis on the fallibility and limitations of our deliberative efforts. Despite our attempts to live up to our best judgments about what is worth doing, we will face inevitable conflicts in values and we will make mistakes. Some of these mistakes and apparent failures rest on the fact that within any life there are many relationships that may sometimes come into conflict. Consider, for example, the self-understanding, values, and responsibilities that will accompany my experiences of being someone's daughter, sister, mother, friend, colleague, teacher, neighbor, and so forth. No simple story will cover these versions of my identity, and new circumstances may create new responsibilities or set up conflicts in my various roles. Suppose I agree to attend an important meeting with colleagues who are planning a special event at my college; but then I discover that my son has a concert on the same day and I have promised to go to all of his concerts. I cannot keep both of my commitments even though both are important, but I can act with integrity if I explain the conflict to my son and my colleagues and find a way to compensate for breaking my commitment to one of them. Walker concludes, "A central use of 'integrity,' then, is to describe not only people who act well from, as it were, a standing position but also people who own up to and clean up messes, their own and others" (Walker 1997, 74).

Finally, we may borrow insights from Paul Ricoeur's (1992, 1993) analysis of narrative identity to further explore the social aspects of identity and integrity. Although we clearly construct first-person narratives to establish our own unified life histories, first-person narrative does not produce the atomistic, self-created individual. Rather, we first understand narrative in third-person stories and we gain some measure of self-understanding from the stories told about ourselves. I have very few memories from early childhood, but I do have the stories that my parents used to tell about me—being afraid of the family dog, being a chatter box, having a sweet and sunny disposition—and when I forget about my occasional bad temper, my brothers will remind me by gleefully retelling stories to the whole family. Even in first-person narrative identity, one describes oneself as a subject who is deeply connected to others in many ways. Thus for example, I can be both narrator and character in my life story, but I can only be coauthor because sections of my life history are entangled in the histories of others—my life is part of the life histories of my parents, siblings, friends, and acquaintances. Furthermore, the beginning and end of my life belong more to the histories of others than to me. My conception, birth, and early childhood are not even part of my own memories and belong to the stories of my parents. Similarly, I can never grasp my own death as an experience or a narrative end; stories of my death will belong to those who survive me. First-person narrative is descriptive but it is also selective and interpretive and therefore partial, excluding some things that could be included and emphasizing, weighting, and valuing the things that are included. Because my life-narrative is always open and unfinished, interpretive and partial, my narrative identity is always open to revision. According to Ricoeur, the realization of personal identity understood in the sense of one's lasting character requires the mediation of others who contribute to the narrative emplotment of character; and integrity understood as reliability and accountability is constituted in responsibility to others.

RETHINKING INTEGRITY AND VULNERABILITY

Let me return now to the problems of Mrs. B (the patient suffering from kidney failure) and Margo (the victim of Alzheimer's disease), in order to see how this rethinking of integrity can help us understand and respond to vulnerable persons. Once we see the social and relational aspects of integrity, we can begin to criticize the idea of integrity as a capacity for "self-creation." Although we will give a certain priority to first-person accounts of narrative identity and critical interests, we should also consider the ways in which an individual's life is lived in relation to others. We should consider that the narrative coherence of a whole life will include events and circumstances that are not under the control of the individual. The idea that I might make an advance directive that completely controls the end of my life-story neglects the changing, relational aspects of human lives.

Thus we might ask in cases of dementia, why should the competent person who is author of an advance directive be the only person with a relevant interest in determining how she is treated if she becomes demented? Our narratives are bound up with the lives and stories of others and we neglect our responsibilities to others when we attempt to determine the future without regard to our future relationships with others. This does not mean that doctors and hospitals should refuse to respect advance-directives, but it does imply, at a minimum, that advance directives should be made in consultation with one's family. It also implies that advance directives might not be the best means to protect integrity and dignity in a future that we can neither predict nor control. As an alternative, we might consider giving power of attorney to a very close friend or family member, someone who knows our values and who could make decisions for us once we are no longer able to make our own coherent choices. This would permit the continued participation of family, caretakers, and physicians who could offer their best judgments of what is worth doing for the demented patient as the dementia progresses.

A more complex description of narrative identity and integrity challenges any simplistic notion of how we define critical interests in a human life. Walker's (1999) criticism of the career self can be applied to this argument. Walker argues that the dominant concept of narrative identity involves a sense of one's life lived according to a rational plan, with a linear story that gets meaning from the climax of adult achievements. We value productive self-governance and denigrate or minimize the experiences of dependence or discontinuity in our lives. Walker suggests that there may be a more adequate conception of life as a journey with lateral connections that enrich and transcend the individual. Instead of integrating all experiences into a coherent story of my life as a whole, I might better think of the meaning of my life as constituted by the way my life can be integrated into other lives and collective experiences. I might better think about the many ways in which I have participated in larger stories that transcend the story of my life—being part of a family (past, present, and future), being a participant in a political movement or a religious community, being part of the ongoing work of educating young people, making some small contribution to the ongoing work of philosophy, but also being cared for in times of need or dependency and being part of the ongoing human work of caring for one another. Given this understanding, I would not place the entire value of my life in my own successful completion of rational plans as a mature adult. I would perhaps understand that part of who I am and part of the meaning of my life is the way my life is integrated into the lives of others, including my reception of their care for me, and that this sort of integration and meaning could continue even in dementia.

Thus in the case of Margo, for example, since the development of dementia in Alzheimer's patients is usually very gradual, there will be a continuing narrative of Margo's life that includes the early onset of her disease, changes in her interests, and accounts of the ways she copes with loss. As Davion's work suggests, Margo will try to integrate her illness into her life and sense of self, negotiating changes and working to maintain meaningful relationships. Unless she chooses to commit suicide as soon as a diagnosis of Alzheimer's disease is confirmed, her experience with Alzheimer's will be an unavoidable part of the story of her life as a whole and not subject to her control. At a certain point in her experience with dementia, she will no longer be the principal narrator of her life. But as Ricoeur's view suggests, we are dependent on others for many aspects of our narrative identity—for stories about our birth and early years, reminders about details that we may have forgotten, corrections when we distort our own narratives or deceive ourselves, and so forth. We are also completely dependent on others to remember us after death and to sustain the memory of who we were. One could easily imagine that Margo's closest family or her caretakers might need to help her maintain her narrative identity through changes in her condition. They might provide continuity to the past, emphasizing her love of reading as it is still expressed in her life, for example, rather than emphasizing the apparent inadequacies of her random page turning. Thus in contrast to Dworkin's view, we would not insist that a life of integrity and dignity is over when a person can no longer shape critical interests.

Finally, we can use this richer notion of integrity to better understand the situation of Mrs. B, the patient suffering from kidney failure. If we give up the idea of integrity as "self-creation" and pay attention to integrity as a social and relational virtue, we can begin to see that Mrs. B is actually struggling to maintain her own integrity in the face of chronic disease and growing dependence. She is talking with friends and health professionals about her discomfort, testing the possibility that she might end treatment, perhaps seeking the responses from others that could help her find good reasons for a decision and peace of mind. If we simply stand back and say: it's up to her, she's the patient, *she* has to decide, or if we say she's being wishy-washy and clearly lacks integrity, then we miss the fact that she is making every effort to "stand for something before others" in a time of vulnerability. If we simply say she is depressed because she wants to end treatment, then again we miss the fact that both the chronic disease and the treatment are discontinuities in her life and may disturb her sense of self. We should be asking ourselves, what is our responsibility here? What can we do to help her reexamine her life and her values and her relationships to others so that she can act with integrity?

If we give up the idea of integrity as "self-creation," we will still respect the informed and competent wishes of an individual, but we will also be better able to assist the vulnerable to maintain meaning and continuity through illness and the process of aging. Integrity is a virtue of agency that ultimately aims at the good life for the individual: a life lived well according to the values, beliefs, and continuity of character that one has developed over time. But acting with integrity as members of a moral community will include learning how to live well together through chronic illness, disability, dependence, and decline.

NOTES

The first draft of this chapter was written as part of an NEH 2000 Summer Seminar, "Bioethics in Particular," directed by Hilde Lindemann Nelson and James Lindemann Nelson at the University of Tennessee in Knoxville.

1. This case was modified slightly from *The Hastings Center Report* 30, no. 6 (2000): 24.

9

Physician-Assisted Suicide and Euthanasia: Weighing Feminist Concerns

Norah Martin

In "Feminist Bioethics and Psychiatry" (Martin 2001) I argue that one of the biggest challenges facing feminist bioethicists is how to deal with the tension between care for suffering individuals and concern for issues of power and oppression. Nowhere is this issue more pressing or troubling than in feminist considerations of physician-assisted suicide (PAS) and euthanasia. Susan M. Wolf's "Gender, Feminism, and Death: Physician-Assisted Suicide and Euthanasia" (1996) raises some important gender considerations with regard to PAS and euthanasia and shows how feminist analysis can be brought to bear on these and related issues. While her concerns should certainly give proponents of PAS pause and point to inadequacies in current laws and proposals, her argument against legalization is ultimately unconvincing and has some disturbing consequences. In particular, it would appear that Wolf recommends requiring suffering individuals who are already victims of oppression to continue to suffer as part of the greater fight to overcome suffering and oppression. Sydney Callahan (1996) also raises feminist concerns in arguments against PAS and euthanasia, many of which echo Wolf's.

In addition to the issue of the tension between care for suffering individuals and the struggle to overcome oppression, there are other concerns of importance to feminists. Wolf and Callahan argue that women will be disproportionately affected by the legalization of PAS because they

131

will be expected to sacrifice their lives to ease the burden that caring for them places on others. Yet concern that women will be disproportionately affected by the legalization of PAS may lead to a conclusion different from that of Wolf and Callahan. As PAS laws are currently conceived it may be that women are discriminated against in that they will be less able to take advantage of them. That is, it may be the case that women's requests to die will be less likely to be heard and acted upon than men's requests, rather than women more often being put in the position of feeling obligated to die and their requests more often being acceded to, as Wolf and Callahan argue. The arguments of Wolf and Callahan, while they raise important points for feminists to consider, do not lead to the conclusion that feminists should be opposed to PAS. Thus, it remains unclear whether feminist concerns should lead to opposition or support of PAS laws and of euthanasia.

In this chapter I shall discuss several problems with Wolf's position and arguments, some of which have been previously discussed by Diane Raymond and Dena Davis. I will draw an analogy between the choice of the terminally ill woman and the non-choice of the character O at the end of *The Story of O*. I will also discuss concerns shared by Wolf and Callahan that may just as easily lead to a conclusion quite different from the one they draw. I do not come to a conclusion as to how to resolve the tension between care for those who suffer and fighting oppression, nor do I come to a definite position on PAS. My intention rather is to highlight the tension in relation to PAS and euthanasia, emphasize its importance in the realm of feminist bioethics, and suggest some new ways to think about it.

WOLF'S ARGUMENT

Wolf rightly points out that debates about PAS and active euthanasia speak of a patient with no gender, race, or insurance status—the same generic patient featured in most bioethics debates. Yet differences among patients may alter the way we think about the questions surrounding PAS and euthanasia. Most of the cases prominent in the American debate feature women. Wolf reminds us that this occurs against a backdrop of a history of cultural images "revering women's sacrifice and self-sacrifice" (1996, 282). Also, the quality of healthcare one gets and one's general health status may affect a patient's vulnerability to considering PAS, including things that differentially plague women, such as depression, poor pain relief, and difficulty obtaining good healthcare. Suicide itself is more often attempted by women, though less often completed, suggesting the possibility that women's requests for PAS may, more often than men's, be an effort to change an oppressive situation rather than a literal request for death. Certainly American society devalues women who are ill, disabled, or even just old. The traditional valorization of women's self-sacrifice may affect women's readiness to request death and the physician's responses to this request. Physicians may be likely to affirm women's negative self-judgments.

Wolf points out that in addition to its concern for women, feminist criticism also suggests three sorts of problems with the way the rhetoric of rights justifies PAS and euthanasia. First, the rhetoric of rights ignores *context*. In what context has the patient made her decision? Her choices may be severely constrained. Some of the constraints may be alterable or removable. By ignoring the question of context, those who focus on rights leave no room for exploring possible alternatives to her request.

The second problem Wolf finds suggested by feminist criticism is that in focusing on rights we extol "the vision of a rights bearer as an isolated monad and denigrate actual dependencies" (1996, 299). In doing so, we fail to ask what sort of family, social, economic, and medical support she is getting. Improving a patient's circumstances may be more appropriate than acceding to her request to die. The final problem Wolf identifies as suggested by feminist criticism is that those who use the rights argument to defend PAS and euthanasia confuse two separate issues: what the patient may do and what the physician may do.

RAYMOND'S CRITICISMS OF WOLF

Diane Raymond points to a number of reasons that should lead us to be cautious in accepting Wolf's arguments. I will not discuss all of them, but rather only those relevant to the overall points I wish to make in this chapter. Raymond suggests that because women are traditionally taken less seriously than men, their requests for death may also be taken less seriously. Wolf herself notes early in her essay that physicians may ignore women's requests for death due to misogynistic beliefs that women are irrational and overly emotional. Wolf never returns to this point, yet it seems at least as likely a possibility as the one she takes more seriously, namely that women are more likely to have their requests granted. Further, Raymond finds Wolf's argument from self-sacrifice to suicide suspicious. One might argue instead that, "given that women's historical role has been to endure selflessly all forms of labor and abuse, particularly in the domestic sphere, suicide may for women be the ultimate transgressive act" (Raymond 1999, 10). The gender ideology discussed in Wolf's essay may in fact suggest a greater reluctance rather than eagerness to grant women's requests for death. According to Raymond, there is evidence to suggest that men are undertreated at the end of life, whereas women are

overtreated. As Raymond points out, Steven Miles and Allison August have
found that in judicial decisions relating to withdrawal of treatment at the
end of life there is a pattern of "acceding to male patients' wishes over
females'" (11). Women's requests to die are held to higher evidentiary
standards. Miles and August point to gendered language in judicial treatments of these cases, which tends to discount women's agency. "[M]en's
statements about end-of-life treatment are held to reflect 'mature, rational
choice' while women's are seen as 'unreflective, emotional, or immature'" (Miles and August 1990, 87; Raymond 1999, 11).

One might question the assertion that women are overtreated at the
end of life whereas men are undertreated given that men have much
greater access to earlier interventions such as standard diagnostic procedures as well as to things like organ transplants. However, the two are
actually consistent with patriarchal ideology in that we hold to a higher
standard of quality of life for men than for women. "If such is the case,"
says Raymond, "then gender ideology, in valorizing female passivity, may
actively collude with the medical profession in keeping dying, suffering
women alive. Likewise, ideological constructions of masculinity as inextri-
cably aligned with agency, activity, and transcendence might lead to
respect for men's medical directives—formal *and* informal—as well as to
gendered distinctions on quality-of-life issues" (1999, 11).

DAVIS'S CRITICISMS OF WOLF

Dena Davis in her "Why Suicide Is Like Contraception" (1998) takes issue
with another of Wolf's concerns. Wolf argues that women's decisions to
commit suicide, and society's acceptance of those decisions as appropriate, may be skewed by "a long history of cultural images revering wom-
en's sacrifice and self-sacrifice" (Wolf 1996 as quoted in Davis 1998, 118).
Davis sees the issue of women's traditional role of self-sacrificer as cutting
in more than one way. While she acknowledges the concerns raised by
Wolf, she sees women's self-sacrifice in another way. For those opposed
to PAS, and other forms of rational suicide,

> The self-sacrifice expected is to undergo long periods of pain and disability,
> perhaps even dementia, rather than to do something as dramatic and uncon-
> ventional as to put an end to one's life. The ill or dying person is being asked
> to forgo acting on her own interests in order to (1) avoid making her relatives
> look like selfish, uncaring brutes in the eyes of the more conventional world;
> (2) refrain from challenging the comfortable belief that life is always worth
> living; and (3) avoid giving to society at large a push down the slippery slope
> in the direction of callousness toward those sick and disabled persons who
> do *not* wish to end their lives. Thus, one could argue that those who oppose

rational suicide are asking women to shoulder yet another traditional female burden: the preservation of society's moral and religious values. The stereo-typical virtues assigned to Victorian women of "piety, purity, submissiveness, and domesticity," which rightly disturb Wolf, can as easily be harnessed by traditionalists to argue against suicide as for it. (Davis 1998, 119)

In other words, women at the end of life may be asked to make one final sacrifice, namely to endure suffering, rather than calling an end to it. They may be asked to do this in order to allow their families to feel good about themselves and to support some of society's most basic beliefs with regard to the value of life. If the society itself is one that has oppressed these women throughout their lives, being required to make such a sacrifice to support that society's values and beliefs could be seen as the final insult.

TENSION BETWEEN CARE AND FIGHTING OPPRESSION

My concern is similar to those articulated by Davis and Raymond; however, I want to frame it differently. I am concerned that in denying suffering women the ability to choose to die, we fail to respond to their suffering and thus sacrifice caring for them in the name of fighting the oppression of women more generally.

Wolf gives us good reason to accept that we should be suspicious of any argument for PAS and euthanasia that fails to attend to the vulnerability of women and other groups. But her claim is much stronger than this. She argues that

[t]o institute physician-assisted suicide and euthanasia at this point in this country—in which many are denied the resources to cope with serious illness, in which pain relief and palliative care are by all accounts woefully mishandled, and in which we have a long way to go to make proclaimed rights to refuse life-sustaining treatments and to use advanced directives working realities in clinical settings—seems, at the very least, to be premature. (1996, 305–306)

In fact, she goes on, it is more than premature; it is a danger to women (1996, 306). But her arguments do not support such a strong conclusion. We are certainly led to the view that considerations of PAS and euthanasia should include the issues she raises and that laws should take these into account. But to argue that because the oppressive nature of our society has led some people to desire death, we should therefore deny their requests to die seems perverse. People are forced to live in conditions that

cause them enormous suffering. Wolf would tell them that they must continue to live with their suffering. Obviously we should work to change
conditions so as to minimize suffering. Certainly PAS and euthanasia laws
should require considerations such as whether the patient has adequate
pain relief, and if she does not to be sure she gets it. But to say categorically that there should be no laws allowing PAS and euthanasia because of
the oppressive nature of our society only compounds that oppression and
suffering. The decision to die may be the only one left for some people.
We prefer abstract principles to caring when we deny them the possibility
of making that choice.

Wolf seems to anticipate this objection in that she suggests that an argument based on care ethics, which might justify PAS, is strange in that

> it asserts that the physician's obligation to relieve suffering permits or even
> commands her to annihilate the person who is experiencing the suffering.
> Indeed, at the end of this act of beneficence, no patient is left to experience
> its supposed benefits. Moreover, this argument ignores widespread agree
> ment that fears of patient addiction in these cases should be discarded, physi
> cians may sedate to unconsciousness, and the principle of double effect
> permits giving pain relief and palliative care in doses that risk inducing respi
> ratory depression and thereby hastening death. Given all of that, it is far from
> clear what patients remain in the category of those whose pain and discom
> fort can only be relieved by killing them. (1996, 302)

This concern, however, takes into account only physical suffering.
Requests for PAS tend to involve more than this. There are various kinds
of psychological suffering involved as well. Moreover, without further
argument it is hard to see a relevant difference between sedating to
unconsciousness for the remainder of life and ending life. Such arguments
could be made, but any that I can think of would have premises that
would be highly questionable from a feminist perspective or would be circular. For example, one could make an argument based on the inherent
value of human life. Any such argument, however, would already be
assuming that PAS would *never* be morally permissible regardless of the
social conditions under which it was practiced.

Wolf advocates a view she calls "principled caring," which involves
examining the reasons women may seek euthanasia or PAS. Women are at
greater risk for inadequate pain relief than are men, Wolf asserts. They
are also at greater risk for depression, poverty, and vulnerability in the
healthcare system, and more likely to fear burdening their family. Such
things constrain rational choice. In particular, Wolf suggests that women
may be in much greater danger of making coerced decisions. That is, their
desire to avoid being a burden and to be self-sacrificing may lead to the
request to die. Women may well be more likely than men not to want to

be a burden to their families. Their families may also treat caring for women more of a burden than caring for men. I agree with Wolf on all of this. However, I argue that while this tendency must be revealed through criticism, and laws certainly must take account of the possibility of coercion, for some women this desire not to be a burden, while socially constructed, is no less real. Just as living in a pro-natalist society does not make a woman's desire for a child any less real, so too, a society that valorizes self-sacrifice does not make a woman's desire not to be a burden any less real. The reality of such desires should be taken seriously even as we work to change the conditions that cause them. We might also question whether this desire is a bad one or whether, in fact, it is one that should be encouraged in men as well.

For women in a patriarchal society in which they are systematically oppressed, there may not be any good options. The desire to die may well be the best option for a woman who is terminally ill and in great pain. Her suffering may be compounded by her realization that she is a burden to others, by medical professionals not taking her concerns seriously, including not taking her pain seriously. While we work for changes in the system of domination and oppression, are we to deny women and others who suffer under the oppression of patriarchy what may be the only way out of that suffering right now? The suffering woman has only months to live. The changes to the system of oppression may be years away. If we are attentive to the possible dangers to women of PAS and euthanasia, why outlaw it entirely? As Raymond puts it, "ironically, if death is, under some circumstances, a benefit, then one of the injustices women, people of color, and the socially and economically deprived suffer is that where PAS and euthanasia are a benefit, they are deprived of it" (1999, 17).

To further illustrate this point, I would like to draw an analogy between the situation of the terminally ill and suffering woman and O at the end of *The Story of O* (Réage 1965). At the end of her novel recounting the progressive debasement of a young French woman named only O, Pauline Réage suggests two possible endings. In one ending O is returned to Roissy, the castle at which her debasement has largely taken place, and abandoned by Sir Stephen, a man who is both the representation of patriarchy and the one for whom O exists (albeit utterly debased). Her abandonment by Sir Stephen is the final suffering and debasement for O. In the other ending, O sees that Sir Stephen is about to leave her and says that she would prefer to die. Sir Stephen gives his consent. She must have Sir Stephen's consent because she belongs to him and thus the decision is not hers to make. A third possible ending, not suggested by Réage, but perhaps more in keeping with the narrative, would be for O to request to die and for Sir Stephen to deny her permission to do so. One could even imagine him saying "No, that would be *wrong*." This third ending would be the final denial of her identity. In the first ending where he leaves and there is no mention of her feeling about it, her identity is already fully erased. In the second, she is still, however weakly, able to articulate what she wants and for once it is actually granted. In the third ending, she is, as in the second, able to articulate what she wants (however constructed by her oppression that desire may be), but that would be precisely the problem from Sir Stephen's perspective. The debasement is not yet complete if she can still state a preference, if she still has a voice with which to make her request.

How is any of this relevant to PAS? Certainly there are disanalogies between O and the terminally ill woman. O may not recognize other options that the reader sees for her, such as escaping from Roissy and from the "bonds of love" (Benjamin 1988) which keep her there. Perhaps a little feminist consciousness raising would have done O a world of good. Perhaps, however, her "false consciousness" has become all that she is. Her own debasement, one might say, is the result of oppression and false consciousness, as is the belief that she would rather die than live without Sir Stephen. Surely, some might argue, we should help her to see that she can live without Sir Stephen, and is better off without him, rather than accede to her request to die. Remember, however, that she is left to live at Roissy, the place of her debasement. There does not seem to be any chance that she will be helped to understand her situation differently, though one might argue that as long as she is alive there is *some* hope. If she dies, then she certainly will never be able to overcome her oppression.

Wolf's line of reasoning would seem to lead to the argument that women's desire to be self-sacrificing and not to be a burden are also the result of oppression and false consciousness. A woman suffering terribly with a terminal illness would not have to suffer if she could get decent pain relief and understand that her feeling of being a burden is socially constructed. Yet unlike O, who arguably has the hope of overcoming her oppression, and thus her suffering, as long as she is alive (or at least we have that hope for her since there is a world outside Roissy, unlike the situation of actual women, as there is currently no world outside of patriarchy), the terminally ill woman has no such hope. She knows she is going to die in the next few months. However socially constructed her nonphysical suffering may be, it is no less real than her physical suffering. Further, her desire to die at the time and under the conditions she chooses suggests a greater autonomy than any false-consciousness analysis could allow. In short, it may be that being able to choose to die is a way of acting on her autonomy when any other way is foreclosed. To prevent her from doing so, as Wolf and others opposed to PAS would, would be to do what Sir Stephen does in the hypothetical third ending—to be aware of her suffering but to refuse to allow it to end in the only way open to her.

Clearly PAS would not be desired or necessary if conditions were significantly different, or at least if conditions were significantly different it would not be desired in ways that should cause feminists concern or that disproportionately affect women. However, even as we work to change conditions, we must recognize that there are women who are suffering *now*. Are we to say that in the name of a future overcoming of oppression by future women these women must suffer? These women seem to have no really good choices.

OTHER CONCERNS

A second concern related to this is the possibility that PAS laws as currently conceived and as currently used in the state of Oregon, the only state in the United States in which PAS has been legalized, actually discriminate against women in that women's wishes to die are less likely to be heard and acted upon than are men's requests to die. The reasons for this are precisely those that Wolf and Callahan point to as reasons that women are more likely to be coerced into dying. Women are generally socialized to be less assertive than men and tend to have less of a sense of entitlement when dealing with mostly male authority systems. Authority systems are more likely to discount women's voices. Callahan cites studies of gender disparities in the legal and medical systems. These studies show that women's medical treatment preferences "were more often ignored because the courts 'treated prior evidence of women's values and choices as immature, emotional, or uninformed, but considered men's prior statements and lifestyle decisions to be mature and rational'" (Jecker 1994, 676; Callahan 1996, 23). Callahan thus concludes "old women will bear the brunt of any inadequacies in the system our society devises for the fragile old at the end of life" (1996, 23). While for Callahan this is a reason to find that PAS will be more likely to be imposed on women, it seems to me that precisely the opposite conclusion could be drawn from the same data. The Oregon assisted suicide law requires that one actively request death on several occasions, that one satisfy one's doctor that one is making a rational decision in requesting death, and that one must have the cooperation of more than one doctor. If women's voices are less often heard and their decisions more often considered rational and emotional, and if they are less assertive in male-dominated authority systems than are men, then it seems likely that women are far less likely to go through the steps of requesting PAS, and if they do, are far less likely to have their requests acted upon. If anything, it seems that women would be unfairly discriminated against in that they would be less likely to be able to take advantage of laws, like the one in Oregon, allowing PAS. As I stated earlier,

Wolf suggests this possibility, but does not pursue it. Raymond raised it as a general concern, but also does not pursue it. Yet this seems an extremely important concern for feminists considering PAS. A question that seems important for us to ask is whether it would be possible to develop assisted suicide laws that would take into account not only the possible dangers to women that Wolf and Callahan point to, but also the possibility that women's requests will be less often heard or acceded to than men's would be. The current PAS law in Oregon certainly does not do that, but rather assumes the existence of an autonomous, genderless, classless, and contextless decision maker whose rationality must be decided upon before the request for physician assistance can be acceded to.

From a feminist perspective it is also worth noting that the Oregon assisted suicide law, based as it is on enlightenment ideals of personal autonomy, does not make any provision for input from loved ones when a suicide decision is made. How are those in close relationships to the patient affected by her decision to opt for death? From a personal autonomy standpoint, such considerations would be irrelevant. From a care perspective, such considerations would be relevant, though obviously problematic, as one could be subject to coercion based on the desires of one's family. As we have seen, this could involve coercing a woman to continue suffering just as easily as it could involve coercing a woman to cease being a burden.

Anne Donchin (2000) has pointed to the problems inherent in conceiving of autonomy within the prevailing paradigm of individualism. She suggests that a relational view of autonomy would be particularly desirable in considering PAS. Whether this suggestion would alleviate the potential problems with the Oregon law will have to be left to future discussions, but it does seem to be one promising avenue to pursue.

A final concern with regard to arguments against PAS and euthanasia that start from the premise of protecting women from coercion is that those who make such arguments may be, albeit unwittingly, taking part in a pattern of gendered reasoning that has disadvantaged women in the past. In their investigation of gender difference in "right to die" judicial decisions, Miles and August (1990) have found a pattern of judicial decisions depicting men as "subject to medical assault" when extraordinary means are used to extend their lives. The indignities suffered in these situations tend to be the focus of concern. Women, on the other hand, tend to be depicted as "subject to medical neglect" and therefore in need of judicial protection (Miles and August 1990, 89). Courts have tended to use paternalistic, protective language in decisions involving women's desires to terminate life-sustaining medical care. The texts of judicial decisions do not describe women as suffering indignities, but rather as being in "fetal positions" or in "infantile states." Such infantilizing terms are not used in discussions of men in similar situations. In short, courts treat women as vulnerable and in need of protection. Thus their previously expressed wishes not to have their lives extended by extraordinary means are far less often heeded than are men's previously expressed wishes.

There is a danger that feminists may replicate this pattern of gendered reasoning that has disadvantaged women in "right to die" cases in discussions of PAS and euthanasia. We need to be cautious not to overly restrict women's choices and freedom in attempting to protect them from potential harm. I see the danger here as being akin to the one faced by women with overly protective fathers, boyfriends, or husbands—at a certain point the potential for harm is outweighed by the restrictions placed on women's freedom. For example, despite the disproportionate dangers to women who are out in a city alone at night, preventing a woman from going out alone at night seems like an unwarranted restriction on her freedom. We want to be sure that the dangers facing women are severe enough to warrant restrictions placed on freedom. In this case, are the dangers to women posed by PAS sufficiently great to outweigh the benefits suffering women might gain were it to be legalized, as it has been in Oregon? On the other hand, of course, in the cases cited by Miles and August, the courts may recognize precisely what feminists are concerned about in the medical arena, namely that women *are* subject to medical neglect and thus are in need of protection. While we need to be careful in arguments against PAS that begin with the premise of protecting women that we are not limiting women's freedom by overprotecting them, at the same time, such protection may be warranted. My point here is that we need to be aware of the dangers on both sides as we think about the impact of PAS and euthanasia on women. Perhaps we should seek to create PAS laws that take account of the particular dangers to women and other vulnerable groups rather than opposing PAS altogether. On the other hand, it may be that laws with sufficient safeguards against misuse would disadvantage those who are less assertive in seeking what they want.

CONCLUSION

In this chapter I have discussed a number of problems to which feminist bioethical discussions of PAS and euthanasia give rise. My point has not been to argue for or against PAS or euthanasia, but rather to further problematize them from a feminist perspective. The tension between caring for individuals who are suffering and working to overcome a system that to a large extent may be responsible for their suffering is my greatest concern. There do not appear to be any simple or easy ways out of this. It appears, rather, that we must do what we can to make sure that women have as many options open to them as possible, while also being alert to potential coercive elements that may accompany apparent options. That PAS may present a danger to women is no more nor less a possibility than that it presents another avenue for women to challenge the forces that oppress them. If we remember that suicide is generally frowned upon in American and other Western societies, and under patriarchy more generally, we may see women who demand their physicians' help in dying as challenging social norms. On the other hand, to the extent that women have always been expected to be self-sacrificing and have been less valued than men, we may see these same women as coerced. What implications this has for law and public policy are, at best, ambiguous. Wolf and others certainly show how problematic PAS and euthanasia are from a feminist perspective. They do not, however, convince us that feminists should be opposed to them per se, but rather that we should be far more concerned than we have been, and that everyone engaged in the debate should take the questions raised by feminist analysis seriously.

10

Talking Back to Feminist Postmodernism: Toward a New Radical Feminist Interpretation of the Body

Bonnie Mann

> If the body is a metaphor for our locatedness in space and time and thus for the finitude of human perception and knowledge, then the postmodern body is no body at all.
>
> —Susan Bordo, *Unbearable Weight*

If there is one thing that is clear in feminist postmodernism as the new millennium begins, it is that bodies are texts. And textual as they are, they are no longer the flesh and blood sites of oppression and liberation feminists theorized thirty years ago. They are sites of play, sites of performance, sites of catachresis. I am interested in a new radical feminist account that both draws from the theoretical developments that turned the body into a text, and re-turns the body to its flesh and blood. This effort will take us into one of the central insights of feminist postmodernism's[1] account of agency, and subject this account to a Marxian turn on its head, in order to bring the body out of its textual playground and back to Earth. "Back to Earth" is meant literally here, as the Earth itself in the "naive" extra-textual sense, is both what brings us back and what we come back to.

This chapter is motivated by a certain dismay at the distance between feminist "high theory" in the United States and the most pressing political and social issues of our times. Particularly, in the face of unprecedented levels of global environmental destruction, we seem to be unable to articulate our relationship to the planet we inhabit in a politically meaningful way. The textual body, or in some accounts the virtual body, seems to have little relation to the body of the Earth, seems in fact to be the realization of that quintessential Euro-masculine fantasy of emancipation from necessity, where "necessity" serves as a negative marker for the relationship of dependence between humans and our environments, between persons and places.

A new radical feminist account of the body will call for a re-marking of this relation, and will draw on the feminist postmodern theory of "subjectivation" to do so. Radical feminists reading feminist postmodern theory have tended to respond defensively and dismissively. I find this response understandable but not particularly fruitful. It is understandable because radical feminism has itself been a prime target of derision and dismissal at the hands of theorists engaged in the development of feminist postmodernism, to such an extent that I think the "critique" of radical feminism has often functioned as an excuse for not reading radical feminist work, or for not taking it seriously. But a responding dismissal is not particularly fruitful. Radical feminist philosophy, like any thinking politics, needs to engage criticism in order to move forward. We need to read feminist postmodern theory closely, but we needn't read it literally. There are many ways to read postmodernism, one of the most promising of which is as an expression of the phenomenology of life under globalization,[2] under threat of environmental destruction. A critical reading can bring postmodern insights out of the discursive universe and into a philosophical engagement with lived bodies, and the body of the planet that sustains them (us).

HOW THE BODY BECAME A TEXT

Before the body became a text, it was, for U.S. feminists, already a complicated thing. Of course, to call the body a "thing" is to lie about it already—is to belie the complexity that 1970s feminists tried to engage. Variously theorized as the site of oppression, or the site of liberation; women's bodies, whether objectified, violated, pleasured, overworked, underpaid, wholly natural, socially constructed, or given by the goddess, were of central concern to second wave feminists. Early second wave women's liberation politics called for social policies that would give women control over their own bodies, particularly when it came to reproductive freedoms and sexuality, but also in connection with "women's" work. Closely on the heels of this call came another, the demand to end violence against women. First the rape crisis movement then the movement against domestic violence addressed the social situation of women who were victims of male violence. The issue of women's control over our bodies was connected with broader issues of sexual socialization, male dominance, economic disenfranchisement, housework, and sexuality as a site of women's oppression. A burgeoning lesbian feminist movement theorized lesbianism as resistance to male domination, and androgyny as embodied resistance or "conscientious objection"[3] to feminine socialization.

In the 1980s, the question of women controlling their bodies got even more complex. Much of this complexity hinged on whether or not many of the things women were doing with their bodies were seen as expressions of women's control over their bodies or lack of it.[4] Was it an expression of women's control over their bodies to sell them into pornography or prostitution? Could a woman choose, was it in fact an expression of her control over her body and thus liberating for her to choose, "violation" in the form of masochistic sex? Could traditional femininity be liberating if a woman chose it? Could the decision to change her sex surgically and hormonally be an expression of her right to control her own body? These questions entered what came to be called "the sex debates" in feminism with a vengeance. To oversimplify a bit, how one answered them determined which side one was on. "No" to all of the above made one a radical feminist—the other side called you "anti-sex" or "cultural feminist" or "victim feminist," and later "essentialist." "Yes" to all of the above made one a pro-sex feminist—the other side called you "sex libertarian" or "anti-feminist." Sitting the fence was another option, one that many feminists who felt allied with neither camp chose.

The 1990s brought a new turn to feminist philosophies of the body. The "pro-sex" feminists "won," at least in academic feminist contexts in the United States. Their focus on "free choice" in a rabidly individualist and voluntarist cultural milieu secured what can only be called a hegemony in U.S. academia for "pro-sex" feminism. Their notions of the body cohered more comfortably with postmodern theories than radical feminist notions. Postmodern theory had become more appealing to many feminists, and a new alliance between postmodernism and feminism[5] was fast replacing the older alliance with Marxism.[6] The feminist alliance with postmodernism has created a dramatic shift in feminist approaches to the question of the body.

One mark of this change is the collapse of the central conceptual paradigm that distinguished sex and gender, a collapse that occurred initially both inside and outside of the new feminist postmodernism. The old feminist distinction between sex (as natural and biological) and gender (as social and cultural) was questioned in social constructionist accounts that recognized gender's influence in how sex was defined, articulated cultur- ally, and lived.[7] The value of these insights for feminism should not be underestimated. Initially change was fought for on the field of gender. But sex always returned as that natural, God-given, immutable fact of women's existence. Women have babies. If they don't have babies, at least they can. This is what sex is, and sex is presocial. Therefore every social policy that could be justified by reference to "real" sexual differences was. It was essential for feminists to question the sanctity of what was defined as pre- social sex. As Catharine MacKinnon put it, "To limit efforts to end gender inequality at the point where biology or sexuality is encountered, termed differences, without realizing that these exist in law or society only in terms of their specifically sexist social meanings, amounts to conceding that gender inequality may be challenged so long as the central epistemo- logical pillars of gender as a system of power are permitted to remain standing" (1989, 233). Gender became the primary of the two terms for feminists, but not as a superstructural formation of natural sex. Neither gender nor sex was seen as natural. Sex was a function of gender.

This critique was extended so much in postmodern accounts that the gendered body today is not only cultural rather than biological, con- structed rather than natural, but textual rather than material, or in some accounts virtual rather than real. Gender is contingent, malleable, and performative. It is not particularly intransigent. Such cultural "perform- ances" as drag demonstrate that there is no "original" or "authentic" gen- der to play around with all gender is, essentially, gender play.[8] The gendered body has become, in feminist postmodern accounts, the quint- essential simulacrum, the copy for which there is no original.[9] Today, the reigning wisdom in academic feminism sees the body as a discursive site. The body has turned into a text.

JUDITH BUTLER AND THE
TEXTUALIZATION OF THE BODY

Though one cannot attribute all of the positions in the above paragraph to Judith Butler, no feminist has been more influential in the development of feminist postmodernism in the United States than she has. Understand- ings, misunderstandings, and reworkings of her work are the bedrock of what counts as "good" feminist thinking in much of academia. At feminist conferences, hardly a session goes by without some positive attention to her writings or favorable mention of her deconstructions of the central categories of second wave feminist thinking.

Butler's work has been key in the importation of the epistemology of the simulacrum into feminist theory. The early feminist epistemology of unmasking, of sorting through appearances to get to the real underneath, has been discredited as "essentialist."[10] Feminist standpoint epistemology was an attempt to respond to this accusation by using social location as a "standpoint" from which at least local and situated knowledge could be articulated.[11] But it is the epistemology of the simulacrum that has become hegemonic for feminism at the turn of the millennium. Here "the real" plays a part only as that which dissolves into the appearances themselves. Behind the appearances, if there were such a place, would be only an abyss of absence.[12]

I want to take a closer look at how this epistemology functions in Butler's (1993) book on the body, *Bodies that Matter: On the Discursive Limits of "Sex."* I am interested in a critical reading of Butler's notions of interpellation, of "constitutive outside" and of her deconstruction of the notion of matter, not simply in order to say what I think she got wrong. Rather, I find her work, read critically, provides important provocation for the development of a new radical feminist philosophy of the body.

In *Bodies that Matter*, Butler sets out to deal with some of the trouble that her former book, *Gender Trouble*, left unaddressed. She is responding to criticism that her earlier work left out "the material body." "The question was repeatedly formulated to me in this way," writes Butler, " 'What about the materiality of the body, Judy?' I took it that the addition of 'Judy' was an effort to dislodge me from the more formal 'Judith' and to recall me to a bodily life that could not be theorized away. There was a certain exasperation in the delivery of that final diminutive, a certain patronizing quality which (re)constructed me as an unruly child, one who needed to be brought to task, restored to that bodily being which is, after all, considered to be most real, most pressing, most undeniable. . . . And if I persisted in this notion that bodies were in some way *constructed*, perhaps I really thought that words alone had the power to craft bodies from their own linguistic substance?" (1993, ix–x). Butler sets out to look more closely at what it means to say that bodies are socially constructed.

She disavows what she calls "linguistic monism," where "socially constructed" means we are simply subjected by language, and agency is done away with entirely. But she is equally at pains to distance herself from a voluntarist notion of the subject, a notion some readers found in the idea of "gender performativity," so central to *Gender Trouble*. If gender is something we perform, then doesn't a "willful and instrumental subject, one who decides *on* its gender" (Butler 1993, x), do the performing? How is it possible within this framework to preserve "gender practices as sites of agency" (x), while avoiding the two extremes, of a voluntarist subject or no subject at all? Butler's answer to this question comes in the form of what she calls "constitutive constraint" (xi).

Butler is indebted here to Foucault and Althusser. Foucault's notion of

assujettissement "is not only a subordination but a securing and maintaining, a putting into place of a subject, a subjectivation" (1993, 34).
Social construction is the process through which the subject is subjected
in the double sense of bound and made. Agency is as much a product of
the bonding as is "oppression." "To claim that the subject is itself produced in and as a gendered matrix of relations is not to do away with the
subject, but only to ask after the conditions of its emergence and operation" (7). Althusser's notion of interpellation is key to Butler's account as
well. "In Althusser's notion of interpellation, it is the police who initiate
the call or address by which a subject becomes socially constituted. There
is the policeman, the one who not only represents the law but whose
address 'Hey you!' has the effect of binding the law to the one who is
hailed. This 'one' who appears not to be in a condition of trespass prior
to the call (for whom the call establishes a given practice as a trespass) is
not fully a social subject, is not fully subjectivated, for he or she is not
yet reprimanded. The reprimand does not merely repress or control the
subject, but forms a crucial part of the juridical and social formation of
the subject. The call is formative, if not performative, precisely because it
initiates the individual into the subjected status of the subject" (121). Butler's own example is of the doctor whose exclamation "It's a girl!" is the
first interpellating speech act that begins the process of "girling the girl"
(7–8).

  Interpellation, a kind of subjectivating definition, works as much
through what is excluded as what is included. "To what extent," Butler
asks, "is materialization governed by principles of intelligibility that
require and institute a domain of radical *unintelligibility* that resists materialization altogether or that remains radically dematerialized" (1993, 35)?
One way to understand this is certainly through what happens to intersexed infants. Between the culturally intelligible "It's a girl!" and "It's a
boy!" is only the culturally *unintelligible*. What is unintelligible will not
be "materialized" in that the material body of the infants will be altered
to conform to one or the other intelligible cultural options.[13]

  The unintelligible functions for Butler as a "constitutive outside" for
the intelligible. Butler's whole notion of "constitutive outside" is the key
to her response to the question of the material body. The criticism has
been, of course, that she has neglected *what is most outside discourse*,
the body, but Butler's response pulls the body back into discourse. "For
there is an 'outside' to what is constructed by discourse, but this is not an
absolute 'outside,' an ontological thereness that exceeds or counters the
boundaries of discourse; as a constitutive 'outside' it is that which can
only be thought—when it can—in relation to that discourse, at and as its
most tenuous borders" (1993, 8). This "outside" will return to disrupt the
coherence of the intelligible, and will return *internally*. "A constitutive

or relative outside is, of course, composed of a set of exclusions that are nevertheless internal to that system as its own nonthematizable necessity. It emerges within the system as incoherence, disruption, a threat to its own systematicity" (39). The "outside" was always the abjected and unacknowledged heart of the "inside."

Butler's deconstruction of the whole notion of "matter" is meant to show that "matter" operates as a constitutive outside for the social, a "presocial" that the social requires for its own self-definition. But "matter has a history" (1993, 29), and it is to the history of matter as a sign that Butler turns her critique. Her account of this history is convincing, and she uncovers "a violation that founds the very concept of matter" (53) and its discursive function "as the site at which a certain drama of sexual difference plays itself out" (49). Far from being the presocial "outside" to constructionist accounts, matter returns as the very notion that is socially constructed in the delimitation of the difference between the social and presocial. And this delimitation is far from innocent, it is complicit in the entire story of heterosexual hegemony. "To return to matter requires that we return to matter as a sign" (49), she argues, since what we say about matter is always already caught up in the chain of signification that constructs it as a concept. After all, "the body posited as prior to the sign, is always *posited* or *signified* as *prior*. This signification produces as an effect of its own procedure the very body that it nevertheless and simultaneously claims to discover as that which *precedes* its own action. If the body signified as prior to signification is an effect of signification, then the mimetic or representational status of language, which claims that signs follow bodies as their necessary mirrors, is not mimetic at all. On the contrary it is productive, constitutive, one might even argue performative, inasmuch as the signifying act delimits and contours the body that it then claims to find prior to any and all signification" (30). In the beginning was the sign, on the second day, the body was born into discourse.[14]

I find Butler's deconstruction of the concept of matter convincing, even moving, and important for feminism. It is not, however, an adequate response to the question she purports to be addressing, which is not about the *concept* of matter at all. The question is about extra-discursive matter. To ask the question of the material body is to ask the question of the relationship between the extra-discursive and the discursive. To "return to matter as a sign" is precisely to misunderstand the question, since matter *as a sign* is not *in* question. The question has to do, rather, with the stubborn fact of the *existence* of matter *extra-discursively*. Butler's use of the notion of "constitutive outside" serves only to *defer* the question of a *real* outside. Instead of grappling with an outside to discourse, she merely does away with the outside by showing how things that are *conceptually* excluded from certain notions, such as matter is to the social, are internally constitutive of such *notions*. Butler has essentially, and rightfully, pointed out that our concept of the social contains a repressed concept of the presocial that is foundational for it. This is not an unimportant accomplishment, because Butler also shows that the unintelligibility of the "constitutive outside" of such concepts functions politically in often heinous ways—and making the unintelligible intelligible is important political work. We think of matter as an innocent and presocial thing, while the concept we think it with, "matter," has been everything but innocent and presocial.

If we accept this, which I certainly do, we are still left with the question of an outside that is *not merely internally constitutive* in Butler's terms, an outside that is not reducible to a moment of exclusion on the inside of the discursive "system," which is, it seems, able to digest just about anything. She has shown that *conceptually*, "matter," like every other *term*, can be deconstructively devoured by discourse theory. She has shown that how we think and live our bodies is discursively constrained. Butler has answered her interlocutors by brilliantly illuminating a relationship *between concepts*, but they have not asked after a relationship between concepts, they have asked after the relationship between a body as what precedes, exceeds, resists, or escapes discourse—and the discursive.

But in a brief passage titled "Are Bodies Purely Discursive," Butler does give an answer to the complaint I raise above. I am essentially accepting the philosophical position that the being of a concept, "matter" and the being of matter itself, are ontologically distinct and that this distinction is important. Neither need be "presocial" in the sense of unimpacted by or implicated in social or political relations of power. The ontological distinction between them does not mean that they are radically separate, but it does mean neither is reducible to the other. To return to our example above of the intersexed infant, the unintelligibility of the infant's body to the doctors or parents results in a material intervention/violation of the infant's body. What Butler calls the "chain of signification" is instrumental in the "re-materialization" (to use what is certainly too neutral and innocent a term) of the infant's body as intelligibly male or female. But the intersexed body was there to begin with, and it is significant that many adults who discover that they were surgically "corrected" as infants experience a deep sense of violation at the revelation (Kessler 1994). My example here is meant to counter Butler's assertion that if "materiality is considered ontologically distinct from language," then "the possibility that language might be able to indicate or correspond to that domain of radical alterity," is undermined (Butler 1993, 68).

She goes on to argue that it is the ontological similarity between the two that provides the ground for a possible relation—language is itself material. The "phenomenality" of the signifying process requires, after all, that language make a material appearance, whether as sound, words on a page, or gestures. But in the next moment, a new "radical difference" is introduced. "Apart from and yet related to the materiality of the signifier is the materiality of the signified as well as the referent approached through the signified, but which remains irreducible to the signified. This *radical difference* between referent and signified is the site where the materiality of language and that of the world which it seeks to signify are perpetually negotiated" (Butler 1993, 69, my emphasis). The "radical difference" here is hard to pin down. It seems to exist in the *irreducibility* of the referent to the signified (i.e., the material body is not reducible to what we mean when we say "material body"), which is not reducible to the sign itself "material body"—though all are material. It is unclear why this "irreducibility" does not constitute an *ontological* difference, and it is equally unclear why, if it did, this would mean that the "referentiality of language," would be undermined.

Indeed, elsewhere Butler raises these same questions, and responds to them very convincingly. In a searing criticism of Lacan, Butler takes on the notion that an ontological difference between the penis and the phallus necessarily sets the phallus free of its debt to the penis, to operate as a privileged signifier. Summarizing Lacan's position, Butler writes,

> The phallus symbolizes the penis, and insofar as it symbolizes the penis, retains the penis as that which it symbolizes; it is not the penis. . . . The more symbolization occurs the less ontological connection there is between symbol and symbolized. . . . Symbolization depletes that which is symbolized of its ontological connection with the symbol itself. (1993, 83–84)

Against this argument, Butler asks, "What is the status of this particular assertion of ontological difference . . . if the penis becomes [always] the privileged referent to be negated?" In spite of their different kinds of being, "the phallus is bound to the penis through determinate negation. Indeed, the phallus would be nothing without the penis" (1993, 84). By what assumption could we conclude that different kinds of being so radically escape one another? What is the status of the assertion that an ontological difference between the being of language and the being of materiality would necessarily seal them off from one another rather than help to explain their relation to one another? Yet such an assertion would maintain the irreducibility of the one to the other, which Butler purports to want to do as well, so why the denial?

Her denial of the ontological difference between language and materiality seems to be what enables Butler to recollapse materiality back into language—to ultimately sidestep the very irreducibility she claims to defend. She defines the question of the relationship between the two as follows:

"To answer the question of the relation between the materiality of bodies and that of language *requires first* that we offer an account of *how it is that bodies materialize*" (1993, 69 my emphasis). Butler's "requires first" serves to establish a priority. From here, where will her account take us? Back to language, which again becomes the privileged and indeed active term of the two—language materializes the body. The example of the intersexed infant certainly shows that language, in the fuller sense of a "chain of signification" and an arbiter of intelligibility, does and can affect the material world in heinous ways. Yet the infant had a body, certainly, before it was surgically altered, that was materialized outside of the "chain of signification"—and this body is not to be reduced to a "constitutive outside," to a mere function of the system of gender intelligibility. This body is what we feel has been violated when we respond with horror to the surgical "sexing" of intersexed infants. We recognize there was something there, however "unintelligible" before the "materialization" of the body into the intelligibility of the chain of signification. But in Butler's account the body is reduced, again, to a mere function of discourse.

It remains unclear why we are bound—"required first"—to approach the question in the way Butler prescribes. Required by whom? If we must ask *first* after the materialization of the body (in language), then the intersexed body of the infant is disciplined out of our inquiry. It would be something like an original, for which there is no copy—and in the world of discourse we can attend only to the copies, for which there are no originals. Why would we not ask after the *material* materialization of the body—or has this materialization been rendered unintelligible by discourse theory? Why would we not ask how language is materialized, and find our answer in the body? Isn't it, after all, the body that materializes language—how would we speak without breath, write without any body at all? The material materializers of the body—breath, water, food, light, and warmth—sustain our speech. This materiality certainly merits our attention. Could it be that Butler's account serves to deconstructively discipline the body into occupying a discursive universe, sealed against the possibility of an ontologically different, and now discursively unintelligible, materiality? Could it be that the tendency Butler takes note of, the tendency of bodies to "indicate a world beyond themselves," is effectively effaced, or in her terms abjected, by the active and determinate role assigned here to language as the materializer of the body?

DISCIPLINING FEMINISM

Since asserting this difference, an ontological difference between words and things, will open me to charges of "essentialism," a lengthy digression is necessary here, to call into question the status of that particular accusation. Particularly in the U.S. context, feminists tend now to identify any talk of the extra-textual body as "essentialist!" where the word in its accusatory form functions to discredit and silence. Even social constructionist approaches to the body, if they do not see the body as sufficiently textual and contingent, are accused of "falling into" essentialist traps.[15]

Emphatic antiessentialism is part of what defines the alliance between feminist thought and postmodernism. The term serves to "mark" something as antithetical to postmodernism, and increasingly, antithetical to feminism. The philosophical and political stakes that make the question of essentialism such a charged one remain largely unaddressed. This is to say it functions as *the antithesis* of postmodern correctness. The accusation "essentialist!" has come to exercise a disciplinary force among feminists, while attempts at critical intervention receive far too little attention.[16] Particularly when it comes to feminist theories of the body, it is important to consider how antiessentialism functions to derail feminist investigations of the lived body, before they have even been seriously undertaken.

I use the descriptive term "emphatic" to differentiate postmodern antiessentialism from earlier feminist and antiracist criticism, which stressed that the wrong sorts of essentializing notions were applied to women or various races. Starting with Beauvoir's manifesto-like proclamation that women are made not born,[17] feminists threw the patriarchal claim that "biology is destiny" under the light of critical scrutiny. Women's hormones, anatomy, and physiology (especially in terms of menstruation and reproduction) did not and could not justify the political and social domination of women by men. Feminists set out to "tell the truth" about women, against what were recognized as essentializing fictions, using language in the process that essentialized women in another way. This later discovery came first from women of color and lesbians who criticized the falsely inclusive use of the category of "woman" much as other feminists had criticized the falsely inclusive categories of "mankind" or "human."[18] Monique Wittig's own manifesto, "Lesbians are not women," functioned as an ironic addition to Beauvoir's earlier claims.[19] These criticisms surfaced initially in the context of feminist political work and were sparked by very concrete issues of power within the feminist movement.[20] They neither defined essentialism so broadly, nor disregarded it on principle[21] as is generally the case today.

The academic theorization of essentialism in the late 1980s and 1990s, however, has become a *quest for theory purified* of essentialism.[22] This took the form initially of academic feminists pitting postmodern theory against older activist-based feminist theory, and finding feminist theory inadequate.[23] Particularly, feminist theory in its "radical feminist"[24] form, was found to be essentialist.[25] "Essentialist!" took on almost battle-cry status in academic feminist circles, and the accusation became one that both shamed and discredited. Efforts to critically intervene in this situation have been passionate and have come from many corners of the feminist movement. Yet these politically diverse voices have been too few and far between to stem the tide of antiessentialist orthodoxy. I quote here just three of myriad such efforts from diverse thinkers in feminism in order to show that the critical response to antiessentialism has been widespread, though apparently having little impact:

> Has essentialism received a bad rap? Few other words in the vocabulary of contemporary critical theory are so persistently maligned, so little interrogated, and so predictably summoned as a term of infallible critique . . . as an expression of disapprobation and disparagement. (Fuss 1989, xi)

> The term essentialism covers a range of metacritical meanings and strategic uses that go the very short distance from convenient label to buzz word. Many who, like myself, have been involved with feminist critical theory for some time and who did use the term, initially, as a serious critical concept, have grown impatient with this word—essentialism—time and again repeated with its reductive ring, its self righteous tone of superiority, its contempt for "them"—those guilty of it. (de Lauretis 1994, 1)

> "Essentialism" is the nemesis of "post-modernist" feminism. It is its chief target of attack, and yet the critique of "essentialism" relies on the very framework post-modernism is at such pains to reject. The meaning of "essentialism" depends on a master narrative of truth. "Essentialism" is to be avoided because it is false, and it is judged to be false from a position, which is outside all positions, on criteria, which would be everywhere and always the same. (Thompson 1996, 334)

Despite these critical voices, today, the term "essentialist" functions more than ever to discipline feminist thinkers in the academy, rather than to inspire careful scholarship.[26] "Essentialist!" has become an interpellation, a performative speech act. I borrow my terms here from Butler herself, but deploy them in an unusual direction, perhaps even catachrestically. The accusatory "essentialist!" has come to function with a self-legitimating authority, to "essentialize the essentialist," whose work need not be carefully read or responded to once this accusation has functioned to dismiss it as "bad feminism."[27]

It is impossible to deny that the concerns motivating feminist antiessentialism, even in its emphatic form, are deep and serious. Particularly, real movement-based political struggles over exclusion and inclusion have fueled the anti-essentialist fire. Yet emphatic antiessentialism has served much less as a political corrective to inequalities of power between women, which remain, in academia, remarkably unchanged, than as an intellectual policing tool that marks *theory* as pure or impure. This situation has far-reaching implications for feminism. Feminist efforts to think, write, speak, campaign, protest, and in general *change* the ways women's bodies are controlled socially and lived personally, *extra-textually*, are curtailed.

DEPENDENCE

It is important to consider what is disciplined out of feminist philosophies of the body by emphatic antiessentialism. A careful consideration of all the aspects of this disciplining is beyond the scope of this chapter, but I would like to at least note one of these aspects here and discuss a second more fully.

Any notion of bodily violation is immediately subject to accusations of essentialism, depending, as it seems to, on an implicit "original" body that has been violated. If the subject is produced in the very act of violation, than the violation becomes more enabling than egregious. This effectively disables feminist claims of harm in discussions of pornography, rape, or domestic violence, as it becomes impossible to identify *who* is being harmed. The political consequences of the disciplining of feminism away from consideration of bodily violation/harm are deep and far-reaching.

In this chapter I am concerned more primarily with the disciplining out of feminist concern with the *biological body*. I return here from my lengthy digression into the status of accusations of essentialism to the question left dangling earlier, the question of the material materialization of the body and language. The biological body seems to have all but disappeared under conditions of postmodernity, where hormone treatment, plastic surgery, and reproductive technologies appear to have done away with biological intransigence once and for all. While feminist efforts to unlink biology from destiny were extremely important to the birth of the feminist movement, and a return to an account of women's social position as causally linked to women's biology is neither desirable nor possible, biology remains an important part of how bodies are lived. We are not (and here my "we" includes all humans) emancipated from our biological bodies in any decisive way, even if they have been rendered unintelligible in certain cultural contexts.

Feminists whose focus on women's bodies has led to charges of essentialism have generally focused on how women's bodies differ from men's, how reproductive, sexual, or hormonal differences might provide a key to

understanding women's social, moral, or political differences from men—
where these differences are understood as positive (i.e., the argument that
women make better moral choices than men). Closely related has been an
account of women's social role in raising and nurturing children as foundational for women's differences from men.[28] These views have been criticized, in my opinion sometimes correctly, but often dismissively, as
"essentialist," with essentialism in this case implying a return to or
approximation of a patriarchal "biology as destiny" perspective.

Many feminists have been rightfully suspicious of efforts to define
human differences biologically, since such efforts have long been key components of European racism. European science has shown itself to be virtually obsessed with finding the anatomical or now genetic explanations
for racial differences and with using supposed biological differences to
justify all manner of social and political injustice. The same suspicion also
marks disability rights activism, gay rights activism, and much feminist
activism as well. All of these groups have every reason to resist any return
to the territory of biology as causally explanatory for social, economic, or
political differences between humans. In the context of feminism, because
women's reproductive capacity or role has been used for centuries to justify women's political disenfranchisement, feminists who ground their
own notions of women's difference in biology are treading on ground that
the rest of us have every reason to call "dangerous."

At the same time, I find the rejection of efforts to explain women's social
or political differences from men biologically does not justify a wholesale
censure of feminist inquiry into the more philosophical questions of what
it means to live as embodied beings *at all*. I am particularly concerned
that an area of inquiry that offers great promise in terms of understanding
what we share with others across all manner of differences is excluded
from what counts as "good feminism." Bodies as texts will yield difference, since the way bodies are inscribed is everywhere local, specific, and
culturally and historically bounded. It is the extra-textual body, the body
that has to breathe, drink, eat, absorb light and warmth, to live—that is
the body-in-common.[29] It is also this extra-textual body that remains
dependent on the Earth for sustenance.

But what is an *extra-textual* body? In what does its irreducibility to the
textual consist? The *textual* body, as we have seen, is a body that is culturally inscribed, written on, so to speak—yet not in the sense of some "original" natural thing, some primary matter on which the social is *later*
inscribed. The body comes to be an intelligible body at all in the very process of its inscription. It is *interpellated*, meaning subjected in the double
sense of being made a subject (agent) and a subject (loyal follower) at the
same moment. It is a body that *performs* its subjection in both senses of
the word, its subjection to authority and its subjective resistance to

authority. Gender is "written" on this body and "read" from it. It is a body that is marked, defined, disciplined into being this or that gender, this or that race, but not from some original genderless, raceless material. Like gender itself, the body is a simulacrum, a copy for which there is no original. It becomes a body through its being gendered, through its being raced. It may be a body that is surgically, hormonally, anatomically altered to fit a foregoing definition or an individual preference—but what is altered cannot be understood to be some authentic, original thing. What is altered is no-thing at all until the alteration makes it into, marks it, as just this sort of body.

By insisting on the irreducibility of the body to language, I am not *opposing* the material body to the textual body. I am not asserting an extra-textual body in the sense of some primary, original, untainted *antithesis* to the social. I am insisting, rather, on a body that can never be wholly claimed or contained by the language that does, indeed, inscribe it, even by a sophisticated deconstructive slight of hand. This body, in fact, materially *produces* language. It is itself as much *materially* produced as it is discursively. I am insisting on bodies that live, again in Butler's words, in "a world beyond themselves," where "this movement beyond their own boundaries, a movement of boundary itself" is "quite central to what bodies are" (1993, ix). In this sense, the body is the boundary between discourse and the material, but boundary is surely the wrong word, it is more appropriately the link between words and things. It is inscribed by discourse, but produces discourse. It is materially produced but produces materially. The body so understood, is reconnected to its place, its environment, the Earth itself.

It is certainly a cultural achievement of enormous proportions to have rendered such a connection unintelligible, but this is precisely the circumstance we find ourselves in under conditions of postmodernity. Postmodern theory celebrates these circumstances uncritically, demonstrating deconstructively that our experience of being set adrift from the world and sealed into language is "true" at the same time the theorist breathes, drinks, and eats to sustain her capacity to deconstruct.

From a different corner of the world of feminist theory, Eva Kittay's most recent book, *Love's Labor: Essays on Women, Equality, and Dependency* (1998), contributes to the effort to make the materiality of the body intelligible. She takes the universality of the human condition of dependence (i.e., that all of us at least begin our lives dependent for our very survival on others), to found new notions of equality in an ethics of care. She focuses on dependency work as a kind of labor that is both necessary and sustaining for human life, though marginalized in areas of social thought that have taken the autonomous individual as their model of normalcy.[30] Kittay's work primarily addresses intersubjective dependence, but has important implications for another kind of dependence, that of all humans on the Earth. Even the "original" dependence of the embryo on the human mother is "nested" in a prior and ongoing dependence of the mother on the Earth itself. Activities such as breathing, eating, drinking all attest to the porosity of the border between self and world, and to this primary dependence. Kittay's epistemological move is to see the experience of human dependence as a place from which we can and should know what is essential to just social policies.

Similarly, our dependence on the Earth can be understood to be a place from which we can and do know, and articulate, the materiality of the body. Ironically, it will be the postmodern notion of subjectivation that will turn us toward a new feminist understanding of the material materialization of the body. This central postmodern insight, whereby discourse is understood to subject the subject, in the double sense of bound and make, must be brought out of the sealed discursive universe and down to Earth. If we understand dependence on the Earth as not simply what bounds the subject, though it does, but what *produces* the subject materially, the postmodern notion of subjectivation can be reworked on a material level. Just as postmodern theory has claimed that discourse constructs the subject, we see that outside of and prior[31] to discourse the Earth itself "constructs" and sustains the subject, moment by moment.

Human beings are so radically dependent on the Earth that we still cannot survive for more than four minutes without "taking in" the Earth as breath. Where is this dependence? It is precisely on the porous boundary, the body, which links us to the immediate places we find ourselves (Casey 1993). The Earth sustains us only by crossing over this porous boundary, only by entering and leaving our bodies. The things that sustain us moment by moment; air, water, food, light, and warmth, do not cease to sustain us because of a fantasy, whether Euro-masculinist or feminist, of emancipation from them. Our life-sustaining relationship to the places we inhabit may be "disciplined out" of feminist theory in the academy, but it can never be disciplined out of our lives.[32] The Earth is not our prison, but a *productive place* we inhabit, that constitutes and enlivens us moment by moment. "Freedom" from the Earth, from this perspective, is suicidal. And indeed, the ongoing ecological destruction of our planet has been pointed out by many to be a kind of suicide.

A radical feminist philosophy of the body starts from this insight, that *places are subject-productive*. This is a bare dependence that is most certainly "universalizing" and "essentialist." It also pulls us out of our containment in a sealed textual universe and back to the Earth that gives us life, breath, and thus speech.

If we move toward new radical feminist interpretation of the body that calls for a reconnection of bodies to the places that sustain them, we must also move toward *prioritization* of place, and a *politicization* of our relationships to place. Some directions such a prioritization and politicization might take us are: to a more widespread focus on feminist environmentalism, feminist geography, and feminist urban planning; to world food politics; to global indigenous human rights activism; to feminist architecture and alternative building practices. The list, as for any list of "what feminists are interested in," could go on endlessly. The point here is that when we start from an understanding of the Earth and all the particular places it provides us as *productive places*, as places that enliven, enable, and materially construct the bodies that inhabit them, as places through and in relationship to which we are subjectivated—made subjects—we are opened to and engaged immediately with the "world beyond." The distance between feminist "high theory" and the pressing social issues of our times is narrowed. The textual universe loses its exclusive hold on us. We return from a fantasy of discursive emancipation from our "imprisonment" in a material body that lives in a material world to acknowledge a material world that makes and remakes us moment by moment. We return, against the grain of the phenomenality of daily life under conditions of postmodernity, to the Earth itself. This Earth is not a prison house, and the body that returns to it is not a text.

NOTES

The term "talking back" used in the title for this chapter is from a section of Judith Butler's *Bodies that Matter* where she tries to distinguish mere repetition from a kind of repetition or "performance" of gender that is "a kind of talking back" or resistance (1993, 132). She is attempting here to talk about resistance as something that takes place in the "slippage between discursive command and its appropriated effect" (122). I mean my use of the term to imply both an appropriation, and a making over, of feminist postmodernism.

1. Butler might say that my very use of the term "postmodernism" in the sweeping way I use it here is an "effort to colonize and domesticate these theories under the sign of the same, to group them synthetically and masterfully under a single rubric, a simple refusal to grant the specificity of these positions that provides an excuse not to read, and not to read closely" (Butler 1990, 4). Postmodernism is admittedly a diverse and self-contradictory field, as is modernism, of course. Postmodern theories have legitimately looked for the "foundations" of modern thought, lumping things together in the process, in order to try to name and criticize what various modernisms have in common. If various postmodern theories have laid down certain common foundations in spite of their differences, and I believe they have, it is also important to "find a way to bring into question the foundations it is compelled to lay down," also in Butler's words, "It is this movement of interrogating that ruse of authority that seeks to close itself off from contest that is, in my view, at the heart of any radical political project" (8). Here I

try to "find a way" to question what has apparently become unquestionable in much academic feminist practice—the textualization of the body.

2. Here I am writing in agreement with such thinkers such as Fredric Jameson, David Harvey, Terry Eagleton, and Seyla Benhabib, who have defined their projects against postmodernism more than with it, yet are deeply engaged in and with the central concerns that postmodern theories raise. I share a central belief with this emergent critical tradition that postmodernism has material conditions. Such notions as "textuality" and "difference" are interpreted in part as "symptoms" (or simply phenomenological descriptions) of experience under conditions of extreme reification. In other words, we really do experience ourselves as set adrift in the sign-world of the text, or caught up in an endless play of difference; but these experiences themselves are symptomatic of the material conditions that they seem to deny. Here there is an "outside" to the power of discourse that relocates discourse "inside" a historical time period and its social and political materialities. Judith Butler sees the view that "historically a set of theories which are structurally similar emerge as the articulation of an historically specific condition of human reflection," as a "Hegelian trope," which serves to falsely unify diverse theories under the assumption that they "symptomatize a common structural preoccupation" (1990, 5). This underlying view in turn "authorizes" the falsely universalizing sign "postmodern." I dispute this view, along with Fredric Jameson, Terry Eagleton, and others. Although I don't believe developments in theory are simply reducible to certain historical causes, I do believe that writers of theory are immersed in material conditions that constitute, at least in large part, certain concerns as more central than others, and that it is valuable to bring the conditions that constitute these concerns under reflective scrutiny.

3. Sheila Jeffreys, in her account of early lesbian feminism, refers to lesbian feminists as "conscientious objectors" to gender. She also argues that "lesbian feminists have always been radical social constructionists in their approach to lesbianism" (1996, 361, 367).

4. I am leaving out the important role played by the enthroning of desire over reason in postmodern theories more generally. "Control" may be a misleading term, since a right to express wayward desire does not necessarily correlate on first glance with a notion of "control"—but even so, having the right to desire in feminist postmodernist accounts, whether or not by way of unbridled expression, certainly meshes with early feminist claims that women should have the power to decide their bodily destiny, in sex and pregnancy.

5. The flurry of publications that established this new relationship took, in its early years, the form of disavowals of the "essentialism" of "cultural feminism" (a new, politically charged term for radical feminism), followed by an articulation of the superior intellectual framework of some progenitor or proponent of postmodern theory. As Theresa de Lauretis wrote at around that time, "Anglo American (feminists) seem for the most part to be engaged in typologizing, defining, and branding various 'feminisms' along an ascending scale of theoretico-political sophistication where 'essentialism' weighs heavy at the lower end (1994)." Some early examples include Linda Alcoff's 1988 *Signs* article, "Cultural Feminism versus Post-Structuralism: The Identity Crisis in Feminist Theory," Alice Echol's 1983

piece in *Powers of Desire: The Politics of Sexuality*, titled, "The New Feminism of Yin and Yang," and her 1984 article in *Pleasure and Danger: Exploring Female Sexuality*, titled "The Taming of the Id: Feminist Sexual Politics," as well as Chris Weedon's 1987 book *Feminist Practice and Poststructuralist Theory*, all enthusiastic about what postmodern theories had to offer feminists."

6. In 1979 Heidi Hartmann had written "The Unhappy Marriage of Marxism and Feminism: Towards a More Progressive Union," amid a flurry of publications about what was, by most feminist accounts, an extremely unsatisfactory "union" (Patchesky 1979; Sargent 1981; Weinbaum 1978). The central complaint Hartmann raised was that "the 'marriage' of marxism and feminism has been like the marriage of husband and wife depicted in English common law: Marxism and feminism are one, and that one is marxism" (424). This outpouring of dissatisfaction, however hopeful initially for reconciliation, ended in a nasty divorce sometime in the 1980s.

7. For both Catharine MacKinnon (1989), a radical feminist influenced most directly by Marxism and the central figure in radical feminist theory in the academy, and Judith Butler (1999), the central figure in the establishment of feminist postmodernism, the collapse of this distinction is key to their theoretical work. Both argue that the intelligibility of sex is constructed through the social conventions of gender.

8. A classic formulation of this idea can be found in Butler's 1991 essay "Imitation and Gender Insubordination." She gives credit to Esther Newton for the insight that drag "enacts the very structure of impersonation by which *any gender* is assumed" (21). This has profound implications for our understanding of gender. "Drag constitutes the mundane way in which genders are appropriated, theatricalized, worn, and done; it implies that all gendering is a kind of impersonation and approximation. If this is true, it seems, there is no original or primary gender that drag imitates, but gender is a kind of imitation for which there is no original; in fact, it is a kind of imitation that produces the very notion of the original as an effect and consequence of the imitation itself" (21).

9. And this body is the "site" of the new feminist epistemology of the simulacrum. Soja's brief rendition of Baudrillard's "4 epistemes" is useful here. The first, where appearances mirror reality, gives way to the second, where appearances are thought to be deceptive and must be sorted through to get to the real underneath (this is the "counter-epistemology" of critical theory and practice according to Soja, and this was early second wave feminist epistemology as well). "Baudrillard's third phase, wherein the image masks the growing absence of a basic reality as a prime referential, can be interpreted as the inaugural moment of contemporary postmodernity and the first step toward the denouement of his fourth phase, when all images become their own pure simulacra, bearing no relation to any reality whatsoever" (1989, 120).

10. Mary Daly's classic formulation of feminist epistemology as a journey from the foreground world of deceptive patriarchal appearances to the background realm of "Wild Reality," first appeared in print in 1978. Another formulation was published in 1989 with MacKinnon's treatise on the practice of feminist consciousness raising. "Consciousness raising is a face-to-face social experience that strikes

at the fabric of meaning of social relations between and among women and men by calling their givenness into question and reconstituting their meaning in a transformed and critical way" (1989, 95). Though very different in starting points and assumptions, both of these accounts involve a sorting through of the givenness of patriarchal relations and the emergence of another (deeper) meaning.

11. For a good account of the history of and debates about feminist standpoint epistemology see *Feminist Epistemologies*, edited by Linda Alcoff and Elizabeth Potter (1993), especially "Rethinking Standpoint Epistemology: What Is Strong Objectivity?" by Sandra Harding and "Marginality and Epistemic Privilege," by Bat-Ami Bar On.

12. Butler is certainly the most well-known feminist in the U.S. academy whose work turns on the abyss of absence at the heart of the real. Though there are moments of ambiguity in Butler's work, and even confusion, this theme remains central throughout. Her critiques of Lacan and Zizek, for example, involve the deconstruction of their notions of "lack" to uncover the prediscursively fixed real (the threat of castration) that is smuggled in under the sign of absence. Butler excavates an even deeper abyss at the heart of "the rock of the real" (Butler 1993, 187–222). The influence of Butler's work, and especially her epistemology, on U.S. feminism, has been dramatic and widespread. There is hardly a session at a feminist academic conference in which Butler's work, particularly in terms of its epistemology, is not favorably mentioned.

13. The precise nature of this intelligibility is described in Suzanne Kessler's study of the medical management of intersexed infants, "The Medical Construction of Gender." Kessler shows that the single factor determining an intersexed infant's "sex assignment" is penis size and functioning, independently of chromosomes or other anatomical factors. Here femaleness is understood to be the absence of maleness, defined as having a decent sized, potentially sexually functional penis (1994, 225).

14. I am playing on Catharine MacKinnon's similar wording to describe the perceived relation between dominance and difference (1989, 220).

15. Catharine MacKinnon comes to mind as a clear example of an almost dogmatic social constructionist who is regularly and almost ritualistically accused of essentialism. Cressida Heyes (2000) argues in her recent book, *Line Drawings*, that feminist antiessentialism is today focused on essentialist moments within social constructionist arguments.

16. One of the earliest attempts I know of to grapple critically with this situation was Diana Fuss's 1989 *Essentially Speaking: Feminism, Nature, and Difference*. This was followed by the 1994 anthology, *The Essential Difference*, edited by Naomi Schor and Elizabeth Weed. Some of the claims I make here, in slightly different terms and with a different emphasis, were made beautifully by the editors and authors of that volume. Schor rightly points out that the political stakes of antiessentialism have to do with feminist intellectuals distancing themselves from lesbian separatism. For a more recent and very thoughtful history of the essentialism debates, analysis of what is at stake, and proposal for a Wittgensteinian way out, see Cressida Heyes (2000) *Line Drawings: Defining Women Through Feminist Practice*. My emphasis in this chapter is on the consequences of emphatic anties-

sentialism for feminist environmentalism, but the many other consequences of this dogmatic intellectual stance should be taken equally seriously.

17. This claim is certainly the most often cited from de Beauvoir's, *The Second Sex.*

18. See for example, Moraga and Anzaldúa's (1981) *This Bridge Called My Back.* Moraga writes, "Lesbian separatist utopia? No thank you, sisters. I can't prepare myself a revolutionary packet that makes no sense when I leave the white suburbs of Watertown, Massachusetts and take the T-line back to Roxbury" (xiii). See also "A Black Feminist Statement: the Combahee River Collective," in the same volume, and Angela Davis, *Women, Race and Class.* These early critical works did not question the category of woman per se, but rather separatist politics and the power of white women to define feminism that amounted to a false inclusion of "other" women in what seemed to them to be a white, middle-class, heterosexual category. Elizabeth Spelman took up these critiques in her *Inessential Woman: Problems of Exclusion in Feminist Thought* in 1988. She wrote against "a tendency in dominant Western feminist thought to posit an essential 'womanness' that all women have and share in common despite the racial, class, religious, ethnic, and cultural differences among us," and set out to "show that the notion of a generic 'woman' functions in feminist thought much the same way the notion of generic 'man' has functioned in Western philosophy: it obscures the heterogeneity of women" (ix).

19. "What is woman? Panic, general alarm for an active defense. Frankly, it is a problem that the lesbians do not have because of a change of perspective, and it would be incorrect to say that lesbians associate, make love, live with women, for 'woman' has meaning only in heterosexual systems of thought and heterosexual economic systems. Lesbians are not women" (Wittig 1988, 438).

20. The editors and authors of the volume cited above, *The Essential Difference*, write this history in a slightly different way, focusing on the conflict between New French Feminism, Irigaray and those influenced by her work; and de Beauvoir and Marxist feminists in Europe. I am telling the story in the context of U.S. feminism, which is engaged with but not reducible to the debates in Europe. In the United States concrete struggles between women over issues of heterosexism and racism were of enormous influence in the essentialism debates. See note 25, below.

21. Cressida Heyes (2000) uses the term "principled anti-essentialism" to differentiate today's broad strokes antiessentialism from the specific critiques that earlier feminists employed.

22. As Heyes (2000) notes, essentialism can be philosophically understood as a quest for purity, where the general concept is purified of any ontological association with its particular instantiations. This fits well with early feminist critiques of essentialism where efforts to critically engage the concept of woman from the diverse realities of women's experience resulted in important antiessentialist positions. It is equally important to note, however, that emphatic antiessentialism ends by demanding another sort of purity, the theoretical purity of a feminism where every trace of essentialism has supposedly been eradicated (see Bordo 1993 217, 243).

23. See note 4, above. In the U.S. academy, those feminists accused regularly
and almost ritualistically of essentialism in its most reviled form included Adrienne
Rich, Robin Morgan, Andrea Dworkin, Catharine MacKinnon, and feminists who
affirmed an ontological connection between women and nature, such as Mary
Daly and Susan Griffin. This list, give or take a few names, appeared in article after
article and functioned as a kind of warning to other feminists. Association with
"essentialism" would mean association with this group of feminists whom academics believed to be discredited to the point of disgrace. Even now, papers at
feminist conferences are full of off-hand remarks about Catharine MacKinnon,
who seems to have inherited the spite formerly directed at the list of women
above, and whose name is thrown out as the "marker" for essentialist (i.e., bad)
feminism. Catharine MacKinnon, an emphatic social constructionist if ever there
was one, occupies this position in what can only be called a wildly ironic twist of
the antiessentialist logic. Not incidentally, all of these women are associated with
1970s and 1980s feminist activism, politicized lesbianism, separatism, and/or anti-
pornography work—feminist positions that have thrown the norms of heterosexuality deeply into question. As Schor claims, this may be one of the keys to
unlocking the political stakes of what I call emphatic antiessentialism and its vehe-
mence.

24. This is also when the term "cultural feminist" was created to stand in for
the self-definition "radical feminist" by those opposed to radical feminist positions.

25. See for example Alcoff and Potter (1988), Jane Flax (1990). In *Feminism
and Foucault* (1988) Sawicki writes explicitly, "I . . . want to contribute to the
movement beyond polarized debate, specifically by further developing the theoretical and practical implications of a *more adequate* sexual politics in the work
of Michel Foucault" (emphasis mine).

26. See Jane Roland Martin (1994) for an account of the "chilly research climate" created by the accusation of essentialism.

27. Naomi Schor and Elizabeth Weed argue that "definitions are by definition,
as it were, essentialist," and claims that antiessentialists have essentialized essentialism by creating a context in which all sorts of essentialism are treated as equally
heinous. She argues that the first task is to "de-essentialize essentialism" (Schor
and Weed 1994, 43). Diana Fuss argues similarly that "there is no essence to
essentialism . . . (historically, philosophically and politically) we can speak only of
essentialisms" (1989, xii).

28. Feminists who seem to have based their theoretical or political work on
women's capacity for motherhood or nurturance, or women's physical or biological characteristics, are the particular targets of this critique. Feminists as diverse as
Carol Gilligan, Luce Irigaray, and Maria Mies have all been accused of this kind of
essentialism.

29. This should not be read to imply that the body will be lived everywhere and
cross-culturally the same, only that it is lived everywhere. To speak of "the body"
is already to speak in a certain cultural context that understands "body" in an indi-
vidualizing framework that will not be intelligible in some different contexts.

30. Kittay writes, "Dependents require care. Neither the utterly helpless new-

born who must be cared for in all aspects of her life nor a frail, but functioning, elderly person who needs only assistance to carry on with her life, will survive or thrive without another who meets her basic needs (1999, 30)," and establishes with the first words of her introduction an "essential" and "universal" fact of human existence from which she builds her critique. "The dependency critique considers . . . the inescapable fact of human dependency and the ways in which such labor makes one vulnerable to domination" (16). The political implications are clear, "How a social order organizes care of these needs is a matter of social justice" (1), and similar political implications will be drawn when this concept is extended to dependence on the Earth itself.

31. I don't mean my "prior" here to be read temporally, although in a certain developmental sense it can be, I mean it more in terms of "priority," first in the order of importance—where breathing, drinking, eating have a clear priority over theoretical activity.

32. Here I am writing in agreement with ecofeminists Maria Mies and Vandana Shiva (1993), whose revaluation of the realm of necessity is the centerpiece of their feminist call for a subsistence economy. In addition to the economic conclusions they draw, however, this insight is important philosophically. They call for a separation of the notions of "emancipation" and "freedom." Emancipation from the natural world has no part in their definition of freedom, which is freedom within the realm of necessity, not in contradistinction to it.

III

RIGHTS

11

Truth and Voice in Women's Rights

Margaret Urban Walker

Truth commissions are a remarkable and novel political institution of our time. A truth commission is an official body "set up to investigate a past period of human rights abuses or violations of international humanitarian law" (Hayner 1994, 598). With the successful Latin American examples of the 1980s, over twenty truth commissions have been formed to date.[1] South Africa's Truth and Reconciliation Commission, described by political theorist Elizabeth Kiss as "the most morally ambitious truth commission to date" (Kiss 2000, 70), set a new standard with its public testimonies of victims and perpetrators, aimed at restoring "the human and civil dignity of the victims," a phrase that occurs repeatedly in its documents and its 1998 Final Report.[2]

In the trend-setting Latin American cases, truth commissions operated in the context of blanket amnesties shielding wrongdoers from criminal prosecution for precisely the offenses the commissions documented, so that truth commissions have been burdened with the reputation of being a "second best" proposition. Even so, their mission of truth-finding and truth-telling is increasingly recognized, around the world, as essential. Truth processes other than truth commissions have been implemented in recent years as well. Following the fall of Communist governments, (then) Czechoslovakia adopted "lustration," barring those who were on membership lists of secret police or various Communist Party organizations from holding public offices for five years. East Germany combined lustration with opening the Stasi (secret police) archives to those on whom the files were kept (see Curry 2000; Garton-Ash 1997; Rosenberg 1995).

While truth processes have proliferated over the past twenty years, the

169

idea of *a right to the truth as a human right* is fairly new. It has emerged out of the practice of truth commissions and other truth processes rather than preceding them. The idea of "rights to truth" implies something stronger than the importance, or value, or positive effect of the truth. It places truths, at least of certain kinds, or under certain conditions, in the category of a something *claimable* for oneself from others, where the claim has both moral legitimacy and urgency, and where the claim presumes the obligations of some parties to effect or enforce it. Rights to truth in cases of gross violations of human rights, like massacre, disappearance, or torture, have been understood as rights of victims, families, and societies *to know or be told the truth* about these matters, as well as rights *to have the truth sought* through impartial investigation.[3] Even in the case of gross violations of human rights, however, not everyone's truths are equally likely to be sought or told. Priscilla Hayner, in the most comprehensive study of truth commissions to date, cautions, "Perhaps the most commonly underreported abuses are those suffered by women, especially sexual abuse and rape" (Hayner 2001, 77). Hayner points to the stigma and shame that may silence women's reports in many settings, but she also notes tendencies to see sexual violation as "secondary" or "added on," or as individual whims, rather than primary violations.

There is a good deal to be learned from, and a good deal to be done about, the persistent impediments to speaking and hearing the truths of women's lives. I will argue that rights to truth must encompass *rights to voice*—to be an authoritative teller of the truth about one's life and experience—as well as rights to know certain truths or to have them sought by others, and that these rights are as important to confronting cases of historically long-standing and systemic oppression as they are in addressing those episodes of violence usually called gross violations of human rights. These are lessons to be drawn from feminist and other liberatory theories that make the possession of "voice" central to social justice and individual freedom. I will also argue that rights to truth—to its being told, but also to telling it—are not only instrumental but are fundamental rights for women and men, for they secure the moral, civil, and political dignity of those, including most women, who have been systemically silenced and epistemically discredited. In these ways they have been denied not only opportunity, equality, or well being, but denied effective moral agency itself.

TRUTHS AND TELLINGS

Rights to truth have been invoked in cases where the truths are those called gross human rights violations, such as extrajudicial killings, torture, disappearance, arbitrary detention, and inhumane treatment. These terrible truths that shatter, suspend, or corrode lives of their victims and others are not "unknown" to all; they are known to perpetrators and to living victims and sometimes to many others. But they are often known incompletely or without detail. In the case of extrajudicial killings and massacres, the living may "know" without being able to verify details or find the remains of their loved ones. And even when some possess the truth, it can be denied, or remain without public legitimation, known but not acknowledged.[4] Many women have been among those who fought for the truth about others they loved, as did the Mothers of the Plaza de Mayo in Argentina and the Mothers of El Salvador, and women marching in the Plaza of Martyrs in Port-au-Prince, Haiti. The South African Commission, concerned that its human rights hearing drew many more women testifying about brutality to others than violations of their own rights, organized hearings specifically for women to come forward.[5] Whether truths are pursued by women or men, and whether they concern women or men, rights to truth have been invoked in a special kind of case, the case of state-sponsored or other organized violence hidden and denied. So it might seem that rights to truth are essentially rights to have certain truths discovered or acknowledged. And it might seem that rights to truth are not fundamental human rights, but rather that claims to truth are instrumental to the protection or exercise of other fundamental rights, like securing justice. I argue, against both of these assumptions, that rights to truth incorporate rights to speak one's truth, and that the standing to speak as well as know is constitutive of moral agency, rather than instrumental to some of its exercises.

Rights to truth do not appear in the U.N. Universal Declaration of Human Rights. Nor do they figure in U.N. conventions concerning torture or genocide. Some U.N. documents, like those on Enforced Disappearance and Extralegal Executions, mandate "investigations," as Amnesty International and Human Rights Watch urge in all cases of gross human rights violations. And a 1997 U.N. recommendation to combat impunity speaks of "full and effective exercise of the right to the truth."[6] Yet among earlier U.N. documents, CEDAW (the U.N. Convention to End All Forms of Discrimination Against Women, opened for ratification in 1980) is interesting in this respect. Although it does not speak of rights to truth, CEDAW requires eliminating "prejudices" about women and women's and men's roles and "customary and all other practices" that support prejudices of women's inferiority.[7] It specially features basic education, as well as career, vocational, family, health, and family planning information. It is more detailed in its coverage of provisions for participation in public and political associations and entities, national and international, than is the Universal Declaration of Human Rights.

I think it is not an accident that so many provisions of CEDAW, growing out of women's movements, go closer to rights to truth, including rights to voice, while also directly addressing rights to work, credit, and economic agency; rights to reproductive control, marital consent, and maternity provisions; and rights to protection from sexual exploitation. I see CEDAW as responsive to a complex of assumptions of feminist activism and theory that are shared with other twentieth-century liberatory movements for rights that address oppressions based on group membership. The assumptions are these:

1. Important truths may not just be "there" for the knowing.
2. Truth is necessarily an interpersonal and social achievement that requires social, discursive, and material conditions.
3. Getting certain truths told requires political will and is a matter of justice.
4. It is an indignity to have one's identity or community represented by lies, and to have to live with those lies.
5. It is a constitutive element of dignity to be a possible bearer of truth about one's experience of oneself and the world.
6. The dignity of human beings is not acknowledged and enacted where human beings do not have *initiative, access, and voice concerning what is true* of their world and in their lives.[8]

On these assumptions it is not only unspoken truths about what are often called "unspeakable" acts of violence and brutality that must be retrieved, released, and publicly acknowledged. It is also crucial for human beings to be able to find and tell truths that are "unspeakable" in other senses. There are truths unspoken out of despair, intimidation, or strategies of self-preservation under desperate conditions. There are truths that await telling because the vocabularies and forms of thought that will retrieve or release them are not yet available, or are not widely understood. There are truths that cannot yet be said in places and by people where they can have real interpersonal, social, and political effects. And there are truths whose tellings and tellers are discredited by the authority of others.

This is why rights to truth matter not only in the cases of wrongs classified as gross violations of human rights. They are critical also to breaking the grip of long-standing systemic and cultural oppressions justified by reference to history and customs. The appreciation of this is one of the achievements of feminist, race, postcolonial, and gay and lesbian theory and politics, which have always been in important part works of truth and politics of truth. It also figures centrally in movements of Native, Aboriginal, or First Nations Peoples. The truth by itself does not set people free, but people's abilities to set themselves free—to claim freedoms and establish their dignity—do depend critically on their initiatives, access, and voice concerning what is true of their world and their lives. To say that we have a moral right to truth is to say that we have urgent and legitimate moral claims in this regard, and that these claims are not only reserved to "moral emergencies" or the kinds of extreme episodes of mass violence that tend to be called human rights disasters.[9]

Contemporary liberatory theories that emphasize *voice* have long recognized the stakes in suppression or denial of histories of injustice and destruction. These theories take seriously *powers to silence* as working parts of oppressive social and political arrangements; they see as fundamental the *powers to speak* that oppressive arrangements are careful to block or destroy. Philosophers María Lugones and Elizabeth Spelman expressed it this way in their brilliant 1983 essay "Have We Got A Theory For You!" Women's having "voice" is necessary both as a way to "increase the chances that true accounts of women's lives will be given, but also because the articulation of experience (in myriad ways) is among the hallmarks of a self-determining individual or community" (Lugones and Spelman 1983, 574). This way of putting it brings out two issues that have intertwined throughout several decades of feminist theories and women's movements: the importance of revealing and responding to the actual truths of women's different lives, as well as the necessity for women to be able to speak those truths out of their own mouths, with a presumption of basic credibility and authority. Rights to truth involve both *rights to know the truth* and *rights to tell the truth*.

PREVENTIONS OF TRUTH AND SPEECHLESS STANDINGS

Although sometimes we speak of the truth when we mean "what really happened" or "what the facts are," a truth is, more precisely, something *told* (that is, asserted or represented). What makes assertions or representations true is something in or about the world, something that in some cases can be established easily (e.g., looking and seeing) or in others can require complex procedures (e.g., techniques of forensic pathology). *What* is true, however, is something that someone *says*, or otherwise *depicts* or *represents*, as being so. A truth is a telling or other representing that has to be told or made or "put forward." Bringing or putting the truth forward requires the *will* or motive to do so, the *means* to do so, the *opportunity* to do so, and the *standing* to do so. Truth commissions after eras of grisly and appalling violence bring forward truths that those who had power did not permit to be told publicly at expense to their power, and did not fear would ever be told. In these situations, there is not only an *absence* of truth, but what we might call, looking at truth as something told or brought forward, a *prevention* of truth.[10]

But everyday, longstanding, historically embedded oppressive practices exhibit these same "preventions" of the truth. Those empowered and entitled by oppressive arrangement do not care about or will not accept the truths about what the arrangement is, why it is oppressive, what suffering and destruction it visits, and what benefits and immunities it allows them to enjoy. So every movement for liberation from injustice, humiliation, or cruelty needs not only to challenge an oppressive system or a practice, but to enunciate the truths, sweeping and small, of what that system really is. Often it is necessary to invent the language and symbolism that is capable of bringing those truths forward. Often it is necessary to overcome powerful feelings of fear or despair in speaking. Even when those with interests in certain truths and the will to speak them do have the expressive means to put them forward, they may still not have access to places where what they will say can be heard or understood in ways that can have an effect. And finally, it is possible to make truths "unspeakable" by disabling the ability of some to have their words "count" in exactly the ways they are intended to, even if they succeed in speaking.

The last form of silencing is the least familiar, but no less important. To have voice is not only to be able to speak, and not only to be able to be heard, but to be able to speak and be heard as saying the kind of thing that you are intending to say. Philosopher Rae Langton explains it this way: "Attempts by the slave to order or forbid [his master] . . . are unspeakable for the slave. Something has silenced his speech, not in the sense of rendering his spoken words inaudible or written marks illegible, but in the sense of . . . preventing those utterances from counting as the actions they were intended to be" (Langton 1993, 316). What is preventing this is not in this case his being gagged, threatened, hidden, or secluded, or his lacking the imagination, concepts, vocabulary, or initiative. It is his *social and legal place*, a standing that is precisely a lack of standing to issue anything that could amount, within that social and legal system, to an order to his master.

Such *speechless standings*, for women, enslaved persons, or members of subject populations can be, and typically have been, written in the black letters of law, as when certain persons cannot give anything that counts as testimony in a court, or have no standing to enter legal actions or complaints. Such standings are also constituted by institutionally backed authorities whose certified expertise includes the power to declare what some people say as chatter, as symptomatic of irrationality or incompetence, as politically proscribed and outlawed speech, or as perversion or filth that in itself shows its source to be discredited. The educational, medical, religious and other authority or expertise of powerful men (and sometimes women) has often been exercised to disqualify the speech of women in these ways. These speechless standings can be constituted as well by reigning definitions of such terms as "politics," or "development," or "family" or "marriage," so that certain people's assertions about these matters do not qualify as relevant views.

In a startling example, Priscilla Hayner reports that commissioners on the Amnesty Committee of South Africa's TRC disqualified an application requesting amnesty for rape without serious consideration because they could not see how rape could be "politically motivated" (Hayner 2001, 79–80). Under statutes for the new International Criminal Court, sexual violations of women are in fact under many circumstances war crimes or crimes against humanity.[11] In February 2001, guilty verdicts on three Bosnian soldiers at the International Tribunal at the Hague for the first time defined rape as a crime against humanity, and found holding women in captivity and raping them a form of enslavement. Still, specifically *sexual* slavery suffered by women in many wartime contexts is not yet acknowledged, nor is the category of genocidal rape yet in law (Simons 2001b; Vidovic 2001). Lawyers defending the three Bosnian Serb soldiers who were found guilty in February 2001 of raping, torturing, and enslaving Muslim women in the town of Foca in Bosnia in 1992, claimed that "rape in itself is not an act that inflicts severe bodily pain" and that prosecutors failed to show that the raped women "were exposed to any severe physical or psychological suffering" (Simons 2001a). Rape as violation, torture, and political strategy remain even now difficult to speak if not unspeakable in some quarters.

The vocabulary of rights, when it is available to someone with the socially recognized and protected standing of a bearer of rights, is itself an example of a socially empowered form of speech without which certain kinds of things are virtually impossible to say. Without the vocabulary that has some of the meaning and function that the vocabulary of "rights" now widely possesses, some assertions can only be seen as preferences, requests, pleas, or complaints, rather than claims that require consideration or demands that must be met. So closely is the concept of "right" connected to the standing to enter claims for consideration, that to paraphrase one well-known philosopher, transposing the gender of his pronouns: To respect a person, or to think of her as possessed of human dignity, simply *is* to think of her as a potential maker of claims.[12] Rights to truth imply claims to being a maker of assertions that embody a point of view and to be a possible bearer of the truth in what one asserts. A variety of material and social resources are needed, however, for that standing to be real and effective.

Because intimidation and violent or costly reprisals are so often the conditions under which women decide what truths to speak, full legal capacity and recourse to civil and criminal law, as well as opportunities for economic survival, are essential for women to tell their truths. Literacy and at least primary education are indispensable for women to get and use the information that allows them to see their lives accurately both as they are in reality and as they might otherwise be, as well as to share this information with others. Further, it won't matter what women have to tell if they cannot be heard telling it in places where it can have an effect. Women's access to *public* speech that is not simply ignored or discounted requires access to public roles, public spaces, and public media or venues of expression. The idea of "public" as opposed to "private" spaces is perhaps too closely tied to Euro-American political formations to be the right one for all contexts. The point is that women's speech needs to be able, where women choose, to enter spheres beyond the personal, familial, domestic, or other borders that often confine it to women's disadvantage.

A right to be a teller of truths involves basic authority to assert, opine, testify, deny, contravert, or refuse, to be perceived as the possessor of a point of view and a possible bearer of truth. But that is not enough. People also need the opportunity to participate in processes that set *forms* of speech and *standards* of credibility. People need opportunities to enjoy some control over, if not access to, the forms and positions of expertise that shape cultural assumptions and social dialogue. I find it increasingly hard to see how, in particular, women's initiative, access, and voice concerning what is true of the world and their lives can be more than remote possibilities without aggressive measures to insure not only political participation, but something closer to proportionate representation in the main local and society-wide institutions of governance that rule women's and men's lives. Inuit people in the new Canadian territory of Nunavut considered, but narrowly defeated, a system of dual-sex political representation (DePalma 1999). France recently adopted a legal requirement for equal numbers of women to be fielded by political parties in almost all elections (Daley 2001). These are measures that address the need to dismantle the disabling of women's speech structurally at both the highest levels of social organization and on a society-wide scale. The same need exists in places of education and culture-making, where bodies of knowledge and the vocabulary and symbolism for socially authorized expression are propagated.

The link between voice and truth has consequences for understanding women's situations and for women's understanding their own situations. One example is the use of "adaptive" or "deformed" preferences (or in an older idiom "false consciousness") to explain women's apparent compliance or complicity with unjust and even painfully oppressive arrangements.[13] When women's behavior that conforms to unjust or oppressive norms is explained as a case of "adaptive or deformed preferences" the women who comply are seen as *actually preferring* what is painful or disadvantageous because they have learned to prefer it. Sometimes it is said that they have "internalized" oppression. But this is not the only explanation of compliant behavior, and it is a very different kind of explanation from one that sees women's compliant behavior as a kind of *adaptation*, that is, a strategy for living with, doing better in, or garnering some control in a hard, dangerous, or defeating situation. If a woman has chosen or learned a strategy by which she protects herself or others while coping with oppressive or demeaning practices, she may continue to find these practices very painful, frustrating, or humiliating *from her own point of view*. She may very well see them as wrong, or cruel, or unjust, or shored up by power rather than by right or good sense. She may see them as the going "game" or "system" that she cannot change and so must work to protect herself and others within it.

The difference between seeing "adaptive preferences" in women's compliant behavior and seeing strategic "adaptations" is the difference, as Uma Narayan has put it, between seeing women as "prisoners" or "dupes" of patriarchy, and seeing them as agents, however seriously constrained, "bargaining with patriarchy," something almost all women in fact do (Narayan 1997, chap. 2; Narayan 2000). This is a very great difference, both as an explanation and as a moral evaluation, in how we understand what women do. One thing that is necessary, however, to distinguish cases where we are seeing realistic adaptations *despite* a woman's preferences from cases where we are seeing actual deformations of her preferences themselves, is to hear women *explain* their choices from *their* points of view. But this is what they cannot do without will, expressive means, access, and voice. Even worse, however, without will, means, access, and voice women may not be able to make these distinctions to themselves, or to make them clearly. This means that without voice it is difficult if not impossible to establish a fact of the matter about women's behavior and preferences. One might reasonably ask whether there necessarily *is* a fact of the matter under these circumstances. The capacities for self-possession and self-revelation that come with having a voice go very deep, to the bases of moral agency.

RIGHTS TO TRUTH: INSTRUMENTAL AND FUNDAMENTAL

Rights to truth and authority in shaping and telling it are instrumental in combating some especially harmful and defeating positions in which women can be placed or exploited by more powerful men and by more privileged women. Rights to truth and telling can enable women to claim their agency by announcing that they are negotiating their positions within unavoidable patriarchal structures the justice of which they do not accept. Rights to truth can be crucial political instruments. Their exercise can block "gendered nationalisms" that manipulate gendered identities, symbols, divisions of labor and resources, or putative "cultural traditions" of sex domination that are mobilized in national struggles to the disadvantage or subordination of women.[14]

What rights to truth protect, however, are not only instrumental goods. They assert one's standing as a knower of the world and oneself, especially of the social world and one's places in it individually and as a member of collectivities. This standing is not only a means to other good things. It is a constitutive element of civil, social, moral, and political humanity. The capacity and standing to speak for oneself about one's self, and especially about one's own actions, is intimately linked to one's moral being, what has sometimes been called a person's dignity. Here, briefly, is one explanation why.

We show how our behavior is human action by expressing our intentions, giving an account of what we are doing from our own point of view. We learn from others to give these accounts of ourselves, and we learn to elaborate, defend, or concede them, by doing so with others. When we are able to do this we are *accountable* for ourselves and to others, and so can be held to account. When women are silenced as self-describers of their actions and choices they lose, or never gain, the status of self-accounting actors in relations of mutual accountability. This is a roundabout way of saying they lose, or never gain, the most basic status of a *moral agent*.[15] Further, when anyone is denied the standing to report for common consideration her or his experience, she or he is effaced even as the holder of a point of view, much less a moral actor with powers of agency, choice, and self-understanding.

Rights to truth and its telling are both instrumental and fundamental. For women who are disadvantaged and oppressed, they are a lifeline to the claiming of other rights. But for women and men they are also the emblem and embodiment of civil, political, and moral humanity.

NOTES

This paper was originally presented as an invited plenary address to the Southeast Women's Studies Association Conference "Women's Rights Are Human Rights" at Florida Atlantic University on March 16, 2001. I would like to thank the organizers of SEWSA for providing the original occasion to work out these ideas. This paper is a slightly revised version of that presentation. A shorter version of this presentation was given at The First Feast, the first annual meeting of the Association for Feminist Ethics and Social Theory in October 2001.

1. Central sources on truth commissions include Hayner 1994, 2001; Steiner 1997; Rotberg and Thompson 2000. Krog 1998 is a riveting first-person account of South Africa's proceedings. See also Wechsler 1990 for the stories of Argentina's and Brazil's ways of addressing a repressive and violent past.

2. The Final Report (1998) of the TRC is available in online form on its website, *www.truth.org.za,* which also displays the founding documents and related material.

3. See Méndez 1997, 261–62, on the "emerging principles" of victims' rights to justice, truth, and compensation, and on the right to know the truth as "a customary international law norm." Neier 1999, 40–41, argues American support of violently repressive regimes in Latin America made "deniable forms of repression" (like disappearance, secret detention and torture, and death squads) essential, and hence defined truth as the main battleground and focus of human rights organizations in the 1980s.

4. The distinction between knowledge and acknowledgment figures prominently in literature on truth processes. The distinction in this context is credited by Lawrence Wechsler to philosopher Thomas Nagel: "It's what happens and can only happen to knowledge when it becomes officially sanctioned, when it is made part of the public cognitive scene" (Wechsler 1990, 4).

5. See Chapter 16, "Truth Is a Woman," in Krog 1998.

6. Quoted in Hayner 2001, 184.

7. This is one of the areas, Article 5 of CEDAW, to which the United States government makes a reservation in signing the treaty, based on U.S. constitutional protections of privacy.

8. Young 1990 is the most comprehensive development of a "participatory" paradigm of justice that underlies much contemporary liberatory theory.

9. Jonathan Glover uses the phrase "moral emergencies" in Glover 2000, 408.

10. As interesting, in episodes of mass violence and severe repression, those with power rely on special euphemistic code languages and expressions so that even *they* often do not in fact tell each other or themselves the precise or whole truth, from bureaucratic euphemisms of the Final Solution to the contemporary code languages of torturers and free-handed security police wherever they operate. See Glover 2000 on distancing strategies, which include euphemism and "cold jokes" concerning torture and killing. See also Jolly 1999, 112–13 on the "use of language as a self-deluding practice of signification" in the speech of assassins and security police who carried out the violent and murderous practices of South African apartheid.

11. See Hayner 2001, 267, note 21. Hayner reports that more recent commissions, like those in Guatemala and Haiti, have placed more emphasis on sexual violations of women.

12. The original passage in Feinberg 1980, 151 reads: "To respect a person, then, or to think of him as possessed of human dignity, simply *is* to think of him as a potential maker of claims."

13. The dangers of adaptive preferences (or in an older idiom "false conscious-

ness") are mentioned repeatedly by contributors in Nussbaum and Glover 1995. See Nussbaum 1995, 91; Glover 1995, 123; O'Neill 1995, 142; Sen 1995, 260; and Okin 1995, 292. Both Martha Nussbaum 2000, chap. 2, and Amartya Sen 1999, 58–64, stress adaptive or distorted preferences in demonstrating the defects of "preference satisfaction" as a measure of well being in utilitarian ethics and economics.

14. Peterson and Runyan 1993, 132–33, discusses gendered nationalism. See also Narayan 1997, chaps. 1 and 2, on gendered nationalism, as well as how feminists may adopt perspectives on women in "traditional societies" that are complicit with conservative or fundamentalist forces in those societies whose aim is to control women through invocations of "tradition" and "culture."

15. Philosopher Annette Baier in the second of her Carus Lectures, on "Intention" (Baier 1997), gives a striking account of the intimate relations between learning to give accounts and being capable of intentional, and so morally assessable action.

12

Globalizing Women's Rights: Building a Global Public Sphere

María Pía Lara

Some decades ago, Habermas's work on the public sphere changed our understanding of how the bourgeois public sphere became an important new dimension in a model for participatory democracy. This, in turn, helped define how new social subjects were creating their own public spaces in the eighteenth and early nineteenth centuries. These emerged from the fusion of literary and political contexts, which were geographically situated in Great Britain, France, and Germany. Habermas's model helped us see the vital connection between the cultural and the political—a connection that allowed societies to understand how this associational life carried greater significance for future developments than just its manifest functions. According to Habermas, "They did provide the training ground for what were to become a future society's norms of political equality" (Habermas 1996a, 424). One of the most interesting things in Habermas's work is that he gave us plenty of examples of the empirical uses and practices of the public sphere, though he uses the term in its normative sense.[1] Some of the empirical practices of the public sphere's reconstruction in Habermas's account allowed us to understand that in shaping the modern concept of the bourgeois' public sphere, the common understandings and the social imaginary helped in shaping a new normative basis that was not fully understood until well into the twentieth century. It is precisely this connection between the innovative practices and our ways of configuring a new conceptual scheme to match those practices, that "unprecedented kinds of spaces require new and unprecedented understandings."[2] The time has come to recognize the significance of these "effects" of globalization and to visualize the emergence of a global public sphere through the culture and products created by a global civil society.

In what follows, I will illustrate how the decentering effects of information and the production of new cultural and political trends have begun to deliver what Anthony Giddens has called the "reverse colonization" (2000, 34), which has a double impact because it has an effect on both parties. I will define this as the "illocutionary effect," a framework for the new global public sphere.[3] It is an effect that allows non-Western countries to influence developments in the West, while, at the same time, to be influenced by the West. These double-sided effects have also begun to challenge the West as poorer, non-Western countries begin to question their exclusion from the possibility of enjoying global justice. Such issues stress their need to be involved in deep processes of democratization and the necessary steps—which would require participation from the West— that would help them achieve those goals.

After Habermas published his work on the public sphere, the criticism that emerged with regard to his basic insights led him to accept a more dynamic picture of how "the exclusion of the culturally and politically mobilized lower strata entails a pluralization of the public sphere in the very process of its emergence" (Lara 1998, 426). Thus, in my view, the constitution of the global public sphere is configured, as it was in Habermas's model, in two ways: First, through a new process by which individuals think of themselves and produce counter-publics. And second, in the ways that they publicly address those "others" through literary works about their new characteristics and their new, desired identities. Culture, then, plays a crucial role in building this new global public sphere.

DEVELOPING DIASPORIC PUBLIC
SPHERES AS GLOBAL SPHERES

By expanding the boundaries of communities across countries and different geographies, the diasporic public spheres have become an important first stage for the notion of a global public sphere. If the bourgeois public sphere was the result of active principles of democratization—equality of status, freedom of expression, new forms of association—then we can conclude that it is in the emergence of diasporic public spheres that the globalizing of the public sphere will become yet another stage of democratization. Such is the result of wider claims for social integration from immigrants, exiles, and poorer countries.

According to Arjun Appadurai, electronic media "decisively change[d] the wider field of mass media and other traditional media" because it reconstructed the concept of mass mediation by offering new resources for the development of social identities (1998, 3). Therefore, just as the bourgeois public began to fashion its own experiments and construct new identities by admiring others' representations of intimacy in novels and biographies, our global subjects have also begun to build their narratives influenced by cinema, television, and other world products. In this way, they are able to write themselves into new scripts that have become "experiments with self-making in all sorts of societies, [and] for all sorts of persons" (3). Thus, novels and narratives become the first vehicles for creating global identities.

I would like to consider the emergence of the global public sphere by highlighting several key moments that have allowed the connection of two important concepts: First, the appearance of diasporic public spheres has connected two or more distinct geographical places that are linked through the voice of a new social subject—one that we will call a "nomadic subject." To illustrate the characteristics of these new global subjects, I will use Carlos Forment's phrase "peripheral people," which describes "political agents, ex-colonials and second class citizens . . . [as well as] their distinct experience, [and] cultural hybridness" (1996, 314). Second, these "peripheral peoples" or "second-class citizens" occupy marginal positions and have been marked by humiliation, discrimination, and prejudice. As Forment has argued, however, they "have become increasingly concerned with 'human rights and civil rights' in their home-land and elsewhere, in order to correct the wrongs they and their counter-parts have experienced" (316). It is, therefore, important to note that these new agents of social change exist because they have been influenced and "shaped" by the liberal notions, narratives, and central institutions of democratic countries. This, in turn, allows them to amalgamate their particular views with those of persons that understand justice and inclu-sion in terms of rights and fairness. Because of its relevance to the connec-tion between the emergence of the bourgeois public sphere and normative notions of egalitarian status, this democratic feature of self-fashioning appears again in this case. It is particularly useful in under-standing normative links within the emergence of the global public sphere, since mass migration (as a global phenomena) has triggered the creation of "diasporic public spheres." Immigrants and exiled people are using such spaces to state their claims for fairer ways of achieving social integration. The normative link that allows for a global definition of these diasporic public spheres lies in the fact that their audiences are not con-figured by the closed frame of the "nation-states," nor are they "local" or "regional spaces" anymore, but, rather, they are the transnational spaces of mobile subjects and they aim to address global audiences. Thus, the global characteristic linking mass media and migration deals primarily with how world spectators interpret and reconstruct their self-images while in exile and in migration. These are images that aim to create new stories and myths about social hope, along with new identities based on postnational projects.

Appadurai has said that the new spaces of the diasporic public spheres are not only spaces of contestation, but of emancipation as well. His study of the cultural dimensions of globalization proposes different types of diasporas. Though he does not explain the differences between them, he provides us with three useful classifications: the diasporas of hope (which, in my view, relate to immigrant workers); the diasporas of terror (which, I believe, refer to people who live as exiles); and the diasporas of despair (which I suppose include all those who wish to return to their countries but cannot do so because of various economic or political reasons). The emancipatory potential of these diasporic public spheres offers "new social projects" for social integration and makes a qualitative "difference" between the phenomenon of migration today and that of the past (Forment 1996, 6).

It is interesting to note that Appadurai seeks to depict the mass media in a positive light by pointing out its power to enlighten and educate. This is an element that was central to Habermas's own account of the emergence of the bourgeois public sphere. If we rescue Forment's claim that democratic and liberal narratives have also deeply influenced the narratives of peripheral people, then we can identify Appadurai's positive understanding of mass consumption as an important element of this global process. Forment explains that "from a set of simple binaries, liberals are able to generate a series of complex dualities, which they then use to compose major and minor stories, harmonizing them in a contrapuntal manner as in a fugue" (1996, 318). The stories, which always involve dramatic tensions and resolutions, tend to counterpose "universal, abstract reason" with "traditional and customary practices"; "legal rights" and "substantive virtues"; "procedural rules" in relation to "individual autonomy" against "collective solidarity." Furthermore, there are even some narratives that extend beyond the typical "antinomies" drawn by the liberal narratives in order to produce a new dimension of justice (318).

Because the public sphere has always been at the center of many varying views, narratives seem to engage readers and spectators in the stimulating task of telling the stories they recover. The processes by which these narratives produce an impact on the public sphere also allow others not only to criticize them, but to imagine new ways of seeing the world. Thus, "through the argumentative retellings that are forever taking place among its practitioners over the changing meaning and significance of its stories," different projects of democracy have begun to give hope to peripheral peoples (Forment 1996, 314).

At the same time, it is important to note that the positive effects of information can help us understand its empirical effects on global civil society and globalization as a new practical agenda. Habermas demonstrates his awareness of these facts in his claim that "the actors in civil society can assume a surprisingly active and momentous role" as the "great issues of the last decades give evidence for this" (1996b, 380–381). As such, the activities in which peripheral people have been involved with the mass media represent more than just a passive participation. Rather, the public is being enlightened by the mixture of democratic narratives, which have been recovered by these peripheral people, to create hybrid stories. We can, therefore, see how the new global narratives can trigger not only "resistance, irony, [and] selectivity," but also a new kind of "agency" (7). So Appadurai's defense of mass consumption of global narratives like films, television shows, documentary news, and exhibits—when offered to the global public sphere—effectively connects with the notion that the public is often more critical than we suppose, and that imagination—collective imagination—is a fertile "ground for action" (7).

The most original feature of these new narratives is their reappropriation of democratic stories, which they "have used . . . to reinterpret a century and a half of imperial-colonial relations" (Forment 1996, 319). These stories, whose vision of equality, fairness, autonomy, and freedom are being used to transform past experiences of "hierarchical domination, social dependency, and lack of recognition" now define the literary and political practices within newer stages of democracy (319). As I mentioned earlier, the equalizing factor illustrates the way in which the fusion of horizons has produced a new tradition, which can be called a "postcolonial narrative," because it envisions a future based on significant new ideas about recognition. These new narratives do not simply aim to end their stories with a false idea of reconciliation or of achieving total transparency, as was done during the Enlightenment. They seek, instead, to accomplish two things: First, they present the complexity of sociopolitical meanings, which are not fixed. And second, they demonstrate the complexity and asymmetry of social relations, which are very much related to different historical interpretations of the meaning of fairness and equality. What matters most in these narratives, then, is that conversation allows the interlocutors to describe and translate their search for new meanings in ways that are best suited to implement social integration.

Just as Rousseau was a key figure in the trend of self-invention through autobiography, in our global era others have already taken vital steps to become relevant figures of diasporic public spheres. During the 1960s, Latin American literature became an important vehicle for the recovery of the identity of "nomadic subjects." We have, for example, the work of writers in exile such as Gabriel García Márquez (living in Mexico), Julio Cortázar (living in France), and many others.[4] Latin American writers invented "magic realism" as a way to find a voice that would allow them to recover their original life experience and their legacy of postcolonial hope. Because the impact of their work in the West was appreciated as unique and valuable and because their influence became global, these writers enjoyed a great deal of success. García Márquez won a Nobel Prize, and with it, Western recognition. His contribution to world literature played an important role in the appearance of "nomadic subjects." Decades later, Salman Rushdie became a key figure in the emergence of diasporic public spheres. This can be attributed to his great contribution to the creation of hybrid stories through major literary works such as *Midnight's Children, Shame, The Moor's Last Sight*, and especially, the book *East-West*, which I consider essential to the comprehension of his concept of the hybrid and of being a "nomadic subject." In the nine stories that constitute the book, Rushdie deals with the convergence and divergence between two cultures that are radically opposed but indissolubly intertwined and fused in a synthesis of various historical epochs. Here, the concept of the "hybrid" is clarified by understanding that this mixture took place for complex and contradictory reasons. Nevertheless, there is comfort in the distance created by being both "in and out" at the same time. It allows critical clarity, the possibility of detachment when one needs to see oneself through the eyes of another culture, and, most of all, insight into "the hybrid" through the cultivation of tolerance as a civic virtue. Rushdie is well aware of the difficult relationship between fact and fiction and of the tragicomic duality experienced by nomadic subjects—a condition he depicts in many of his stories. In these he describes what it is like to feel both a sense of belonging and not belonging in different cultures. They tell us that the only possible way to attain an identity is to make conscious choices in every stage of life rather than accept the given and the particulars of one's own contingencies and historical condition. It is not a coincidence that Rushdie's *Satanic Verses* attempted to create a new concept of "tolerance" through humor and satire (related to the idea of one's own beliefs and particularities). He has written about his hopes that our future will be an "age in which we finally grow out of our need for religion," because so often religion is at the root of our intolerance (Rushdie 1999).

Thus, Rushdie has influenced the literary world and is greatly appreciated in the world's public sphere. His work, which is the product of a diasporic public sphere, has allowed other writers like himself to have their work read. Together they have opened a literary path for eloquent tales about "hybridity" and the conditions of being nomadic. Books such as *The God of Small Things* by Arundhati Roy[5] and *Interpreter of Maladies* by Jhumpa Lahiri—both recipients of important literary awards—offer evidence that the new voices of peripheral peoples are seeking to grow out of barriers between nations and generations.

We can use Edward W. Said, who lives in the United States, as an example of an exile to discuss a second historical stage in the emergence of the diasporic public spheres. His work illustrates the idea of finding new ways to study foreign cultures by connecting diasporic public spheres with the mainstream public. In an influential study he titled *Orientalism* (1979), Said initiated a new way to consider our perception of social identities. He shows that the concept of so-called Orientals was, in fact, the West's way of understanding itself. Said points out that by defining "Other" as the opposite of "us," as we have seen in liberal stories that counterpose one other, the West made a model of what it meant to be civilized and rational. In this model, the East represented the "Other." The uncivilized. The irrational. Thus he explored the field of culture by focusing on the West's study of "Orientalism," which employed basic ontological and epistemological presuppositions to build a "discourse" (in the Foucaultdian sense). From this was created a narrative that became a "systematic discipline by which European culture was able to manage—and even produce—the Orient politically and imaginatively during the post-Enlightenment period" (Said 1979, 3).

The first interesting characteristic of *Orientalism* is that Said was well aware of the strategy the West used and he understood the relevance of all the stories that related to such a view. He, therefore, not only studied the novels of many authors such as Nerval and Flaubert, he also examined the ways those writers "imagined" the "Orientals" as well as the impact of those novels and of other literary studies on the imagination of the West and on the way the West visualized and mythologized other cultures. The second important element is Said's connection of culture to power. By emphasizing the connection between the different fields in which "Orientalism" was studied, Said showed how the West expanded its scope of geopolitical interests beyond the aesthetic, scholarly, economic, sociological, historical, and philological barriers.

It is true, however, that Said's work was polemical. After its publication he was even accused of feeding a tradition of anti-Western ideas. It is my opinion that his work was a first step in linking diasporic public spheres to peripheral peoples, and that his description of the Western idea of civic identity was "culturally" constructed. Said's book sheds light on the notion of the "diasporic public sphere" as a significant new concept.[6] It helps us visualize the way Said's views "traversed the imperial East-West divide"—the perimeter of "us" and "them"—the way they entered the "the life of the West, and yet retained some organic connection with the place" from which he came (Said 1979, 336). With this interconnection, Said has offered an example of a fusion of horizons as the new site of a nonessentialist type of learning that can take place between two "sides." Therefore, despite its controversy, Said's work contains emancipatory goals and connects itself to this new tradition of peripheral peoples, alongside other works that have already greatly contributed to the reversal of colonialism.

The conclusion drawn by Said's work can be seen as the "reverse effect of colonization" because it demonstrates the way in which the West constructed stereotypes while developing a framework for "civic characteristics" with which to represent itself as the embodiment of rational and civil society. The conclusion about "Orientalism" made by those who contested Said, however, clearly shows its Foucauldian influence if we understand it to be a discourse of power over the Orient and a system of knowledge that produced a myth and a "rational" framework for the identity of Oriental peoples that was disseminated into the general population. But even moving beyond its purely controversial effects, Said's work reaches the perimeter of the paradoxical ways in which Westerners have built their identities. This is because it deals with the way in which Western culture has influenced even non-Western systems of creating identities through notions of others as opposites of what we consider "good" in ourselves. A close inspection of these strategies will surely allow us to find ways to redress the effects of stereotypes by exposing them in the public sphere. Said's ability to trace this particular exclusionary tendency to the way studies were conducted in the post-Enlightenment provides an important historical precedent for understanding just how exclusionary our definitions of the "civic characteristics" of Western democracies have been. As Said argued, "The culturally sanctioned habit of deploying large generalizations by which reality is divided into various collectives: languages, types, colors, mentalities, each category being not so much a neutral designation as an evaluative interpretation," classified in a "rigidly binomial opposition of 'ours' and 'theirs,'" and made "'our' values liberal, humane, correct; which were [also] supported by the tradition of belles-lettres, informed scholarship, [and] rational inquiry" (1979, 227).

This critical dimension of Said's work must be related to its normative opposite—that is, the claim that it is important to find new public ways to discuss inclusion, along with a more respectful approach to the study of cultures. As Said has argued, if the construction of social identities always "involves the construction of opposites and 'others' whose actuality is always subject to the continuous interpretation and reinterpretation of their differences from 'us'" (1979, 332) then it is imperative that we move beyond binary distinctions into a different way of creating identities that involves the idea of "hybrid identities." Any "hybrid identity" should begin by focusing on the mixture, not only of Western characteristics, but also of the influence felt by the West from other places.[7] We can see this influence in literary trends—in narratives such as movies that are now among the leading films of the world. For example, Chinese films,[8] the newly "discovered" Iranian cinema,[9] and, more recently, some highly successful Mexican movies.[10] Eastern culture and aesthetic have deeply influenced Western fashion over the past few decades. Eastern knowledge, medical treatments, and exercises have become fundamental in the development of new health and fitness trends in the West. Even Eastern religions have been adopted by Westerners who rediscover their cultural and religious icons as symbols of freedom and peace (the Dalai Lama, for example). In general, the East and the South (as they have been called by Westerners) are finally being appreciated as important sources of inspiration in the creation of Western identities as well.

We should be able to acknowledge that it is impossible to find one-sided elements of purity in our identities when they are defined by codes of goodness, rationality, and virtuosity. We should also recognize the awkwardness of defining our particularities as one-sided codes of ethnicity, race, and sense of belonging, when we fail to notice the effects of other mixtures that have already occurred in all our cultures.

If works like Rushdie's and Said's teach us how to redress the effects of colonization and alert us to the dangers of opposing binary definitions of civic virtues of noncivic people, we should now learn that paradoxes and antinomies do not provide the only literary tropes with which to redefine ourselves. These examples of global narratives should help us reach beyond the perimeter of an exclusionary "us" against "them" by giving us a new concept of "hybrid identities."

Having said this, I would like now to focus on the third stage of the development of the narratives of colonialism, which has enlarged the scope of hybrid stories. This time, I will pinpoint the South as it is linked to the West. The key figure here is a woman. The narratives on which we will focus contain, in a "striking contrast to liberal orthodoxy," an "especially rich, complex, and appreciative set of stories about the importance of communal solidarity, collective memory, social honor, rendering service to one's own community, and becoming personally engaged in struggles for social justice as a way of renewing and remaking one's self" (Forment 1996, 320). This third stage can be thought of as a laboratory in which "hybrid peoples" have begun to use progressive stories to reinvent their traditions and, by doing so, to transform themselves. An excellent example of this third stage is Rigoberta Menchú's autobiography, *My Name is Rigoberta Menchú and This Is the Way that My Conscience Was Born* (1985). It is a highly mixed joint project between Menchú, an Indian Maya political exile, and Elizabeth Burgos, a white intellectual woman liv-

ing in exile in France. Together they have woven a narrative that depicts
the injustices suffered by an entire community, the Maya-Quichés of Guatemala. The accounts of Menchú's suffering in her so-called biography are
a mixture of what, by Western standards, would certainly be considered
forms of humiliation and even of mass ethnic extermination. Within her
story, she uses her own persona to embody and portray the suffering of
her people—she describes them as the experiences of an individual. In
this way, instead of creating a typical account of the story of an ethnic community, Menchú gathers the stories of the various abuses inflicted on her
people into a new story of her own creation. Thanks to David Stoll's
research, we know that Menchú was educated by nuns, who said she was
a fast learner (Stoll 1998). Yet, in her book, she depicts herself as illiterate
and uses Burgos as her "translator." Her descriptions are also a mixture
of her Western and Mayan influences. Each chapter is delivered with an
elegant simplicity that makes them seem like poetry. It is a voice that she
knows will echo the exotic "strangeness" of how her people might sound
to Westerners.[11] We also know from Stoll that she did not lose as many
members of her family as she claims, in her story, to have lost; nor did
they die in the way she has written. These are, in reality, the stories of
other Mayan-Quiché families. In the book, her family—like the people
they represent—are killed by their savage oppressors, the Guatemalan
army. Menchú then goes on to tell her story as a peasant woman working
under extreme conditions and exploited by hostile landowners. She also
depicts significant elements of racial discrimination in a chapter that tells
the story of her work as a maid when she moved to the city. Her account
weaves different stories of "deliverance from oppression and captivity,"
which she follows with her "hidden transcripts" (Scott 1990), and then
chronicles her overt forms of resistance as a member of a rebel organization (CUC). Finally, Menchú ends her book with the story of her exile in
Mexico and a promise of redemption and the renewal of her commitment
to find the means to a freer and more just society. Thus, the stories in her
fictional autobiography are claims to rights—human rights and specific
cultural rights (which can be understood within the framework of democratic institutions). When she speaks of recognition, she is explicitly connecting it to the idea of democratic rights. Menchú knows that only within
the bounds of democratic institutions can discrimination be fought.

The striking originality of this example of a "hybrid" autobiography
demonstrates the ways in which Menchú interweaves her Mayan culture
with her Western influences. As we have seen, the injustices she (and her
people) suffered are recounted within the framework of democratic narratives. Yet, at the same time, she revisits the ancient poem "El Popol Vuh"
in every one of her chapters to illustrate its connection to her people. She
describes her culture and her people's rituals, linking them to her own

upbringing from girlhood to adulthood. Menchú is also empowered by her own ability to communicate her people's ideas about who they are and wherein lie their duties. She writes of the love they feel for their land, the way they relate to the Other. These appear now to be commendable virtues of solidarity, strong bonds with which to construct a collective memory, and a shared feeling of social honor. The paradox here lies in the way she fuses the "I" with the "we." When she describes all the suffering and oppression her people have endured, she becomes an individual, and she is capable of recovering all the normative claims implicit in earlier liberal narratives about social justice. The outcome is a narrative with a "postcolonial" texture within the context of a diasporic public sphere in Mexico. Thus, according to Western standards, Rigoberta Menchú's biography—or "autobiography"—is the best vehicle she could use to attract the attention of the global civil society and of public opinion.[12] Through it, Menchú was able to exercise international pressure to stop the killings of her people, arrange for institutional measures to protect her people's rights, and gain social recognition.

Later, in Rigoberta Menchú's acceptance speech for the 1992 Nobel Peace Prize, we find the same traits of a postcolonial narrative. Once again, she connects her hopes for a future democracy while lamenting her forced exile. She states that Indians are willing to combine "tradition" with "modernity," but warns the world that this will not be done at "any price" (Menchú 1994, 21). Menchú also stresses the need to understand that the motto "unity in diversity" is not merely a rhetorical device, but rather a new way of understanding the inclusion of Indian peoples into the paradigm of the world's social justice (Canby 1999, 28–29). Furthermore, she explicitly acknowledges the need to situate Indian claims for social integration as an important part of the agenda of world democratization with the help of international institutions (Menchú 1994, 25). Finally, she urges the "international community" to actively engage more directly with Guatemala, particularly to support its transition to democracy. Her last words are a reminder of the fact that the need for justice has become a global need, and a mention of the many places where both democracy and peace are needed in order to combat injustice.

A global society needs current studies of cultures and new ways to use the positive effects of reimagining ourselves so that we can question and censure previous prejudices from the West. As seen with Rushdie's and Said's work, Menchú's story constitutes a third stage of this movement toward "hybrid" narratives that search for new ways to express a "reappropriation of the historical experience of colonialism, revitalized and transformed into a new aesthetic of sharing and often [of] transcendent re-formulation"(Said 1979, 351).

One final phase, in our view, of the process of building a global public sphere can be defined as the stage in which the effects of a "reverse colonization" have begun to shape Western initiatives in supporting other countries' transitions to democracy. This can be accomplished by offering them a concrete, legal way of understanding the need to extend the positivization of international law. The first key figure in such a process is the Spanish judge Balata Garzon, who has made it his job to indict the military forces behind the dictatorships of Guatemala, Chile, and Argentina. After the arrest of General Augusto Pinochet in London, we have begun to see what a journalist from the *New York Times* has described as a "'New World Moral Order'—one ruled by ideas like civil society, humanitarianism and, first and foremost, human rights" (Rieff 1999, 37).

The first important impact of Garzon's strategy of indicting Pinochet while visiting England has been named by international journalists "the Pinochet effect." The term describes the "multiplying initiatives against authoritarian tyrants since the British police accepted Garzon's claim" (Cembrero 2000, 2). Our second figure here, then, is the group of international journalists who played a crucial role in expanding the political significance of the "Pinochet effect" as the most important action that "has reverberated beyond Latin America, as, for example, the indictment of Suharto, the former president of Indonesia, was partly encouraged by the surprisingly successful efforts in Chile to investigate General Pinochet" (Faiola 2000, 9).

The "Pinochet effect" inspired legal scholars to revise their international precedents, as, for example, Human Rights Watch did in their work titled "The Pinochet Precedent."[13] As Roberto Garreton, a legal advisor for the UN Commission on Human Rights, has argued, the significant consequence of such an effect is that "the message to new democracies is that you can't be afraid; in order to evolve as a nation and society, you have to face the past. These people cannot be above the law" (cited in Faiola 2000, 9).

The dynamic exchange of tremendously positive narratives on the subject of global justice, written by international journalists, has already opened a new legal agenda. As Clifford Krauss, another journalist from the *New York Times*, has written, "Suddenly, the taboo subjects of disappearances and torture became the daily grist of the news media as journalists covered the charges made against [Pinochet] by prosecutors in Spain, Belgium, France and other quarters. Local rights groups resuscitated themselves and torture victims began to organize" (2000). The "Pinochet effect," therefore, led Latin American societies to return to the essential task of connecting their transitions to democracy with their authoritarian past. Furthermore, they began such processes by publicly disclosing the identities of the criminals that led their countries to commit acts of genocide and to violate international law.

One cannot separate these movements from those that attempt to try human rights abusers in international tribunals such as those set up for the Balkan War crimes[14] and the genocide in Rwanda.[15] These joint efforts to, first, translate claims of justice to an international level, and second, to raise awareness in the global public sphere, have only succeeded partially. There is, however, an important sense in which the success is complete: in the symbolic sense. Justice has been redefined as having no borders, and no one is exempt from legal responsibility when committing crimes against other human beings. In much the same way, the "Pinochet effect" has led peripheral societies to uncover real-life stories as well as their own countries' histories in front of the world's public eye. They have put into action procedures that will result in the formal condemnation of those responsible for the atrocities and have found ways to give emotional relief to the victims' families. As public opinion puts pressure on these global interconnections, we will see that we have only begun this vital new stage of the globalization of justice and of expanding the civic community.

NOTES

1. I argued about this problematic more extensively in Lara 1998.

2. This extraordinary feature has been well understood by Charles Taylor, whose essay titled "Contemporary Sociological Theory: On Social Imaginary" can be found at www.nyu.edu/classes/Calhoun/Theory/Taylor-on-si.htm. This is the text Taylor used for a course at the New School for Social Research in New York in the fall semester of 2001.

3. I have used this terminology following Habermas's speech act theory to explain how "alter" and "ego," once they have been engaged in a process of communication, when successful, begin to see the normative effects of understanding each other (Lara 1998).

4. Among them Alfredo Brice Echenique, Mario Vargas Llosa, Augusto Roa Bastos, Mario Benedetti.

5. Describing Roy's political career, Celia W. Dugger, a columnist of the *New York Times* said: "She has stepped into the limelight with a gusto for intellectual combat that has made her perhaps even more famous than her only novel so far, 'The God of Small Things' " (Dugger 2001).

6. Bill Ashcroft notices this diasporic effect when he claims that "Edward Said has an evocative term for this process, which he calls 'the voyage in.' It is particularly useful because it takes a huge diasporic movement of peoples from colonized countries to the metropolitan centers as a geographical and historical metonym of the essentially political engagement we can call 'interpolation'" (2001, 48).

7. An interesting example of this kind of study is done by Roxanne L. Euben (1999).

8. I am thinking of film directors such as Yang Zhimou, Ang Lee, and many others.

9. A cinema that has captured the attention of world audiences because of its poetic and original character on the one hand, and, on the other, because of the way in which it has circumvented censorship to tell stories of suffering under authoritarian rule and of harsh, hierarchichal male domination. The films of Jafar Panahi provide excellent examples. One of his most recent and compelling movies is *The Balloon*.

10. Mexican movies, especially *Amores Perros* have been recognized as a new important cinema linking obvious problems that relate life in Mexico to Western ideas.

11. Even the title of her book reveals this poetic simplicity, but one needs to focus on the way she describes the Mayan-Quiché's view as linked organically to the earth, the cosmos, and their forces.

12. Ashcroft notices the problems that Menchú's narrative brings to light: "In her account the predominance of the enunciation and the insistence upon a communal narrative both confirm the fundamentally allegorical structure of historical narrative" (2001, 123).

13. This is an account of the procedures for prosecuting former dictators.

14. See Cohen (1999, 2001a, 2001b); Crossete (2001); Erlanger (1999); Fisher (2001).

15. See McKinley (1998).

13

Vulnerable Women and Neoliberal Globalization: Debt Burdens Undermine Women's Health in the Global South

Alison M. Jaggar

WHAT IS NEOLIBERAL GLOBALIZATION?

Interpreted broadly, the term "globalization" refers to any system of transcontinental travel and trade. In this broad sense, globalization has always existed; after all, the foreparents of every one of us walked originally out of Africa. However, contemporary globalization is distinguished by its integration of many local and national economies into a single global market, regulated by the World Trade Organization (WTO). This treaty organization was established in 1995 to determine the rules for global trade. WTO rules supersede the national law of any signatory nation and are rationalized by a distinctive version of liberal political theory, namely, neoliberalism.

Although its name suggests that it is something novel, neoliberalism in fact marks a retreat from the liberal social democracy of the years following World War II. It moves back toward the nonredistributive laissez-faire liberalism of the seventeenth and eighteenth centuries, which held that the main function of government was to make the world safe and predictable for the participants in a market economy. Following are some main tenets of contemporary neoliberalism.

"Free" Trade

Neoliberalism promotes the free flow of both traded goods and of capital. However, not only does it not require the free flow of labor, the third crucial factor of production, but it also seeks actively to control that flow.[1] Although immigration from poorer to wealthier countries is currently at record levels, much of it is achieved in the teeth of draconian border controls that often cost would-be immigrants their lives.

Opposition to Government Regulation

Neoliberalism opposes government regulation of such aspects of production as wages, working conditions, and environmental protections. Indeed, legislation intended to protect workers, consumers, or the environment may be challenged as an unfair barrier to trade. In the neoliberal global market, weak labor, consumer, or environmental standards may well become part of a country's "competitive advantage."

Refusal of Responsibility for Social Welfare

Neoliberalism presses governments to abandon the social welfare responsibilities that they have assumed over the twentieth century, such as providing allowances for housing, healthcare, education, disability, and unemployment. Social programs, such as the Canadian healthcare system, may even be challenged as de facto government subsidies to industry.[2]

Resource Privatization

The final feature of contemporary neoliberalism is its push to bring all economically exploitable resources into private ownership. Public services are turned into profit-making enterprises, sometimes sold to foreign investors, and natural resources such as minerals, forests, water, and land are opened up for commercial exploitation in the global market.

Many people have come to equate "globalization" with neoliberalism and they regard the costs of this system as inevitable consequences of modernization and progress. This equation discourages attempts to question the justice of neoliberal globalization or to envision alternatives to it. This chapter sketches some consequences of this system for women's health and offers some reasons for questioning its democratic legitimacy.

GLOBAL NEOLIBERALISM IS BAD FOR (MOST) WOMEN'S HEALTH

The consequences of neoliberal globalization have been almost entirely good for some people, almost entirely bad for others, and mixed for many more. Those who have reaped most of globalization's rewards have tended to belong to the more privileged classes in the global North or to elite classes in the global South.[3] Those who have been harmed overall by neoliberal globalization have usually been people who were already poor and marginalized, in both the developing and the developed worlds. Since women are represented disproportionately among the world's poor and marginalized, neoliberal globalization has been harmful especially to women—although not to all or only women. This section sketches a few of the ways in which the various features of global neoliberalism, mentioned above, have tended to worsen the health of many women in the global South relative to more privileged women, to many men of their own social class, and even absolutely.

"Free" Trade

The most obvious consequence of trade liberalization is that it has increased enormously the gap between the world's rich and poor, so that this gap has now reached what the *United Nations Human Development Report* for 1999 called "grotesque" proportions. In 1960, the countries with the wealthiest fifth of the world's people had per capita incomes thirty times that of the poorest fifth; by 1990, the ratio had doubled to sixty to one; by 1997, it stood at seventy-four to one. By 1997, the richest 20 percent had captured 86 percent of the world's income while the poorest 20 percent captured a mere 1 percent (Wallach and Sforza 1999, 4).[4] For many—perhaps most—poor people in the world, neoliberal globalization has resulted in their material conditions of life deteriorating not only relative to the more affluent but also absolutely. The 1999 *United Nations Human Development Report* states that, for more than eighty countries, per capita incomes are lower than they were a decade ago; in sub-Saharan Africa and some other least developed countries, per capita incomes are lower than they were in 1970.

Economic inequality is increasing not only between the global North and South but also within them. In June 2000, for instance, the U.S. Federal Reserve reported that the net worth of the richest 1 percent of U.S. households rose from 30 percent of the nation's wealth in 1992 to 34 percent in 1998. Meanwhile, the share of the national wealth held by the bottom 90 percent of U.S. households fell from 33 percent in 1992 to 31 percent in 1998 (*Denver Rocky Mountain News*, June 11, 2000). The Economic Policy Institute asserted that the median inflation-adjusted earnings of the average worker were 3.1 percent lower in 1997 than in 1989 and by the end of the 1990s the poorest 20 percent of U.S. citizens were making less in real terms than in 1977.[5] Homelessness in the United States has reached unprecedented proportions, affecting even people with full-time jobs.

In the global North, women, especially women of color, have been disproportionately impoverished by the movement of many hitherto well-paid jobs to low wage areas in the global South. In the North, these jobs have often been replaced by so-called McJobs, "casual," contingency or part-time positions, often in the service sector, which are typically low paying and lack health or retirement benefits. The reduction in the U.S. real hourly wage since the 1970s affects all U.S. low-paid workers but it especially affects women and, among women, especially women of color, because they disproportionately hold those jobs. The U.S. Census Bureau recently reported that the earnings *gap* between men and women widened for the second consecutive year in 1999.[6]

The feminization of poverty was a term coined originally to describe the situation of women in the United States, but the United Nations reports that the feminization of poverty has now become a global and growing phenomenon, with women making up 70 percent of the world's 1.3 billion poor (UNIFEM 2001). Even this statistic may understate the extent of women's poverty, because it is based on the studies of consumption in female-headed compared to male-headed households and so ignores the fact that, within all families, women and girls are less likely to receive available resources such as food and medical care.[7]

Poverty affects women's health in myriad ways. Poor nutrition associated with poverty directly creates special health problems for pregnant and lactating women and has contributed to increasing maternal mortality in many poor countries. Because women are poorer, they are more vulnerable to the so-called diseases of poverty, such as TB, diphtheria, yellow fever, malaria, and cholera, all of which have increased in the 1990s (Harvard Working Group 1996). Women's impoverishment relative to men in their own countries affects their health indirectly as well as directly. For instance, when women are perceived as an economic drain on families, rather than as economic contributors to them, they and their daughters are less likely to receive available resources such as food and medical care. Moreover, impoverishment makes women more vulnerable to domestic violence, sexual harassment, and rape.

Economic inequality among countries as well as within them also has negative consequences for women's health. A steady "brain drain" of doctors, dentists, nurses, and other trained medical workers flows from the poor to the rich countries, to the detriment of patients in the poor countries. For instance, Filipino nurses are a familiar feature of hospital life in the United States and the *New York Times* recently reported U.S. efforts to recruit nurses from China. Sixty percent of Ghanaian doctors are said to practice abroad.

The AIDS epidemic is one of the most dramatic health consequences of global economic inequality. The worst ravages of this epidemic are in the developing countries, where 93 percent of people with HIV/AIDS lived by the end of 1997, and especially in sub-Saharan Africa, where 80 percent of all deaths occur (UNIFEM biennial report: *Progress of the World's Women* 2000). The higher incidence of HIV among people living in the developing world has special significance for women's health, because a higher percentage of adults living with HIV/AIDS in these areas than in the global North are women. While 49.75 percent of all people infected with HIV in sub-Saharan Africa were female, 27.52 percent of those infected in Asia and the Pacific were female and 24 percent of those infected in Latin America and the Caribbean were female. The percentage of women to men with HIV/AIDS is lower in the global North, but it is increasing there too, reaching 20.4 percent by 1998. In the United States, Black women are 15 percent more likely to test positive for AIDS than white women, following the global pattern that the most impoverished women are the most vulnerable. Women are now contracting the AIDS virus at a higher rate than any other group, both in the Third World and also in North America (Sivard 1995, 26).

In sub-Saharan Africa, women's increasing rate of AIDS infection is in large part a consequence of poverty, which has forced men to migrate to the cities in search of work and has forced women to sell street sex in order to stay alive and feed their families. Elsewhere in the global South, AIDS among women is linked with the recent enormous growth in sex tourism, itself an outgrowth of global economic inequality.[8] Especially in the global South, however, little money is available to cope with this epidemic.[9]

Antiregulation

The WTO pays lip service to the need for protecting consumers, labor, and the environment but in practice its rulings have weakened previous standards.[10] Women's health is clearly threatened by WTO's stand on a number of regulatory issues, including the following.

Abandonment of the Precautionary Principle

The WTO rejects the Precautionary Principle, which puts the burden of proof on the manufacturers to show that food and pharmaceuticals are safe. Instead, the WTO requires that any country wishing to ban the import of food or drugs for health reasons should bear the burden of proof for showing that the product in question is unsafe. The full health implications of the WTO's rejection of the Precautionary Principle are yet to emerge, but any resulting harm is likely to be felt disproportionately by women. In part, this is because women tend to be poorer and so less able to restrict their purchases to foods thought to be safer, such as so-called organic foods. In part it is because children are especially susceptible to health problems resulting from unsafe foods and it is invariably women who are assigned the responsibility of caring for sick and disabled children.

Lack of Protection for Labor Rights

The WTO's disregard for labor rights probably affects women disproportionately, not only because laws banning sex discrimination and sexual harassment are unenforced but also because women are disproportionately represented among the low-paid "sweatshop" workers whose rights to a decent wage and a safe working environment are unprotected.

Failure to Protect the Environment

The WTO's disregard for environmental protection also has consequences for women's health. For instance, water pollution increases rural women's workload by forcing them to travel farther and farther in search of clean water (sometimes as far as twenty kilometers from their homes) and to deal with the health problems that result from families having to drink polluted water.

Cutbacks in Social Welfare

The worldwide cutbacks in social programs are the most obviously gendered feature of global neoliberalism. They have tended to affect women's economic status even more adversely than men's, because women's responsibility for caring for children and other family members makes them more reliant on such programs. In the global South, cuts in public health services have contributed to a rise in maternal mortality; less hospital care is available and patients are discharged earlier—to be cared for at home by female family members. Reductions in social services have forced women to create survival strategies for their families by absorbing these reductions with their own unpaid labor. The effect of these strategies has been felt especially in the global South, where more work for women has resulted in higher school dropout rates for girls. In addition, the introduction of school fees in many Southern countries has made education unavailable to poorer children and especially to girls; women currently constitute 64 percent of all illiterate adults.[11] Longer hours of domestic work and less education obviously contribute to women's impoverishment by making it harder for them to attain well-paying jobs.

Resource Privatization

The increasing privatization of natural resources, such as land, forests, minerals, and water, has led to increasing exploitation, depletion, and pollution of the environment and to the further impoverishment of women. Multinational corporations have patented many indigenous seeds and medicines in what Vandana Shiva has aptly called a theft of the commons (Shiva 1996; Shiva et al. 1997). The WTO has defended so-called intellectual property rights (IPRs), which guarantee corporations' global patents on seeds and medicines, including indigenous seeds and medicines.[12] These patents are criticized in the *United Nations Human Development Report* for 1999 because they preclude poor countries' access to food and medicine, with inevitably adverse health consequences for women, who tend to be even poorer than men.

Neoliberalism's assaults on women's health are overlapping and often mutually reinforcing. Neoliberalism has had adverse consequences for the health of all poor people but especially for women, whose already unsatisfactory health status has deteriorated even further.

WHY DOES THE GLOBAL SOUTH ACCEPT NEOLIBERALISM?

When neoliberal globalization has been so harmful to the health of many people in the global South, it is natural to wonder why they continue to participate in this system. Much of the answer lies in the past.

Neoliberal policies were introduced in many Southern countries in the 1980s as conditions of borrowing money from international lending institutions or of rescheduling existing debts. Many developing countries engaged in massive borrowing in the 1970s, when interest rates were low, but, when interest rates rose sharply at the end of that decade, most debtor countries had difficulty paying the interest on their loans. In the early 1980s a world debt crisis resulted, threatening the failure of major U.S. banks and perhaps a collapse of the world economic system. In order to forestall default by large debtors such as Mexico, international lending institutions such as the International Monetary Fund and the World Bank rescheduled many debts. At the same time, they imposed new loan conditions mandating so-called policies of structural adjustment or SAPs. These neoliberal economic policies "adjust" the "structures" of local economies so they can be integrated into the global economic system, thus enabling them to gain the foreign currency necessary for servicing external debts. SAPS thus are designed to orient local economies away from production intended to satisfy the needs of local people and toward producing goods for export.[13]

Any local economy that is integrated into the global economy becomes vulnerable to the vicissitudes of world trade. For example, SAPs encouragement of cash crop agriculture has forced many countries in the global South to become permanently dependent on Northern machines and fertilizers, as well as on world prices for their crops. Thus, SAPs have created guaranteed markets for Northern manufactured products, technologies, and consumer goods and simultaneously have ensured a "captive" supply of cheap exploitable labor, cheap raw materials, and agricultural products. In a world where the terms of trade for raw materials and agricultural products have historically tended to worsen (with a few conspicuous exceptions, such as oil), such interdependence has inevitably made the North richer and the South poorer.

Although SAPs were promoted as necessary to economic development in the global South, they have harmed rather than helped development in many debtor nations. The growth rates of most debtor countries have been significantly reduced, living standards in many have deteriorated, and some have become trapped in a vicious cycle of stagnation and decline. Some of the countries that are worst off are the most integrated into the global economy; for instance, exports account for close to 30 percent of the GDP of impoverished sub-Saharan Africa, compared to less than 20 percent for industrialized nations. Many Southern countries are now in a state of economic collapse and their debt burden has multiplied many times over. By 1997, the total debt stock owed by the developing world to the developed world was $217 *trillion*, up from $1.4 trillion in 1990.

Although SAPs have been counterproductive from the point of the view of the global South, they have been highly successful from the point of view of the global North, because they have ensured that an increasing proportion of the debtor countries' resources have gone to paying off foreign debts. Even by the mid-1980s, the Third World was paying out annually about three times as much in debt repayments as it received in aid from all developed country governments and international aid agencies combined. Ten years later, the developing countries are paying the rich nations $717 million per day in debt service; $12 billion annually flows north out of Africa.

The need to service their debts provides much of the explanation why many countries in the global South have joined the WTO, despite the fact that the neoliberal rules of this organization tend to favor the interests of Northern countries and corporations over those of poor people and countries. Deeply indebted nations, which need foreign exchange to service their debt, cannot afford to be left out of the global trading system.

Thus, the existence of long-standing debt is one of the chief mechanisms maintaining global neoliberalism. It binds Southern debtors and Northern creditors together in a system advantageous primarily to the privileged classes of the global North. Because this system is harmful to most women's health, Southern debt should be an important concern for both medical ethics and feminist ethics. I wish to conclude by suggesting that many supposed Southern debt obligations are not morally binding because they were not legitimately undertaken.

NEOLIBERAL GLOBALIZATION AND DEMOCRATIC CONSENT

Liberal democratic theory holds that all citizens are collectively responsible for decisions made by their democratically elected governments. Even citizens who disagree with particular government policies are said to have consented to them indirectly if not directly because they agreed to the rules of the electoral game.[14] Like most bioethicists, most liberal political philosophers hold that such consent is binding only if it is informed, rational, and uncoerced. In practice, however, people's rationality is always imperfect, our information incomplete, and our available options restricted; hence the validity of consent is always a matter of judgment. I shall argue that, when many Southern countries undertook their supposed debts, their citizenry was largely uninformed and their options were virtually nonexistent.

Consent to the Debt as Coerced

Many Southern countries were forced to borrow because their wealth was stolen. One reason why citizens in the global South cannot be said to have undertaken their supposed debts voluntarily is that neoliberalism was not introduced into a global state of nature, composed of nation-states that were politically sovereign and economically independent. Instead, it was introduced into a world previously made unequal by colonialism—which also often exacerbated inequalities among and between men and women. Despite the lip service paid by the European Enlightenment to such ideals as universal freedom and equality, European expansion was characterized by violence, slavery, and genocide. These destroyed many non-European societies and drastically weakened many others, forcibly converting them into sources of cheap raw materials, food, and labor, as well as markets for the manufactured goods of the colonizing countries. The import of manufactured goods from Europe and the United States undermined production by local artisans and sup-

pressed the manufacturing potential of the colonies. Thus, it made formerly self-sufficient communities economically dependent. Patterns of
colonization varied but typically they created powerful local elites whose
interests were linked to maintaining an open economy. At the same time,
much of the population was severely impoverished and the seeds were
planted of land misuse and environmental degradation.[15] In short, colonialism drained massive resources and wealth away from the colonies and
destroyed their economic self-sufficiency.

After political independence, the erstwhile colonies were left dependent on the metropolis for manufactured goods and also for training
indigenous professional and skilled people. Seeking to end their economically disadvantageous position as suppliers of raw materials, many Southern countries sought to develop their own industries. However, so much
wealth had been siphoned off from their nations during the colonial
period that they lacked sufficient capital to invest in new plant or infrastructure and were forced to borrow. It was because they had been impoverished by previous centuries of Northern colonialism that these countries
cannot be said to have undertaken their debts voluntarily—even if they
consented formally to accept the loans. Basically, they are forced to borrow back wealth that was stolen from them—and to borrow it from (the
descendants of) the robbers.

Consent to Southern Debt as Uninformed or Nonexistent

The people who bear the overwhelming burden of paying Southern
debt are the poorest citizens of the poorest countries in the world—
especially Southern women. These citizens are held economically responsible for debts undertaken by their governments, often before they were
born. Every baby born in the developing world today owes about $500 at
birth.

In most heavily indebted countries, however, electorates were uninformed about the meaning or even existence of foreign loans. Debts were
often assumed by local elites, who spent them on unproductive prestige
projects or siphoned them into personal foreign bank accounts. Many
debtor countries were run by autocratic rulers, who were supported by
wealthy First World countries as a bulwark against popular insurgencies
regarded as "communist," and they often used borrowed funds on the
military repression of their own populations. Thus, much of the money
lent to Third World rulers in the 1970s and 1980s by wealthy First World
states not only did not support economic development but in fact undermined it by subverting democracy.

Given this history, it is plausible to argue that poor people in the global
South have no responsibility to pay back money that they did not ask to

borrow, from which they enjoyed no benefits, and through which they were even repressed. It is especially unreasonable to expect Southern women to be responsible for the debts because, even if they had the formal equality of the vote, they had even less input than men into taking on the loans and benefited even less from them. We have seen that women in the global South, as a group, receive less food, health care, and education than men, and they benefit even less from military expenditures.

Absence of Democracy in Global Economic Institutions

So far I have contended that the entry of many Southern countries into the neoliberal global economic system occurred under considerable duress and was therefore less than fully voluntary. I now wish to argue that a situation of duress continues, since these countries have little or no influence over the conduct of the global economic system, despite being bound by its rules.

The political weakness of what was then called the Third World was already evident in the 1980s, when SAPs were imposed on many debtor nations. At that time, the International Monetary Fund and the World Bank were the main institutions governing the global economy and their policies were heavily influenced by a small group of wealthy countries. At both the World Bank and IMF, the number of votes a country receives is based on how much capital it gives the institution, so rich countries have disproportionate voting power.[16] Although it is intuitively reasonable that lenders should be able to determine the conditions under which they lend their money, we have seen that much of the wealth of the world's rich countries was derived, directly or indirectly, from a long history of conquest and colonial exploitation. Since this wealth was acquired illegitimately, I suggest that those who currently claim ownership of it lack the moral right to control its disposal, much less to use it in ways that worsen the lives of those from whom it was taken.

The birth of the WTO created a supranational organization whose rules, as we have seen, supersede the national laws of its members on issues of trade. Joining the WTO limits the sovereignty of member nations over an enormous range of issues, since the WTO construes trade so broadly as to include many matters of ethics and public policy. The WTO is formally democratic in that each of its 142 member countries has one representative or delegate who participates in negotiations over trade rules, but democracy within the WTO is limited in practice in many ways. Wealthy countries have far more influence than poor ones, and numerous meetings are restricted to the G-7 group, the most powerful member countries, excluding the less powerful even when decisions directly affect them. Moreover, even though sovereign states are the only official members of the WTO, this organization's dispute resolution system allows powerful multinational corporations to challenge trade barriers or domestic regulations, sometimes seeking to reverse decisions lost in the political arena at home. The dispute resolution system of the WTO violates most democratic notions of due process and openness. Cases are heard before a tribunal of "trade experts," generally lawyers, who are required to make their ruling with a presumption in favor of free trade, and the burden is on governments to justify any restrictions on this. The WTO dispute resolution system permits no amicus briefs, no observers, no public record of the deliberations, and no appeals.

The present organization of the global economy undermines democracy by increasing the political exclusion of the poorest and most marginalized people across the world. It especially excludes women, who are among the poorest and most marginalized of all. Even though the proportion of women representatives recently has increased in most national legislatures, except those of Eastern Europe, the significance of this gain is diminished when the authority of national legislatures is reduced. The virtual absence of women from the decision-making processes of such bodies as the World Bank, the International Monetary Fund, and the World Trade Organization reflects the very limited influence exercised by women at all levels of global politics.

CONCLUSION

Despite its rhetoric of freedom and prosperity—freedom of enterprise, freedom from the red tape of government regulation, freedom from onerous taxation, and, above all, freedom of trade—the present system of neoliberal globalization has brought little freedom, democracy, or prosperity to most women in the global South. Instead, the current neoliberal framework traps billions of people in situations of political and economic deprivation, increasing their health vulnerability and condemning them (and their families) to lives of illness and premature death. Despite the fact that present global economic arrangements are rationalized in liberal terms, the broader liberal tradition has the conceptual resources for challenging their democratic legitimacy through its basic idea that legitimate obligations must be grounded in consent that is informed and uncoerced.

NOTES

This chapter was written at the suggestion of Annette Dula and conceptualized in the course of discussions with her. I am extremely grateful for Annette's suggestions, as well as for the comments of my colleague, Michiko Hase. I am also indebted to Stephen Biggs, who undertook much of the empirical research on which the chapter is based. I develop these ideas further in Jaggar (2002).

1. This lop-sided interpretation of "free trade" obviously enables business owners to move production to areas of the world where costs are lowest, perhaps due to lower wages, fewer occupational safety and health requirements, or fewer environmental restrictions, while simultaneously controlling the movement of workers who may wish to pursue higher wages.

2. "Defence and security" are among the very few government expenditures excluded from being judged "subsidies," an exclusion that has permitted the development of a lucrative arms industry. Since the Persian Gulf War, the United States has become the world's top arms exporter, well exceeding "the total arms exports of all 52 other arms exporting countries combined" (Peterson and Runyan 1999, 120).

3. The collapse of the Soviet bloc has made the older terminology of First, Second, and Third Worlds inapplicable and it is now often replaced by talk about the global North and the global South. Roughly, the "global North" refers to highly industrialized and wealthy states, most of which are located in the northern hemisphere—though Australia and New Zealand are possible exceptions. The "global South" refers to poorer states that depend mostly on agriculture and extractive industries and whose manufacturing industry, if it exists, is likely to be foreign owned. Many (though far from all) of these states are located in the southern hemisphere and their populations tend to be dark-skinned, whereas the indigenous populations of Northern states are mostly (though not exclusively) light-skinned. Northern states often have a history as colonizing nations and Southern states often have been colonized. The binary opposition between global North and South is a useful shorthand but, like all binaries (and like the older terminology of numbered Worlds) it is problematic if taken too seriously. Many states (e.g., Japan and Russia) do not fit neatly into it.

4. Meanwhile, drawing on a 1998 (October 12) report in *Forbes* magazine, the *United Nations Human Development Report* declared that the assets of the world's three richest people (Bill Gates, Warren Buffett, and Paul Allen, whose combined assets totaled $110 billion) exceeded the combined GNP of all the least developed countries on the planet. Within a year, this information was out of date; in 1999, the *New York Times* reported that the assets of the first two of these were worth more than $140 billion (Wallach and Sforza 1999, 4).

5. A report from the Center on Budget and Policy Priorities (cited in the *New York Times*, September 5, 1999) found that the richest 1 percent of U.S. citizens earned as much after taxes as the poorest 100 million—as contrasted with 1977, when the top 1 percent earned "only" as much as the bottom forty-nine million.

6. Median income for women who work full time, year-round fell from $26,433 to $26,324 while median income for full-time employed men rose from $36,126 to $36,376 (*New York Times*, September 17, 2000, A12).

7. Ten years ago, Amartya Sen used demographic data to estimate that between sixty and one hundred million women were "missing" in the world, partly as a result of direct violence but often as a result of systematic neglect. (Sen

1990). The figure of sixty million is larger than the combined combat death tolls from the First and Second World Wars.

8. The countries in Latin America and the Caribbean that are most renowned for sex tourism—the Bahamas, Jamaica, Barbados, and the Dominican Republic—have not only the highest percentages of infected people in Latin America and the Caribbean but also the highest percentage of females infected. In Jamaica, girls aged fifteen to nineteen are three times as likely to contract HIV/AIDS as boys in the same age group (Brittain 2002, 5).

9. African countries reacted very coolly to a recent U.S. offer of $1 billion annually in loans to buy AIDS drugs, claiming that it would only increase their indebtedness (Lacey 2000). Of course, such a loan would also bring huge profits to the United States pharmaceutical companies that manufacture the drugs and that appeal to Intellectual Property Rights in order to block the production of cheaper versions for the developing world.

10. For instance, the WTO ruled against Europe for banning hormone-treated beef and against Japan for prohibiting pesticide-laden apples. "In every case brought to the (WTO) that challenged environmental or public safety legislation, the challengers won. . . . When it was Venezuelan oil interests versus the US Environmental Protection Agency's air quality standards for imported gasoline, the oil interests won. When it was US cattle producers against the European Union's ban on hormone treated beef, European consumers lost" (Weisbrot 2001).

11. UNICEF reports that in Malawi the elimination of modest school fees and uniform requirements in 1994 caused primary enrollment to increase rapidly by about 50 percent: from 1.9 million to 2.9 million. The main beneficiaries were girls.

12. The WTO's insistence on protecting IPRs shows that neoliberalism's hostility to regulation and protectionism is really hostility only to certain sorts of regulation and protection.

13. SAPs typically require debtor countries do most of the following:

- To reduce government expenditures, especially spending on social welfare programs. (People pay for services or go without.)
- To eliminate food subsidies.
- To cut jobs and wages for workers in government industries and services.
- To privatize state enterprises and deregulate other industries, possibly selling them to foreign investors.
- To make their resources, such as minerals, forests, and land, available for commercial exploitation. In the South, they have often encouraged shifting from small subsistence farms to large-scale cash crop agriculture, using "modernized" technology.
- To reduce protection for domestic markets, opening them up to foreign investors and stimulating local demand for western goods.
- To devalue local currencies so that they are worth less relative to the dollar. This lowers export earnings and raises import costs by making exports from the local economy cheaper relative to other nations and imports to it more relatively expensive. When the currency of debtor nations is devalued, they are able to buy fewer imported goods with their local currencies, while those

who have stronger currencies, such as dollars, are able to afford larger quantities of their local goods. When nations in the global South devalue their currency, the typical result is a scarcity of Northern manufactured products, including medicines, educational materials, spare parts, and agricultural machinery, because debtor nations can buy less with their devalued currencies.

- To create "Free Trade" or "Production" or "Export Zones," in which protective labor and environmental legislation are unenforced. Labor-intensive production processes are withdrawn from the North and exported to these zones (e.g., garments go for finishing to Central American "free trade zones").

14. This argument is not unproblematic, especially when democracy is less than perfect—as it always is; for this reason, liberal democratic theory also holds out the possibility of civil disobedience for citizens who have strong conscientious objections to particular policies.

15. For instance, European colonization of Africa disrupted farming and herding systems that for centuries Africans had adapted to changing environmental conditions. Europeans seized the best agricultural land for growing coffee, sugarcane, cocoa, and other export crops, and colonial cash cropping ravaged the soil, reducing large areas to desert and semi-desert. Meanwhile, small farmers were pushed onto marginal land that previously had been inhabited only by small groups of nomadic pastoralists. Similarly, Spanish colonizers seized much of the best land in Mexico, pushing indigenous people onto the poor soil of, for instance, the Chiapas Highlands.

16. Each has about 150 members with a twenty-four-member board of executive directors. Five of these directors are appointed by five powerful countries: the United States, the United Kingdom, France, Germany, and Japan. The president of the World Bank is elected by board and traditionally nominated by the U.S. representative, while the managing director of the IMF is traditionally European.

Works Cited

Abelson, Reed. 1999. "A Push from the Top Shatters a Glass Ceiling." *New York Times* August 22.

Addelson, Kathryn Pyne. 1991. *Impure Thoughts: Essays on Philosophy, Feminism and Ethics*. Philadelphia: Temple University Press.

Addelson, Kathryn Pyne. 1994. *Moral Passages: Toward a Collectivist Moral Theory*. New York: Routledge.

Alcoff, Linda, and Elizabeth Potter.1988. "Cultural Feminism versus Post-Structuralism: The Identity Crisis in Feminist Theory." *Signs: Journal of Women in Culture and Society* 13, no. 3: 405–436.

Alcoff, Linda, and Elizabeth Potter. 1993. *Feminist Epistemologies*. New York: Routledge.

Alcoff, Linda Martìn, and Laura Gray-Rosendale. 1996. "Survivor Discourse: Transgression or Recuperation?" In *Getting a Life: Everyday Uses of Autobiography*, ed. Sidonie Smith and Julia Watson. Minneapolis: University of Minneapolis Press.

Anderson, Elizabeth. 1995. "Knowledge, Human Interests, and Objectivity in Feminist Epistemology." *Philosophical Topics* 23, no. 2: 284–304.

Appadurai, Arjun. 1998. *Modernity at Large. Cultural Dimensions of Globalization*. Minneapolis: University of Minnesota Press.

Appiah, K. Anthony. 1994. "Identity, Authenticity, Survival: Multicultural Societies and Social Reproduction." In *Multiculturalism: Examining the Politics of Recognition*, ed. Amy Gutman. Princeton, N.J.: Princeton University Press.

Asante, Molefi K. 1998 [1987]. *The Afrocentric Ideal*. Philadelphia: Temple University Press.

Ashcroft, Bill. 2001. *Post-Colonial Transformation*. New York: Routledge.

Baier, Annette C. 1997. *The Commons of the Mind*. Peru, Ill.: Open Court Publishing Company.

Baldwin, James. 1978. *Just Above My Head*. New York: Dial Press.

Barclay, Linda. 2000. "Autonomy and the Social Self." In *Relational Autonomy: Feminist Perspectives on Autonomy, Agency, and the Self*, ed. Catriona Mackenzie and Natalie Stoljar. New York: Oxford University Press.

Bartky, Sandra. 1990. *Femininity and Domination*. New York: Routledge.

Beauchamp, Tom L., and LeRoy Walters. 1999. *Contemporary Issues in Bioethics*. 5th ed. Belmont, Calif.: Wadsworth Publishing Company.

Beauvoir, Simone de. 1952. *The Second Sex*. New York: Random House.

Benhabib, Seyla, Judith Butler, Drucilla Cornell, and Nancy Fraser. 1995. *Feminist Contentions: A Philosophical Exchange*. New York: Routledge.

Benjamin, Jessica. 1988. *The Bonds of Love: Psychoanalysis, Feminism, and the Problem of Domination*. New York: Pantheon Books.

Benson, Paul. 1994. "Free Agency and Self-Worth." *Journal of Philosophy* 91: 650–668.

Benson, Paul. 2000. "Feeling Crazy: Self-Worth and the Social Character of Responsibility." In *Relational Autonomy: Feminist Perspectives on Autonomy, Agency, and the Self*, ed. Catriona Mackenzie and Natalie Stoljar. New York: Oxford University Press.

Blum, Lawrence. 1998. "Recognition, Value, and Equality: A Critique of Charles Taylor's and Nancy Fraser's Accounts of Multiculturalism." *Constellations* 5: 1.

Bordo, Susan. 1993. *Unbearable Weight: Feminism, Western Culture and the Body*. Berkeley: University of California Press.

Brittain, Victoria. 2002. "AIDS Turns Back the Clock for World's Children." *Guardian Weekly*, May 9–15.

Brodribb, Somer. 1992. *Nothing Mat(t)ers: A Feminist Critique of Postmodernism*. Melbourne: Spinifex Press.

Brumberg, Joan Jacobs. 2000. *Fasting Girls: The History of Anorexia Nervosa*. New York: Vintage Books.

Bubeck, Diemut. 1995. *Care, Gender, and Justice*. Oxford: Clarendon Press.

Bunch, Charlotte. 1990. "Women's Rights as Human Rights: Toward a Re-Vision of Human Rights." *Human Rights Quarterly* 12, no. 4: 486.

Butler, Judith. 1990. "Feminism and the Question of Postmodernism," presented at the Greater Philadelphia Philosophy Consortium.

Butler, Judith. 1991. "Imitation and Gender Insubordination." In *Inside/Out: Lesbian Theories, Gay Theories*, ed. Diana Fuss. New York: Routledge.

Butler, Judith. 1993. *Bodies that Matter: On the Discursive Limits of "Sex."* New York: Routledge.

Butler, Judith. 1997. "Merely Cultural." *Social Text* 15, no. 3–4: 265–277.

Butler, Judith. 1999 [1990]. *Gender Trouble: Feminism and the Subversion of Identity*. New York: Routledge.

Calhoun, Cheshire. 1989. "Responsibility and Reproach." *Ethics* 99: 389–406.

Calhoun, Cheshire. 1992. "Emotional Work." In *Exploration in Feminist Ethics: Theory and Practice*, ed. Eve Browning and Susan Coultrap McQuin. Bloomington: Indiana University Press.

Calhoun, Cheshire. 1995. "Standing for Something." *Journal of Philosophy* 92, no. 5: 235–260.

Callahan, Sydney. 1996. "A Feminist Case Against Euthanasia." *Health Progress* (November–December): 21–29.

Callahan, Sydney. 2000. "The Role of Emotion in Ethical Decisionmaking." In *Life Choices: A Hastings Center Introduction to Bioethics*, 2nd ed., ed. Joseph H.

Howell and William F. Sale. Washington, D.C.: Georgetown University Press, 23–35.

Canby, Peter. 1999. "The Truth about Rigoberta Menchú." *New York Review of Books* 66, no. 6 (April): 28–29.

Card, Claudia. 1996. *The Unnatural Lottery: Character and Moral Luck*. Philadelphia: Temple University Press.

Casey, Edward S. 1993. *Getting Back into Place: Toward a Renewed Understanding of the Place World*. Bloomington: Indiana University Press.

Castañeda, Hector-Neri. 1988. "Knowledge and Epistemic Obligation." *Philosophical Perspectives* 2, Epistemology: 211–233.

Cembrero, Ignacio. 2000. "The Pinochet Effect." *El País*, February 6: 2.

Code, Lorraine. 1987. *Epistemic Responsibility*. Hanover: Brown University Press.

Code, Lorraine. 1991. *What Can She Know? Feminist Theory and the Construction of Knowledge*. Ithaca, N.Y.: Cornell.

Code, Lorraine. 1995. *Rhetorical Spaces*. New York: Routledge.

Cohen, Roger. 1999. "Tribunal Is Said to Cite Milosevic for War Crimes." *New York Times* May 27.

Cohen, Roger. 2001a. "A Time To Judge What Began and Ended in Kosovo." *New York Times,* July 1.

Cohen, Roger. 2001b. "From Bosnia to Berlin to The Hague, on a Road Toward a Continent's Future." *New York Times* July 15.

Collins, Patricia Hill. 2000. *Black Feminist Thought: Knowledge, Consciousness, and the Politics of Empowerment*, 2nd ed. New York: Routledge.

Couser, G. Thomas. 1997. *Recovering Bodies: Illness, Disability, and Life Writing*. Madison: University of Wisconsin.

Coward, Rosalind. 1985. *Female Desires: How They Are Sought, Bought, and Packaged*. New York: Grove Press.

Crenshaw, Kimberly. 1991. "Demarginalizing the Intersection of Race and Sex: A Black Feminist Critique of Antidiscrimination Doctrine, Feminist Theory, and Antiracist Politics." *Feminist Legal Theory: Readings in Law and Gender*, ed. K. T. Bartlett and R. Kennedy. Boulder, Colo.: Westview Press, 57–80.

Crossete, Barbara. 2001. "Today Milosevic, but Soon Justice Without Borders May Turn on Big Powers." *New York Times*, July 1.

Curry, Jane L. 2000. "Old 'Sins,' New Nations: The Politics of Forgiveness vs. Retribution." Paper presented at Forgiveness: Traditions and Implications. The Tanner Center for the Humanities, University of Utah, April 12–15, 2000.

Daley, Suzanne. 2001. "France Looks for More Women in Politics." *New York Times*, February 4.

Davion, Victoria M. 1991. "Integrity and Radical Change." In *Feminist Ethics,* ed. Claudia Card. Lawrence, Kans.: University Press of Kansas.

Davis, Dena S. 1998. "Why Suicide Is Like Contraception." In *Physician Assisted Suicide*, ed. Margaret P. Battin, Rosamond Rhodes, and Anita Silvers. New York: Routledge.

Davis, Lennard J. 1995. *Enforcing Normalcy: Disability, Deafness and the Body*. London: Verso.

Deming, Barbara. 1985. *A Humming Under My Feet: A Book of Travail*. London: Women's Press.

DePalma, Anthony. 1999. "A New State for Inuit: Frigid but Optimistic." *New York Times*, January 29.

Dillon, R. S. 1995. Toward a Feminist Conception of Self-Respect. In *Dignity, Character and Self-Respect*. New York: Routledge.

DiQuinzio, Patrice, and Iris Marion Young. 1995. "Introduction: Special Issue on Feminist Ethics and Social Policy." *Hypatia* 10, no. 1: 1–7.

Dolan, Bridget, and Inez Gitzinger. 1994. *Why Women? Gender Issues and Eating Disorders*. Atlantic Highlands, N.J.: Athlone Press.

Donchin, Anne. 2000. "Autonomy, Interdependence, and Assisted Suicide: Respecting Boundaries/Crossing Lines." *Bioethics* 14, no. 3: 187–204.

Dreger, Alice Domurat. 1998. *Hermaphrodites and the Medical Invention of Sex*. Cambridge, Mass.: Harvard University Press.

Duberman, Martin. 1991. *Cures: A Gay Man's Odyssey*. New York: Dutton.

Dugger, Celia W. 2001. "An Indian Novelist Turns Her Wrath on the U.S." *New York Times*, November 2.

Dworkin, Ronald. 1993. *Life's Dominion: An Argument About Abortion, Euthanasia, and Individual Freedom*. New York: Vintage Books.

Eagleton, Terry. 1996. *The Illusion of Postmodernism*. Oxford: Blackwell Publishers.

Eakin, Paul John. 1999. *How Our Lives Become Stories: Making Selves*. Ithaca, N.Y.: Cornell University Press.

Echols, Alice. 1983. "The New Feminism of Yin and Yang." In *Powers of Desire: The Politics of Sexuality*, ed. Ann Snitow, Christine Stansell, and Sharon Thompson. New York: Monthly Review.

Echols, Alice. 1984. "The Taming of the Id: Feminist Sexual Politics." In *Pleasure and Danger: Exploring Female Sexuality*, ed. Carole S. Vance. Boston: Routledge.

Epling, W. Frank, and W. David Pierce. 1996. *Activity Anorexia: Theory, Research, and Treatment*. Mahwah, N.J.: Lawrence Erlbaum Associates.

Erlanger, Steven. 1999. "Word of Indictment Stuns the Serbs and Blights Hopes." *New York Times*, May 27.

Euben, Roxanne L. 1999. *Enemy in the Mirror: Islamic Fundamentalism and the Limits of Modern Rationalism—A Work of Comparative Political Theory*. Princeton, N.J.: Princeton University Press.

Faiola, Anthony. 2000. "Pinochet Effect Exposes Once-Untouchable Ex-Dictators." *Herald Tribune*, August 7.

Fallon, Patricia, Melanie A. Katzman, and Susan C. Wooley, eds. 1994. *Feminist Perspectives on Eating Disorders*. New York: Guildford Press.

Feinberg, Joel. 1980. "The Nature and Value of Rights." In *Rights, Justice and the Bounds of Liberty*. Princeton, N.J.: Princeton University Press.

Fisher, Ian. 2001. "Where Justice Takes a Back Seat to Just Ending War." *New York Times*, July 15.

Flax, Jane. 1990. *Thinking Fragments: Psychoanalysis, Feminism and Postmodernism in the Contemporary West*. Berkeley: University of California Press.

Forment, Carlos. 1996. "Peripheral Peoples and Narrative Identities: Arendtian Reflections on Late Modernity." In *Democracy and Difference*, ed. Seyla Benhabib. Princeton, N.J.: Princeton University Press.

Foucault, Michel. 1980a. *The History of Sexuality*. Vintage: New York.

Foucault, Michel, ed. 1980b. *Herculine Barbin: Being the Recently Discovered Memoirs of a Nineteenth-Century French Hermaphrodite*. New York: Colophon.

Foucault, Michel. 1997. "Technologies of the Self." In *Michel Foucault: Ethics, Subjectivity, and Truth*, ed. Paul Rabinow. New York: New Press.

Frank, Arthur. 1991. *At the Will of the Body: Reflections on Illness*. Boston: Houghton Mifflin.

Frank, Arthur. 1995. *The Wounded Storyteller: Body, Illness, and Ethics*. Chicago: University of Chicago Press.

Fraser, Nancy. 1997. "From Redistribution to Recognition? Dilemmas of Justice in a 'Post-Socialist' Age." In *Justice Interruptus: Reflections on the Post-Socialist Condition*. Minneapolis: University of Minnesota Press.

Friedman, Marilyn. 1997. "Autonomy and Social Relationships: Rethinking the Feminist Critique." In *Feminists Rethink the Self*, ed. Diana Tietjens Meyers. Boulder, Colo.: Westview.

Frye, Marilyn. 1992. *Willful Virgin: Essays in Feminism*. Freedom, Calif.: Crossing Press.

Fuss, Diana. 1989. *Essentially Speaking: Feminism, Nature and Difference*. New York: Routledge.

Garton-Ash, Timothy. 1997. *The File*. New York: Random House.

Gibbard, Allan. 1990. *Wise Choices, Apt Feelings: A Theory of Normative Judgment*. Cambridge, Mass.: Harvard University Press.

Giddens, Anthony. 2000. *Runaway World*. New York: Routledge.

Gilligan, Carol. 1987. "Moral Orientation and Moral Development." In *Women and Moral Theory*, ed. Eva Feder Kittay and Diana Tietjens Meyers. Totowa, N.J.: Rowman & Littlefield.

Glover, Jonathan. 1995. "The Research Program of Development Ethics." In *Women, Culture, and Development*, ed. Martha C. Nussbaum and Jonathan Glover. New York: Oxford University Press.

Glover, Jonathan. 2000. *Humanity: A Moral History of the Twentieth Century*. New Haven, Conn.: Yale University Press.

Gottlieb, Lori. 2000. *Stick Figure: A Diary of My Former Self*. New York: Simon and Schuster.

Gutmann, Amy. 1994. "Introduction." In *Multiculturalism: Examining the Politics of Recognition*, ed. Amy Gutmann. Princeton, N.J.: Princeton University Press.

Habermas, Jürgen. 1996a. "Further Reflections on the Public Sphere." In *Habermas and the Public Sphere*, ed. Craig Calhoun. Cambridge, Mass.: MIT Press, 421–484.

Habermas, Jürgen. 1996b. *Between Facts and Norms. Contributions to a Discourse Theory of Law and Democracy*, trans. William Rehg. Cambridge, Mass.: MIT Press.

Hacking, Ian. 1986. "Making Up People." In *Reconstructing Individualism: Autonomy, Individuality, and the Self in Western Thought*, ed. Thomas C. Heller et al. Stanford, Calif.: Stanford University Press.

Harding, Sandra, ed. 1993. *The "Racial" Economy of Science*. Bloomington: Indiana University Press.

Hartmann, Heidi. 1979. "The Unhappy Marriage of Marxism and Feminism: Towards a More Progressive Union." *Capital and Class* 8: 1–33.

Harvard Working Group on New and Resurgent Diseases. 1996. "Globalization, Development, and the Spread of Disease." In *The Case Against the Global Economy and for a Turn toward the Local*, ed. Jerry Mander and Edward Goldsmith. San Francisco: Sierra Club Books.

Harvey, David. *The Condition of Postmodernity: An Inquiry into the Nature of Cultural Change*. Cambridge: Blackwell Publishers, 1990.

Hausman, Bernice. 1995. *Changing Sex: Transsexualism, Technology, and the Idea of Gender*. Durham, N.C.: Duke University Press.

Hawkins, Anne Hunsaker. 1993. *Reconstructing Illness: Studies in Pathography*. West Lafayette, Ind.: Purdue University Press.

Hawkins, Anne Hunsaker. 1998. "Pathography and Enabling Myths: The Process of Healing." In *Writing and Healing: Toward an Informed Practice*, ed. Charles M. Anderson and Marian M. MacCurdy. Urbana: National Council of Teachers of English, 222–245.

Hayner, Priscilla B. 1994. "Fifteen Truth Commissions—1974 to 1994: A Comparative Study." *Human Rights Quarterly* 16: 597–655.

Hayner, Priscilla B. 2001. *Unspeakable Truths: Confronting State Terror*. New York: Routledge.

Heldke, Lisa M., and Stephen H. Kellert. 1995. "Objectivity as Responsibility." *Metaphilosophy* 26, no. 4: 360–378.

Hennessy, Rosemary. 2000. *Profit and Pleasure: Sexual Identities in Late Capitalism*. New York: Routledge.

Hesse-Biber, Sharlene. 1996. *Am I Thin Enough Yet? The Cult of Thinness and the Commercialization of Identity*. New York: Oxford University Press.

Heyes, Cressida J. 1997. "Anti-Essentialism in Practice: Carol Gilligan and Feminist Philosophy." *Hypatia* 12, no. 3: 142–163.

Heyes, Cressida J. 2000. *Line Drawings: Defining Women through Feminist Practice*. Ithaca, N.Y.: Cornell University Press.

Heyes, Cressida J. 2003. "Feminist Solidarity after Queer Theory: The Case of Transgender." *Signs* 28, no. 3.

Hirschmann, N. J., and C. D. Stefano 1996. "Revision, Reconstruction, and the Challenge of the New." In *Revisioning the Political: Feminist Reconstructions of Traditional Concepts in Western Political Theory*. Boulder: Colo., Westview Press.

Hoagland, Sarah Lucia. 1988. *Lesbian Ethics: Toward New Value*. Palo Alto, Calif.: Institute of Lesbian Studies.

Honneth, Axel. 1990. *The Fragmented World of the Social: Essays in Social and Political Philosophy*. Albany, N.Y.: SUNY Press.

hooks, bell. 1992. *Black Looks: Race and Representation*. Boston: South End Press.

Houston, Barbara. 1992. "In Praise of Blame." *Hypatia* 7, no. 4: 128–147.

Jaggar, Alison M. 2002. "A Feminist Critique of the Alleged Southern Debt." In *Wissen/Macht/Geschlecht: Philosophie und die Zukunft der "Condition Feminine,"* ed. Birgit Christensen, Angelica Baum, Sidonia Blaettler, Anna Kusser, Irene Maria Marti, and Briggitte Weisshaupt. Zurich: Chronos.

Jameson, Fredric. 1988. "Cognitive Mapping." In *Marxism and the Interpretation of Culture*, ed. C. Nelson and L. Grossberg. Urbana: University of Illinois Press.

Jameson, Fredric. 1991. *Postmodernism or the Cultural Logic of Late Capitalism*. Durham, N.C.: Duke University Press.

Jecker, Nancy. 1994. "Physician-Assisted Death in the Netherlands and United States: Ethical and Cultural Aspects of Health Policy in Development." *Journal of the American Geriatrics Society* 42, no. 6: 672–678.

Jeffries, Sheila. 1996. "Return to Gender: Post-modernism and Lesbian and Gay Theory," in *Radically Speaking: Feminism Reclaimed*. Ed. by Diane Bell and Renate Klein. North Melbourne, Australia: Spinifex Press.

Jolly, Rosemary. 1999. "South Africa's Truth and Reconciliation Commission, Modernity and Their Discontents." *APA Newsletter on Feminism and Philosophy* 98: 109–15.

Kessler, Suzanne J. 1994. "The Medical Construction of Gender: Case Management of Intersexed Infants." In *Theorizing Feminism: Parallel Trends in the Humanities and Social Sciences*, ed. Anne C. Herrmann and Abigail J. Stewart. Boulder, Colo.: Westview Press.

Kim, Jaegwon. 1994. "What Is 'Naturalized Epistemology'?" In *Naturalizing Epistemology*, 2nd ed., ed. Hilary Kornblith. Cambridge, Mass.: MIT Press.

Kiss, Elizabeth. 2000. "Moral Ambition Within and Beyond Political Constraints." In *Truth v. Justice: The Morality of Truth Commissions*, ed. Robert I. Rotberg and Dennis Thompson. Princeton, N.J.: Princeton University Press.

Kittay, Eva Feder. 1999. *Love's Labor: Essays on Women, Equality, and Dependency*. New York: Routledge.

Kleinman, Arthur. 1988. *The Illness Narratives: Suffering, Healing, and the Human Condition*. New York: Basic Books.

Kornblith, Hilary. 1983. "Justified Belief and Epistemically Responsible Action." *Philosophical Review* 92, no. 1: 33–48.

Krauss, Clifford. 2000. "Pinochet, at Home in Chile: A Real Nowhere Man." *New York Times*, March 5.

Krog, Antje. 1998. *Country of My Skull: Guilt, Sorrow, and the Limits of Forgiveness in the New South Africa*. New York: Times Books, Random House.

Kruks, Sonia. 2001. "The Politics of Recognition: Fanon, Sartre, and Identity Politics." In *Retrieving Experience: Subjectivity and Recognition in Feminist Politics*. Ithaca, N.Y.: Cornell University Press.

Lacey, Marc. 2000. "President Urges Nigeria to Fight Tyranny of AIDS." *New York Times*, August 28.

Langton, Rae. 1993. "Speech Acts and Unspeakable Acts." *Philosophy and Public Affairs* 22: 293–330.

Lara, María Pía. 1998. *Moral Textures: Feminist Narratives in the Public Sphere*. Berkeley, Calif.: University of California Press.

Lauretis, Theresa de. 1994. "The Essence of the Triangle or, Taking the Risk of Essentialism Seriously: Feminist Theory in Italy, the U.S., and Britain." In *The Essential Difference*, ed. Naomi Schor and Elizabeth Weed. Bloomington: Indiana University Press

Levenkron, Steven. 1978. *The Best Little Girl in the World*. Chicago: Contemporary Books.

Ligos, Melinda. 2000. "The Fear of Taking Paternity Leave." *New York Times,* May 31.

Lloyd, Elizabeth. 1995. "Objectivity and the Double Standard for Feminist Epistemologies." *Synthese* 104.

Lorde, Audre. 1980. *The Cancer Journals.* Argyle, N.Y.: Spinsters Ink.

Lugones, María C., and Elizabeth V. Spelman. 1983. "Have We Got a Theory for You! Feminist Theory, Cultural Imperialism and the Demand for 'The Women's Voice'." *Women's Studies International Forum* 6: 573–581.

Mackenzie, Catriona, and Natalie Stoljar, eds. 2000. *Relational Autonomy: Feminist Perspectives on Autonomy, Agency, and the Social Self.* New York: Oxford University Press.

MacKinnon, Catharine. 1993. "Crimes of War, Crimes of Peace." In *On Human Rights: The Oxford Amnesty Lectures 1993,* ed. S. Shute and S. Hurley. New York: Basic Books.

MacKinnon, Catharine. 1989. *Toward a Feminist Theory of the State.* Cambridge: Harvard University Press.

MacSween, Morag. 1995. *Anorexic Bodies: A Feminist and Sociological Perspective on Anorexia Nervosa.* New York: Routledge.

Martin, Biddy. 1993. "A Lesbian Identity and Autobiographical Difference[s]." In *The Lesbian and Gay Studies Reader,* ed. Henry Abelove, Michele Aina Barale, and David M. Halperin. New York: Routledge, 274–293.

Martin, Norah. 2001. "Feminist Bioethics and Psychiatry." *Journal of Medicine and Philosophy* 26, no. 4: 431–441.

McKinley, James. 1998. "Ex-Rwandan Prime Minister Gets Life Term for Genocide." *Herald Tribune,* September 5.

McRuer, Robert. 1997. *The Queer Renaissance: Contemporary American Literature and the Reinvention of Lesbian and Gay Identities.* New York: New York University Press.

Menchú, Rigoberta. 1985. *Me llamo Rigoberta Menchú y así me nació la conciencia.* Mexico: Siglo Veintiuno.

Menchú, Rigoberta. 1994. "Discurso en la recepción del Nobel de la Paz". In *Pueblos Indígenas, Derechos Humanos e Interdependencia Global,* ed. Patricia Morales. México: Siglo Veintiuno, 16–29.

Mèndez, Juan. 1997. "Accountability for Past Abuses." *Human Rights Quarterly* 19: 255–282.

Meyers, Diana Tietjens. 2002. *Gender in the Mirror: Cultural Imagery and Women's Agency.* New York: Oxford University Press.

Mies, Maria, and Vandana Shiva. 1993. *Ecofeminism.* London: Zed Books.

Miles, Steven, and Allison August. 1990. "Courts, Gender and 'The Right to Die'." *Law, Medicine and Health Care* 18: 85–95

Mills, Charles W. 1998. *Blackness Visible: Essays on Philosophy and Race.* Ithaca, N.Y.: Cornell University Press.

Minow, M. 1990. *Making All the Difference: Inclusion, Exclusion and American Law.* Ithaca, N.Y.: Cornell University Press.

Minow, Martha, and Todd Rakoff. 1998. "Is the 'Reasonable Person' a Reasonable Standard in a Multicultural World?" In *Everyday Practices and Trouble Cases,* ed. Austin Sarat et al. Evanston, Ill.: Northwestern University Press.

Mohr, Richard D. 1992. *Gay Ideas: Outing and Other Controversies.* Boston: Beacon.

Moi, Toril. 1999. "What Is a Woman?" In *What Is a Woman? and Other Essays.* Oxford: Oxford University Press.

Moore, Lisa C. 1997. *Does Your Mama Know? An Anthology of Black Lesbian Coming Out Stories.* Decatur, Ga.: Redbone Press.

Moraga, Cherríe, and Gloria Anzaldúa, eds. 1981. *This Bridge Called My Back: Writings by Radical Women of Color.* Watertown, Mass.: Persephone Press.

Morris, David B. 2001. "Narrative, Ethics, and Pain: Thinking with Stories." *Narrative* 9, no. 1 (January): 55–77.

Nagel, Thomas. 1979. *Mortal Questions.* Cambridge: Cambridge University Press.

Narayan, Uma. 2000. "Minds of Their Own: Choices, Autonomy, Cultural Practices and Other Women." Ms. copy provided by author.

Narayan, Uma. 1997. *Dislocating Cultures.* New York: Routledge.

Neier, Aryeh. 1999. "Rethinking Truth, Justice, and Guilt After Bosnia and Rwanda." In *Human Rights in Political Transitions: Gettysburg to Bosnia,* ed. Carla Hesse and Robert Post. New York: Zone Books.

Nelson, Hilde Lindemann, ed. 1997. *Stories and Their Limits: Narrative Approaches to Bioethics.* New York: Routledge.

Nelson, Hilde Lindemann. 2001. *Damaged Identities, Narrative Repair.* Ithaca, N.Y.: Cornell University Press.

Nelson, Lynn Hankinson. 1994. "Critical Notice: Lorraine Code's *What Can She Know?*" *Canadian Journal of Philosophy* 24, no. 2: 295–326.

Nussbaum, Martha C. 1992. "Human Functioning and Social Justice: In Defense of Aristotelian Essentialism." *Political Theory* 20, no. 2: 202–246.

Nussbaum, Martha C. 1995. "Human Capabilities, Female Human Beings." In *Women, Culture, and Development,* eds. Martha C. Nussbaum and Jonathan Glover. New York: Oxford University Press.

Nussbaum, Martha C. 2000. *Women and Human Development: The Capabilities Approach.* New York: Cambridge.

Nussbaum, Martha C., and Jonathan Glover, eds. 1995. *Women, Culture, and Development.* New York: Oxford University Press.

Okin, Susan Moller. 1989. *Justice, Gender, and the Family.* New York: Basic Books.

Okin, Susan Moller. 1995. "Inequalities Between the Sexes in Different Cultural Contexts." In *Women, Culture, and Development,* ed. Martha C. Nussbaum and Jonathan Glover. New York: Oxford University Press.

Oliver, Kelly. 2001. *Witnessing: Beyond Recognition.* Minneapolis: University of Minnesota Press.

O'Neill, Onora. 1995. "Justice, Capabilities, and Vulnerabilities." In *Women, Culture, and Development,* ed. Martha C. Nussbaum and Jonathan Glover. New York: Oxford University Press.

Orbach, Susie. 1986. *Hunger Strike: An Anorectic's Struggle As A Metaphor for Our Age.* New York: Norton.

Patchesky, Rosalind. 1979. "Dissolving the Hyphen: A Report on Marxist-Feminist Groups 1–5." In *Capitalist Patriarchy and the Case for Socialist Feminism,* ed. Zillah Eisenstein. New York: Monthly Review Press.

Pellauer, Mary D. 1985. "Moral Callousness and Moral Sensitivity." In *Women's Consciousness, Women's Choices*, ed. Barbara Hilkert Andolsen. Minneapolis: Seabury Press, 33–50.

Peterson, V. Spike, and Anne Sisson Runyan. 1999. *Global Gender Issues*. Boulder, Colo.: Westview Press.

Piper, Adrian. 1996. "Passing for White, Passing for Black." In *Passing and the Fictions of Identity*, ed. Elaine K. Ginsberg. Durham, N.C.: Duke University Press.

Raymond, Diane. 1999. "'Fatal Practices': A Feminist Analysis of Physician-Assisted Suicide and Euthanasia." *Hypatia* 14, no. 2: 1–25.

Réage, Pauline. 1965. *The Story of O*. New York: Ballantine Books.

Rich, Adrienne. 1979. "When We Dead Awaken: Writing as Revision." In *On Lies, Secrets, and Silence: Selected Prose 1966–1978*. New York, W. W. Norton and Company, 33–49.

Ricoeur, Paul. 1992. *Oneself as Another*. Chicago: University of Chicago Press.

Ricoeur, Paul. 1993. "Self as Ipse." In *Freedom and Interpretation: The Oxford Amnesty Lectures 1992*, ed. Barbara Johnson. New York: Basic Books.

Rieff, David. 1999. "The Precarious Triumph of Human Rights." *New York Times Magazine* (August 8): 37–41.

Roland Martin, Jane. 1994. "Methodological Essentialism, False Difference, and Other Dangerous Traps." *Signs* 19, no. 3: 630–657.

Rosenberg, Tina. 1995. *In Haunted Lands*. New York: Random House.

Rotberg, Robert I., and Dennis Thompson, eds. 2000. *Truth v. Justice: The Morality of Truth Commissions*. Princeton, N.J.: Princeton University Press.

Rushdie, Salman. 1999. "Rethinking the War on American Culture." *New York Times*, March 5.

Russell, Denise. 1995. *Women, Madness and Medicine*. Cambridge, Mass.: Polity Press.

Said, Edward W. 1979. *Orientalism*. New York: Vintage Books.

Sargent, Linda, ed. 1981. *Women and Revolution: A Discussion of the Unhappy Marriage of Marxism and Feminism*. Boston: South End Press.

Sawicki, Jana. 1988. "Identity Politics and Sexual Freedom: Foucault and Feminism," in *Feminism and Foucault: Reflections on Resistance*. Ed. by Irene Diamond and Lee Quinby. Boston: Northeastern University Press.

Scheman, Naomi. 1997. "Queering the Center by Centering the Queer: Reflections on Transsexuals and Secular Jews." In *Feminists Rethink the Self*, ed. Diana Tietjens Meyers. Boulder, Colo.: Westview Press.

Scholinski, Daphne. 1997. *The Last Time I Wore a Dress*. New York: Riverhead Press.

Schor, Naomi, and Elizabeth Weed. 1994. *The Essential Difference*. Bloomington: Indiana University Press.

Schwartzberg, Steven. 1996. *A Crisis of Meaning: How Gay Men Are Making Sense of AIDS*. New York: Oxford University Press.

Scott, James C. 1990. *Domination and the Arts of Resistance. Hidden Transcripts*. New Haven, Conn.: Yale University Press.

Sedgwick, Eve Kosofsky. 1990. *The Epistemology of the Closet*. Berkeley: University of California Press.

Sen, Amartya. 1990. "Millions of Women Are Missing." *New York Review of Books* (December): 20.

Sen, Amartya. 1995. "Gender Inequality and Theories of Justice." In *Women, Culture, and Development*, ed. Martha C. Nussbaum and Jonathan Glover. New York: Oxford University Press.

Sen, Amartya. 1999. *Development as Freedom*. New York: Anchor Books.

Shiva, Vandana. 1996. *Protecting Our Biological and Intellectual Heritage in the Age of Biopiracy*. New Delhi: Research Foundation for Science, Technology and Natural Resource Policy.

Shiva, Vandana, Afsar H. Jafri, Gitanjali Bedi, and Radha Holla-Bar. 1997. *The Enclosure and Recovery of the Commons: Biodiversity, Indigenous Knowledge and Intellectual Property Rights*. New Delhi: Research Foundation for Science, Technology and Ecology.

Simons, Marlise. 2001a. "Bosnian War Trial Focuses on Sex Crimes." *New York Times*, February 18.

Simons, Marlise. 2001b. "3 Serbs Convicted in Wartime Rapes: First International Judgment to Condemn Sexual Slavery," *New York Times* February 23.

Sivard, Ruth Leger. 1995. *Women: A World Survey*. Washington, D.C.: World Priorities Inc.

Soja, Edward W. 1989. *Postmodern Geographies: The Reassertion of Space in Critical Social Theory*. London: Verso.

Spelman, Elizabeth. 1977. "On Treating Persons as Persons." *Ethics* 88, no. 2: 150–161.

Spelman, Elizabeth. 1988. *Inessential Woman: Problems of Exclusion in Feminist Thought*. Boston: Beacon Press.

Stanley, Julia Penelope, and Susan J. Wolfe, eds. 1980. *The Coming Out Stories*. Watertown, Mass.: Persephone.

Steiner, Henry J., ed. 1997. *Truth Commissions: A Comparative Assessment*. Cambridge, Mass.: The World Peace Foundation.

Stoll, David. 1998. *Rigoberta Menchú and the Story of All Poor Guatemalans*. Boulder Colo.: Westview Press.

Taylor, Charles. 1989. *Sources of the Self*. Cambridge: Harvard University Press.

Taylor, Charles. 1994. "The Politics of Recognition." In *Multiculturalism: Examining the Politics of Recognition*, ed. Amy Gutmann. Princeton, N.J.: Princeton University Press, 25–73.

Taylor, Charles. 2000. "Contemporary Sociological Theory: On Social Imaginary." Accessed from www.nyu.edu/classes/calhoun/Theory/Taylor-on-si.htm.

Thomas, Carol. 1999. "Narrative Identity and the Disabled Self." In *Disability Discourse*, ed. Mairian Corker and Sally French. Buckingham: Open University Press, 47–55.

Thompson, Denise. 1996. "The Self-contradiction of 'Post-modernist' Feminism," in *Radically Speaking: Feminism Reclaimed*. Ed. by Diane Bell and Renate Klein. North Melbourne, Australia: Spinifex Press.

Thomson, Rosemarie Garland. 1997. *Extraordinary Bodies: Figuring Physical Disability in American Culture and Literature*. New York: Columbia University Press.

Tirrell, Lynne. 1993. "Definition and Power: Toward Authority Without Privilege." *Hypatia* 8, no. 4: 1–34.

Tuana, Nancy. 1996. "Fleshing Gender, Sexing the Body: Refiguring the Sex/Gender Distinction." *Southern Journal of Philosophy* 35: 53–71.

Tully, James. 2000. "Struggles Over Recognition and Redistribution." *Constellations* 7: 4.

UNIFEM. 2001. "Eradicating Women's Poverty." Accessed March 30, 2002, from www.unifem.undp.org/ecpov.htm.

Van Deusen, Julia. 1993. *Body Image and Perceptual Dysfunction in Adults*. Philadelphia: Sanders.

Vidovic, Katerina. 2001. "War Crimes and Women in Croatia." Presented March 16 at Women's Rights are Human Rights, Southeast Women's Studies Association Conference.

Walker, Margaret Urban. 1991. "Moral Luck and the Virtues of Impure Agency." *Metaphilosophy* 22: 14–27.

Walker, Margaret Urban. 1997. "Picking Up Pieces: Lives, Stories, and Integrity. " In *Feminists Rethink the Self*, ed. Diana Tietjens Meyers. Boulder, Colo.: Westview Press.

Walker, Margaret Urban. 1998. *Moral Understandings: A Feminist Study in Ethics*. New York: Routledge.

Walker, Margaret Urban. 1999. "Getting Out of Line: Alternatives to Life as a Career." In *Mother Time: Women, Aging, and Ethics*, ed. Margaret Urban Walker. Lanham, Md.: Rowman & Littlefield.

Wallach, Lori, and Michelle Sforza, 1999. *Whose Trade Organization? Corporate Globalization and the Erosion of Democracy*. Washington, D.C.: Public Citizen.

Wechsler, Lawrence. 1990. *A Miracle, a Universe: Settling Accounts with Torturers*. Chicago: University of Chicago Press.

Weedon, Chris. 1987. *Feminist Practice and Poststructuralist Theory*. Oxford: Blackwell.

Weinbaum, Batya. 1978. *The Curious Courtship of Women's Liberation and Socialism*. Boston: South End Press.

Weisbrot, Mark. 2001. Accessed March 30, 2002, from www.zmag.org/CrisesCurEvts/Globalism/wtoweis.htm.

Weston, Kath. 1991. *Families We Choose: Lesbians, Gays, Kinship*. New York: Columbia University Press.

White, Evelyn C., ed. 1994. *The Black Women's Health Book: Speaking for Ourselves*, rev. ed. Seattle: Seal Press.

Williams, Bernard. 1981. *Moral Luck*. Cambridge: Cambridge University Press.

Williams, Patricia. 1997. *Seeing a Color-Blind Future*. New York: Farrar, Straus and Giroux.

Witt, Doris. 1998. "What (N)ever Happened to Aunt Jemima: Eating Disorders, Fetal Rights, and Black Female Appetite in Contemporary American Culture." In *Contemporary Feminist Theory: A Text/Reader*, ed. Mary F. Rogers. Boston: McGraw Hill.

Wittig, Monique. 1988. "The Straight Mind." In *For Lesbians Only: A Separatist Anthology*, ed. Sarah Lucia Hoagland and Julia Penelope. London: Only Woman Press.

Wittig, Monique. 1992a. "One Is Not Born a Woman." In *The Straight Mind and Other Essays*. Boston: Beacon Press.

Wittig, Monique. 1992b. "The Straight Mind." In *The Straight Mind and Other Essays*. Boston: Beacon Press.

Wolf, Susan. 1994. "Comment." In *Multiculturalism: Examining the Politics of Recognition*, ed. Amy Gutmann. Princeton, N.J.: Princeton University Press, 75–85.

Wolf, Susan M. 1996. "Gender, Feminism, and Death: Physician-Assisted Suicide and Euthanasia." In *Feminism and Bioethics: Beyond Reproduction*. Oxford: Oxford University Press.

Young, Iris Marion. 1990. *Justice and the Politics of Difference*. Princeton, N.J.: Princeton University Press.

Young, Iris Marion. 1997. "Unruly Categories: A Critique of Nancy Fraser's Dual Systems Theory." *New Left Review*, issue 222: 147–60.

Index

About the Contributors

Robin N. Fiore is assistant professor of philosophy at Florida Atlantic University, Boca Raton, Florida, and is associate faculty in the comparative studies Ph.D. program for public intellectuals and in women's studies. She received her doctorate from Georgetown University, Washington, D.C.

Heidi E. Grasswick is originally from Canada, and is an assistant professor of philosophy at Middlebury College in Vermont. She is also a regular contributor to both the women's and gender studies and the environmental studies programs at Middlebury. She works primarily in the fields of feminist epistemology and social epistemology. Her current research focuses on the intersection of ethics and epistemology, and feminist attempts to come to understand the relationship between these two fields. She holds a Ph.D. in philosophy from the University of Minnesota.

Cressida J. Heyes is an associate professor of philosophy at the University of Alberta, where she writes and teaches in feminist philosophy, queer theory, and political thought. Her first book, *Line Drawings: Defining Women through Feminist Practice*, was published by Cornell University Press in 2000, and she recently completed an edited volume entitled *The Grammar of Politics: Wittgenstein and Political Philosophy*, also from Cornell. She is currently working on a series of essays on sexual subjectivities and feminist communities, one of which is forthcoming in *Signs* 28, no. 2, 2003 as "Feminist Solidarity after Queer Theory: The Case of Transgender."

Cheryl L. Hughes received her Ph.D. in philosophy from the University of Massachusetts, Amherst. She is currently an associate professor of philosophy at Wabash College with teaching and research interests in nineteenth- and twentieth-century continental European philosophy, ethics, and social and political philosophy. She has published articles in *Continental Philosophy Review, Hypatia,* and *Philosophy and Social Criticism* and she serves as principal editor of the Social Philosophy Today book series.

Alison M. Jaggar is a professor of philosophy and women's studies at the University of Colorado at Boulder. Her books include: *Feminist Frameworks*, co-edited with Paula Rothenberg (1993); *Feminist Politics and Human Nature* (1983); *Living with Contradictions: Controversies in Feminist Ethics* (1994); and *The Blackwell Companion to Feminist Philosophy*, co-edited with Iris M. Young, (1998).

María Pía Lara is a professor of philosophy at the Universidad Autónoma Metropolitana in Mexico City. She is the author of *Moral Textures: Feminist Narratives in the Public Sphere* (1998), and editor of *Rethinking Evil: Contemporary Perspectives* (2001). She has recently finished her book *Globalizing Justice* (forthcoming) and is currently working on another book on evil and reflective judgment.

Bonnie Mann is a longtime feminist activist and Ph.D. candidate at SUNY, Stony Brook. Her dissertation, "Feminism and the Sublime," is a critical engagement with feminist postmodernism.

Norah Martin is an associate professor of philosophy at the University of Portland in Oregon. She received her doctorate from the State University of New York at Stony Brook. Her most recent work has been in psychiatric ethics; she also works in the areas of philosophy of mind and philosophy of science.

Diana T. Meyers is a professor of philosophy at the University of Connecticut, Storrs. Her most recent monographs are *Self, Society, and Personal Choice* (1989); *Subjection and Subjectivity: Psychoanalytic Feminism and Moral Philosophy* (1994); and *Gender in the Mirror: Cultural Imagery and Women's Agency*, and her most recent edited collections are *Feminists Rethink the Self* (1997) and *Feminist Social Thought: A Reader* (1997). She is the author of the forthcoming *Encyclopedia Britannica* entry on Philosophical Feminism.

Hilde Lindemann Nelson is associate professor in the philosophy department at Michigan State University, and visiting professor (2001–02) at the Center for the Study of Medical Ethics and Humanities at Duke University.

For five years an editor at the *Hastings Center Report,* she is the coauthor, with James Lindemann Nelson, of *The Patient in the Family* (1995) and *Alzheimer's: Answers to Hard Questions for Families* (1996). She has edited two collections—*Feminism and Families* and *Stories and Their Limits: Narrative Approaches to Bioethics* (both 1997)—and coedited *Meaning and Medicine: A Reader in the Philosophy of Health Care* (1999). She coedits the Reflective Bioethics Series for Routledge and the Feminist Constructions Series for Rowman and Littlefield. Her most recent book is *Damaged Identities, Narrative Repair* (2001).

Kate Parsons is an assistant professor of philosophy at Webster University in St. Louis, Missouri. She is the director of the University's Center for practical and interdisciplinary ethics and teaches courses in ethics, feminist theory, and social and political philosophy. Parsons is co-editor of *Rights and Reason: Essays in Honor of Carl Wellman* (2000) and is currently working on a project that explores the intersections between philosophies of the body, feminism, and dance.

Misha Strauss is a Ph.D. candidate in the department of philosophy at Georgetown University. During 2001–2002, she was a visiting instructor of philosophy at Michigan State University. In addition to her dissertation, her current works in progress include Hannah (age 4) and Tobin (age 2).

Margaret Urban Walker is Lincoln Professor of Ethics, Justice, and the Public Sphere in the School of Justice Studies at Arizona State University. She is author of *Moral Understandings: A Feminist Study in Ethics* (1998). A collection of her essays is forthcoming from Rowman & Littlefield in 2003. Her current project is a book on reparative responses to wrongdoing.

Abby Wilkerson is a philosopher teaching in the writing program at George Washington University, and the author of *Diagnosis: Difference: The Moral Authority of Medicine* (1998). In her current research, she is analyzing political resistance to medicalized identities. She is also a columnist for *Philosophers on Holiday,* the philosophical travel and leisure zine.

Iris Marion Young is a professor of political science at the University of Chicago, where she is also affiliated with the Center for Gender Studies and the Human Rights Program. Her most recent books are *Inclusion and Democracy* (2000) and *Intersecting Voices: Dilemmas of Gender, Political Philosophy and Policy* (1997).

About FEAST

MISSION STATEMENT

Feminist Ethics and Social Theory (FEAST) is a professional organization dedicated to promoting feminist ethical perspectives in philosophy; moral, social, and political life; law; and public policy. Our aim is to further the development and clarification of new understandings of ethical and political concepts and concerns, especially as these arise out of feminist commitments. Through meetings, publications, and projects, we hope to increase the visibility and influence of feminist ethics, as well as feminist social theory and political theory, and to provide support to emerging scholars from diverse and underrepresented populations.

FOR MORE INFORMATION

For information about membership, upcoming conferences, and listserv, see the FEAST Web page at www.afeast.org